Visiting ‘Abdu’l-Bahá

This book is dedicated to

early pilgrims

who recorded their impressions, thoughts and emotions
when meeting the Centre of the Covenant,
thus allowing us in this day to feel at least a little
of what it was like to be face to face with
'Abdu'l-Bahá

Visiting 'Abdu'l-Bahá

Volume 2
The Final Years, 1913–1921

Earl Redman

GEORGE RONALD
OXFORD

George Ronald, Publisher
Oxford
www.grbooks.com

A catalogue record for this book is available from the British Library

ISBN 978-0-85398-634-8

Cover design: Steiner Graphics

CONTENTS

PREFACE

This book concludes what is essentially a trilogy about 'Abdu'l-Bahá as seen through the eyes of the pilgrims and other visitors to the Master in 'Akká and Haifa and those who met Him in Europe and America. Volume 1 of *Visiting 'Abdu'l-Bahá* covers the years from 1897 to 1911. 'Abdu'l-Bahá's travels between 1910 and 1913 are covered in *'Abdu'l-Bahá in Their Midst,* and this volume covers the remainder of the Master's physical life through 1921.

As in volume 1 of *Visiting 'Abdu'l-Bahá*, this volume is based largely on the notes of pilgrims and others who visited the Master in the Holy Land. As such, Shoghi Effendi, Guardian of the Bahá'í Faith, warned that pilgrim notes cannot be misconstrued as Bahá'í scripture. In *The World Order of Bahá'u'lláh*, he wrote:

> Much of the confusion that has obscured the understanding of the believers should be attributed to this double error involved in the inexact rendering of an only partially understood statement. Not infrequently has the interpreter even failed to convey the exact purport of the inquirer's specific questions, and, by his deficiency of understanding and expression in conveying the answer of 'Abdu'l-Bahá, has been responsible for reports wholly at variance with the true spirit and purpose of the Cause. It was chiefly in view of the misleading nature of the reports of the informal conversations of 'Abdu'l-Bahá with visiting pilgrims, that I have insistently urged the believers of the West to regard such statements as merely personal impressions of the sayings of their Master, and to quote and consider as authentic only such translations as are based upon the authenticated text of His recorded utterances in the original tongue.[1]

Though they must be viewed as 'personal impressions', another letter written on behalf of the Guardian, clarified how pilgrim notes could be used: 'On the other hand, each pilgrim brings back information and suggestions of a most precious character, and it is the privilege of all the friends to share in the spiritual results of these visits'.[2]

This volume, then, primarily describes the history and activities of 'Abdu'l-Bahá and the Haifa area through the eyes of those who experienced them.

ACKNOWLEDGEMENTS

As they did for volume 1, Lewis Walker and Dr Duane K. Troxel contributed immensely to the creation of this book. Lewis, at the United States National Bahá'í Archives, initially supplied me with over 2,500 pages of pilgrim notes, while Duane, of The Heritage Project of the National Spiritual Assembly of the United States, supplied me with little-known publications, audio files, and searchable electronic versions of many books, all of which greatly aided my work. The materials provided by these two dedicated researchers are what made this book possible.

Maurice Sabour-Pickett put his detail-spotting accountant's skills to good use eradicating typos, grammatical errors and other unwanted bits. Byron McCord also read through the text and offered some very good suggestions. And as she has done for my previous books, May Hofman again offered many comments, suggestions, mistake-catches and sage advice during the editing process. Her help has been invaluable over the years.

My wife, Sharon O'Toole, must again be acknowledged for her constant support, encouragement and suggestions.

1913–1914

The return of 'Abdu'l-Bahá

In 1913, even before 'Abdu'l-Bahá was back in Haifa, the tide of pilgrims and other visitors again began to flow. No sooner had the Master reached Alexandria than Emogene Hoagg asked permission to visit Him.

> When permission arrived she was ill and bedridden, but insisted on starting out immediately nonetheless. Her husband refused to allow her to travel alone, so she invited a friend to accompany her, and they set out for Alexandria, Egypt, where 'Abdu'l-Bahá and His secretaries had rented a house for a period of rest before proceeding to the Holy Land. When Emogene arrived, she was still weak and ill. She asked the Master if He would be good enough to give her a remedy. He sent her two baked apples, with instructions to eat them at once. She did; seeds and all. Then she went to bed and slept soundly. The next morning she was quite well.[1]

More pilgrims were already there awaiting Him in Haifa. In early autumn 1913, Mullá 'Alí-Muḥammad (Ibn-i-Aṣdaq),[2] a Hand of the Cause appointed by Bahá'u'lláh, received a telegram from 'Abdu'l-Bahá, then in Egypt, inviting him and his family to come to Haifa. It was a large party that set out in October on the long journey from Iran to Palestine. They travelled through Qazvin, Rasht, Baku, Tiflis, Istanbul, finally reaching Beirut on 11 November. Their ship had to anchor offshore, but soon a boat approached and its occupant called out asking if there were any 'followers of Abbás Effendi'. The man, named Tarbash, carried the pilgrims to the dock and the group spent three days in Beirut with the local Bahá'ís.[3]

Back on the ship, but before sailing, another rowing boat approached with 16-year-old Shoghi Effendi and a group of students. The combined groups spent the time before sailing together. Shoghi Effendi told them how blessed they were to be going to the Holy Shrines, but also told them that 'Abdu'l-Bahá was, disappointedly, still in Ramleh, Egypt.[4]

The next morning, the ship arrived off Haifa, but because of the stormy conditions, the captain informed them that they were returning to Beirut. Ibn-i-Aṣdaq, however, insisted that they were going ashore and finally two boats were lowered over the side and part of the party disembarked. It was a rough trip and as Ibn-i-Aṣdaq, who had stayed aboard to wait for the second trip, watched the two struggling boats disappear between the swells, he feared they would be lost. But all made it to shore safely and were quickly taken to the house of the Master where the Greatest Holy Leaf welcomed them. Thirteen-year-old Rúhá Aṣdaq remembered the Greatest Holy Leaf with 'Those beautiful eyes, that gaze, that gait, that dignity, I can never forget.'[5]

In late November, as 'Abdu'l-Bahá began to prepare for His return, He sent Emogene Hoagg, Alice Beede, Mrs Wise and Mrs von Lilienthal to Haifa to prepare for His arrival.[6] Over the next three weeks, all the pilgrims visited the Holy Shrines and basked in the warmth of their association with the Greatest Holy Leaf. But everyone greatly missed 'Abdu'l-Bahá. Ibn-i-Aṣdaq had to make a trip to Alexandria and the Greatest Holy Leaf spent a mysterious hour in conversation with him before he left. The Hand of the Cause reached 'Abdu'l-Bahá's presence on 25 November.[7] Then, suddenly two days later, 'Abdu'l-Bahá announced that His entourage was to depart for Haifa the very next day, but He Himself would come several days later. Ahmad Sohrab was so shocked at this abrupt order that he dashed off to ask the Master himself. Ahmad found Him reading a letter by electric light. 'Abdu'l-Bahá looked up and 'started patiently – like a loving father to a spoiled child – to explain the wisdom of his sudden decision. "I will come to Haifa as soon as you leave, but I must come all alone. Rest thou assured that I shall be there soon, real soon."'[8]

All the pilgrims in Ramleh left on 29 November, but Ahmad Sohrab and a few others were allowed to remain with the Master. The departing pilgrims probably included Ibn-i-Aṣdaq, who brought the word that the Master would soon return, though He was very frail and exhausted.

The Holy Household became a frenzy of activity. 'Abdu'l-Bahá's favourite food was prepared and the Greatest Holy Leaf hid some newly made garments for the Master, saying He would only give them away if He found He had extras. The only problem was that no one knew exactly when He would arrive and they kept scanning the horizon. Then, on 5

December, the Greatest Holy Leaf saw a ship moving toward the harbour. 'O vessel. What is it you bring that makes you sway so gracefully?' she asked.[9] Shortly thereafter, the ship entered the harbour. The Master had requested that the believers not meet the ship. One small group did try to row out to the ship, but when informed of the Master's wishes, they returned to shore. 'Abdu'l-Bahá said He would leave the ship at 5 o'clock. Two warships, one German and one French, coincidentally fired their cannons at exactly that hour as though to announce His arrival.[10]

Soon His carriage arrived at the gate. When 'Abdu'l-Bahá walked toward the house He was met with a joyous embrace by the Greatest Holy Leaf and His daughters. To Rúhá, He appeared very weak and tired and to prove her observation, He went directly to His room. Rúhá's sister Talí'ih began to faint and was caught by an American pilgrim.[11] Soon, 'Abdu'l-Bahá returned and welcomed those who were there to welcome Him saying:

> After the end of three years, again I return to the Holy Land. Were it not for the assistance and protection of the Blessed Beauty, I would never have any hope of returning from such a long journey. I went as far as Los Angeles, which is situated on the western coast of America and directly opposite the land of Acca. Should a person drill a hole in that land he would come out here. Everywhere I went, my thoughts were in Acca. I travelled in many countries. I saw deserts and valleys, but no place could equal this. Indeed, the views here are indescribable. There are many places in other countries, which are famous for their grandeur; but here the views are of divine delicacy and of the gentleness of the Creator.[12]

The next morning, 'Abdu'l-Bahá appeared out of a pouring rain and told the gathered friends that He had returned to Haifa because Ibn-i-Aṣdaq had begged him to. Then He began speaking about Ismu'lláhu'l-Aṣdaq, Ibn-i-Aṣdaq's father, and the great services rendered by father and son.[13]

Though she listened to His talks, Rúhá Aṣdaq didn't remember much of what the Master said, writing that:

> I could never stare into the face of the Master and even if I tried I could not fathom the grandeur and majesty of His face. I was like a light bird freed from its surroundings and making its flight to the

heavens. The tone of His voice had a heavenly sound and the reassuring and encouraging words stirred my entire being. I thought, 'Lord, what bounty is it that has been granted us? What have I done and how have I come to deserve such an honour to be alive this day and to have been brought up by such a father and mother? How am I to repay this bounty?' All I knew was that this hour and special bounty would never leave my thoughts.[14]

On 7 December, 'Abdu'l-Bahá took all the pilgrims, believers and members of His household to the Holy Threshold of the Shrine of Bahá'u'lláh. It was His first visit since His return. 'Abdu'l-Bahá initially entered alone and remained inside for a long time. Mírzá Maḥmúd-i-Zarqání, who had travelled across America and Europe with the Master recording all His activities, wrote a poem that attempted to capture the reunion, after a three-year separation, between the Manifestation of God and the Centre of His Covenant:

He who wrote on the pages of being the lines of grace,
He who raised the banner of God in the universe,
He Who established everywhere the tabernacle of universal peace,
Reposed His brow upon the threshold of the possessor of favours...
With the utmost reverence and adoration, He prostrated himself at
the Most Sacred Threshold, at the feet of the King of Eternity,
The Mystery of Bahá, the Most Great Branch,
Meek and humble He supplicated and wept.
Behold the Blessed Beauty responded from the Glorious Throne:
'O Mightiest Branch of being, Moonlight of the Ancient Covenant,
Verily, hast Thou revealed the Divine Secrets.
The world hath been quickened by Thy pure breath,
The Celestial Concourse filled with Thy melodies,
And the song of Thy servitude was heard wholeheartedly,
O Radiant Countenance, O Mystery, rejoice!
O Divine Speaker, O Noble Branch, rejoice!'[15]

'Abdu'l Bahá spent 15 days in 'Akká meeting with people as the news of His return spread throughout the area. Bahíyyih Khánum said, 'They thronged to His house congratulating Him and themselves, saying, "Where did you go and leave us without a friend and brother?" He had brought presents from Europe for them all, and warm overcoats for the poor old men of 'Akká.'[16] He also brought a pair of binoculars for each of the male members of the Holy Family. Greatly enjoying His own pair, 'Abdu'l-Bahá delighted in looking at Mount Carmel from Bahjí and vice versa. His own personal souvenir from America was a 5¢ coin.[17]

Six-year-old Rúḥu'lláh, Ibn-i-Aṣdaq's grandson, felt the power of being in the presence of 'Abdu'l-Bahá. Always a well-behaved little boy, one day he ran into a room to his mother, not realizing that the Master was also there. Seeing 'Abdu'l-Bahá, he quickly began to retreat until the Master called him and told him to sit at His feet. 'Abdu'l-Bahá ordered some tea and sweets for Rúḥu'lláh, then kissed him on the head and called him a 'well-mannered man'.[18]

When Shoghi Effendi returned from school in Beirut, everyone was impressed by the young man. While others played, he read or listened to the Greatest Holy Leaf. He 'had a handsome face, sad and elegant with a sweet, heart-warming and spontaneous smile which on occasion would turn into reverberating laughter.'[19]

The most mesmerizing person in Haifa, other than 'Abdu'l-Bahá, was the Greatest Holy Leaf. Rúhá Aṣdaq wrote a pen portrait of this great lady:

> The Greatest Holy Leaf personally took charge of the affairs of the Master's house, including the kitchen. She would manage everything related to the Holy Household, neighbouring believers and pilgrims. When otherwise unoccupied, even as moths drawn to candlelight, we all gathered around her to listen to her stories of the hardship experienced during their banishment and imprisonment. One day a pilgrim took out a pen and paper to record her memories. She immediately stopped and said, 'Whatever I say is in the way of relating incidents. Do not take notes. I do not wish these to become like the stories of Zaynab and Fáṭimih. Those things which are completely documented should be taken note of. If you want to take note of that which I narrate and quote me later, I will not utter a word.[20]

Before going on pilgrimage, Rúhá had thought of Western believers as 'haughty and arrogant people', so she was surprised to see their 'sincerity and reverence in the Holy Shrines, their insatiable thirst for deepening in the Faith . . . and their disposition to follow the instructions of the Master'. Rúhá remembered one American woman who was always very well dressed and who wore make-up. Then she heard ʻAbdu'l-Bahá talk about 'the beauty of simplicity in appearance and she immediately understood it to mean that he did not approve of excessive make-up'.[21]

One day Mírzá Jalál, a son-in-law of the Master, went to the ʻAkká Telegraph Office to send some of the Master's many cablegrams. He gave the manager one for San Francisco, but after much searching the man couldn't find the city in his rate books. Finally, he asked which country the city was in. 'Persia', Mírzá Jalál replied jokingly. 'The manager, not knowing any better, went on searching. At last he gave up. "I cannot find this", he said. "Tell me, where is Montreal?" "In India." After ten minutes he was in despair. "These cities are not in my books," he said gravely.' At that point Mírzá Jalál confessed to his joke and, taking the rate book, found the cities, chastising the manager for his lack of geographic knowledge.[22]

On 14 December, Ahmad Sohrab described the Master's walks through Haifa:

> Clad in his long, flowing robe, with his soft, dark yellow aba and white turban, and white beard, and compelling figure and soul-searching eyes, and towering forehead, he walks as an imperial sun playing hide and seek. They stop their play and salute Effendi. There are many boys coming out of school. They see Effendi from afar. They wait with a deep reverence, and as he passes on, their hands are on their lips and heads. There are a number of men sitting in the restaurant or café. One of them sees Effendi coming and communicates to the rest. Immediately they are on their feet to pay their homage. The shop keepers are busy wrangling with their customers in their crude, small stores. Oh, they see Effendi and silence is cast over them. They all pay him their respect. The soldiers standing in front of the barrack and the government buildings are on their feet with their muskets to offer him their thanksgiving. The wild Arabs driving their camels in the streets, the modern young men with their European clothes, the learned Sheiks with their silk garments, the poor men with their multicolored patched robes, the veiled women with their babes in their arms, all bow down before Effendi, salute him, kiss his hands, and honor him as their superior master. You ask them, 'Why do you

do this?' It is their love for him which prompts them. Not even the governor of the city is held in such respect and honor by the people. Now and then the Beloved stops in his march as he sees a poor man approach him. He knows him and inquires about his health. To each and all he says: 'How are you? How is your health? Are you well? Are you happy? May God assist and protect you.' And then their faces are wreathed in smiles and laurels of happiness appear on their brows.[23]

On 22 December, there was a large number of pilgrims in Haifa. The group was so large that they didn't fit into 'Abdu'l-Bahá's house and had to divide into two groups, so that the Master had to give two talks that evening.[24]

Finally came a day when 'Abdu'l-Bahá was walking along the beach with Ibn-i-Aṣdaq and said, 'The sea is so calm'. The Hand of the Cause immediately knew it was time to go home. So, on 20 January, after 72 days in the Holy Land, most of it in the presence of 'Abdu'l-Bahá, the family of Ibn-i-Aṣdaq returned to Persia.[25]

In late December, Emogene Hoagg, Mrs von Lilienthal and Alice Beede were still in Haifa and had been joined by Mr and Mrs Holbach, who arrived from England on the 23rd.[26] Shoghi Effendi was back from school for Christmas. Emogene wrote on 27 December that she had been several times to the Tomb of Bahá'u'lláh. On one visit, she encountered the wife and a son of Mírzá Muḥammad-'Alí, the Covenant-breaker. The son insisted quite officiously that she have tea with them. She wrote, 'He seemed possessed to talk to the Americans.'[27]

In his diary letters, Ahmad Sohrab described what is now known as the Eastern Pilgrim House and its construction:

God inspired the heart of Mírzá Jaffar Shirazi [Mírzá Ja'far Rahmání] to come out and beg the Master to give him the privilege of building the first distinctly Bahai Pilgrim's Home in this part of the world. Permission was granted him, and he started to look around for the best available lot on the breast of Mount Carmel. Finally, this charming site was selected, having a most commanding view of the sea, and near the Tomb of the BAB. Then the foundation was laid, and was finished in due time and solemnly dedicated by the Beloved to the Cause. The building has cost about $8,000, a good deal of money in the east. This man alone paid all the expenses . . .

When the building was finished it was opened to the Bahai pilgrims of all nations and religions, especially the Oriental people. As there are no accommodations complete enough to entertain Western pilgrims, they live in the hotels . . . This Pilgrim's Home has four sleeping rooms; a large reception room; a general big hall where a long table is in the center, for the purpose of eating; an entrance hall; a corridor; a kitchen; and a lovely porch . . .

The Home is in possession of two fine watch dogs . . . Although they are friendly and hospitable towards the friends, yet a flood of barkings is set loose when any stranger is seen, especially in the night.

Another interesting object is a very beautiful parrot. They have taught it to say many words . . . Early in the morning when the pilgrims leave their rooms, it says very distinctly:

'Declare, Declare, Declare, Ya Baha El Abha!'

'Say, O! Thou Mystery of God!' and other wonderful greetings. Often one is startled out of his sleep by its voice repeating the commanding word: 'Declare' ever so many times, and at the end, 'Ya Baha El Abha!' that I have mistaken it at first for a human voice . . .

The present Pilgrim's Home is of course only for men. There is no place yet for the women pilgrims. This is naturally the cause of much inconvenience.[28]

1914: JANUARY–JUNE

Maude Holbach and her husband

Maude Holbach and her husband arrived in Haifa on the steamer *Khedivial* on 23 December 1913 and 'Abdu'l-Bahá received them with 'delightful and heavenly courtesy'. Maude was an English Bahá'í and travel writer who had visited the Holy Land in 1909 and had heard about the Faith, but had not investigated it. It wasn't until she returned to England and was in the Bodleian Library in Oxford, where she discovered a book about the Faith, that she gained an appreciation for it. Soon afterwards, she visited Lady Blomfield and saw a portrait of 'Abdu'l-Bahá, whom she recognized instantly, though she had never seen Him before. In late 1912, Maude went on a lecture tour of America and was surprised to find that the Master was in the same city she was, New York. On 23 November, she attended the Day of the Covenant celebration at the Great Northern Hotel and finally met the Magnet who so strongly attracted her. Later, she was also able to be in His presence in Paris.[1]

The Holbachs had an unusually long pilgrimage for Westerners, remaining in Haifa and 'Akká until 24 April.[2] Their goal was to write a historical work on the Faith.[3] They stayed at the Roman Catholic Hospice and when looking through the guest book, found the signature of Thornton Chase, who had been on pilgrimage in 1907.[4]

The Holbachs had many meetings with the Master during their four-month stay. On 3 January, Maude shared with 'Abdu'l-Bahá portions of an article she had written about the Faith for a publication called *Nineteenth Century*. He was pleased with the portions translated and praised her for her 'accuracy and faithful work'.[5] Ten days later, the Holbachs asked 'Abdu'l-Bahá about the Ma<u>sh</u>riqu'l-A<u>dh</u>kár. He said:

> When these institutions, college, hospital, hospice and establishments for the incurables, University for the study of higher sciences and giving post-graduate courses and other philanthropic buildings, are built, its doors will be opened to all the nations and religions.

> There will be absolutely no line of demarcation. Its charities will be dispensed irrespective of color or race . . . Thus for the first time religion will become harmonized with science, and science will be the handmaid of religion, both showering their material and spiritual gifts on ALL humanity.[6]

The Holbachs spent considerable time with Ḥájí Mírzá Ḥaydar-'Alí and listened in rapture while he told of his eventful life.[7] One day, Maude told 'Abdu'l-Bahá about an old German and his blind wife who lived near the Carmelite monastery. The German had only thin clothes and Maude asked the Master to send him a coat. 'Abdu'l-Bahá immediately went and found a coat for him. Then the Master spoke of a Roman Catholic priest who strongly opposed the Bahá'í Faith. Maude said that she had been surprised when she heard that 'Abdu'l-Bahá had contributed a sum of money to the Roman Catholic institution there. He responded by saying, 'Well, we were commanded by Bahá'u'lláh to assist all the communities without the exclusion of anyone. We do not consider their deeds and actions but we never lose sight of the fact that mankind are the children of God and their wants must be relieved without the distinction of race or religion.'[8]

Eastern pilgrims were very impressed with the Holbachs. At one point, there were 16 Eastern pilgrims there and Sohrab noted that they had 'a lovely conversation with Mr and Mrs Holbach in the garden of the Beloved. They were most impressed by and elated over the meeting of our Western Bahá'ís and will carry back to their homes pleasant memories of these unique and spiritual days.'[9]

One day, the authenticity of Christian holy places in Palestine was mentioned while the Holbachs were having lunch with the Master. 'Abdu'l-Bahá told them that

> the sepulchre of Jesus was not known until St. Helena [mother of the Emperor Constantine] had search made. He said: 'What is known is that a piece of ground was bought specially for the Tomb of Jesus and that is known as Golgotha. But the traces of this place were completely lost. When St. Helena went to Jerusalem she tried to have this place discovered. The Jews showed her the place that is now pointed out. They got a good sum for their guidance.[10]

Maude had written an article for the *Christian Commonwealth* entitled 'The Bahai Movement, with some recollections of meetings with Abdul Baha' that was published on 28 January. In it, she wrote of meeting 'Abdu'l-Bahá:

> After meeting Abdul Baha in New York and Paris, I am now fortunate enough to see him in his native East; not, it is true, in the land of his birth, but in the Holy Land – the Land of the Prophets, to which by spiritual succession he rightfully belongs. India is waiting eagerly for his promised visit, but his strenuous life in America and long journeying have told on his body, though his spirit is never weary. Those who love him hope that he will here, in his own home and among his own family from whom he has so long been separated, take the rest he so sorely needs, although even here it is difficult for him to rest. Over fifty pilgrims from Persia awaited his arrival at Haifa, and his loving spirit cannot send away those who have come so far and at so great a sacrifice without giving them all the spiritual teaching and happiness of his presence that they desire. The Bahai community at Haifa and Acre numbers many wives and children of the martyrs who died for their faith in Persia; all these are more or less depending on the bounty of Abdul Baha and his family, who one and all live only for the Cause, and work unceasingly, by deeds of loving-kindness to those near and far, to promote that oneness of humanity that shall begin the New Era of the Most Great Peace.[11]

In response, 'Abdu'l-Bahá dictated a message to the *Christian Commonwealth* about the possibility of a World Congress of Religions in which He said:

> I have read in a recent number of the Christian Commonwealth that there will be held a World Conference of Faith and Order, at which delegates of all Christian denominations shall be present. This news gave me great joy . . . However, were it possible to bring about those ideal forces which shall make the realization of a World Conference of Religions, it shall yield immensely greater results to the human race.[12]

Maude wrote about about her experience with 'Abdu'l-Bahá in another letter published both in the *Christian Commonwealth* and the *Star of the West*:

> I write this by a window that looks across an orange garden to the slopes of Mount Carmel, which rises almost abruptly beyond the red-roofed houses of the German colony. The 'Mount of God' is but a hill in comparison with the mighty Alps, yet how great is its fascination, how beautiful it appears now in the moonlight! From time immemorial it has been the home of the prophets. It is here that Abdul-Baha dwells today, and the simple Germans who left their native land to await 'the second coming' of their Lord upon this mountain, are his neighbors! . . .
>
> Since his return from Egypt, five weeks ago, Abdul-Baha has more than once visited Akka and remained some time . . . During one of his visits there he sent for the American Bahais who are making a pilgrimage to the Holy Land, that with him they might visit the Tomb of Baha'o'llah. Another day the Persian pilgrims were sent for, of whom a contingent have now returned to their native land . . .
>
> It was my privilege to be present at two farewell gatherings given in their honor . . . At the first the men assembled at the Tomb of the Bab, which occupies a commanding position on the slope of Mount Carmel, and is a striking object from my window soon after dawn, when the rays of the rising sun illumine it. The tomb is surrounded by a garden on a terrace on the mountain side and the building has several chambers. In the largest of these about fifty to sixty Bahais were assembled on the occasion to which I refer – Jews, Zoroastrians, Mohammedans, and Christians – to listen to an address by Abdul-Baha. While he was speaking tea was served by the giver of the feast. Then all proceeded to an inner chamber, which in turn led to the tomb proper, and here the Tablets were chanted by one of the pilgrims, a very learned mullah and great orator. The reverence of the Oriental Bahais for Abdul-Baha must be witnessed to be understood. When he came down the mountain side clad in his flowing robe and white turban, and followed by his disciples from far and near, the scene was truly Biblical.[13]

The Holbachs also spent a week and a half with 'Abdu'l-Bahá in 'Akká and Bahjí.

The passing of Mírzá Abu'l-Faḍl

Mírzá Abu'l-Faḍl died in Cairo on 21 January 1914, and on 13 February the American pilgrims held a memorial service for him at the Shrine of the Báb. 'Abdu'l-Bahá attended the service, then spent the night in the home of 'Abbás-Qulí near the Shrine. On 18 February, the pilgrims gathered at 'Abdu'l-Bahá's house in Haifa and heard the news of a memorial meeting for Mírzá Abu'l-Faḍl that had been held in Baku, Russia. The Bahá'ís there had stopped work for three days and nights in his memory. The Persian Consul had attended the meeting, praising their 'unity and harmony' and said that the Bahá'í community was 'the cause of honor to the government and to the nation of Persia'.[14]

Mírzá Abu'l-Faḍl was one of the most learned Bahá'ís of his time. Before becoming a Bahá'í, he had been one of the foremost Muslim scholars. He knew of the Bahá'í Faith before 1875, but it was that year that an illiterate blacksmith, who was a Bahá'í, brought his understanding of his own faith into question. The unlettered Bahá'í asked the well-known scholar about a Muslim tradition that said that each drop of rain is brought to earth by an angel. Mírzá Abu'l-Faḍl said it was true. The blacksmith then wanted to verify that no angel would visit a house in which there was a dog. Again, the scholar said it was true. Then the illiterate Bahá'í sprung his trap on the haughty scholar, asking, 'Then, how is it that rain falls on the houses that have dogs?'[15] A year later, Mírzá Abu'l-Faḍl became a very humble Bahá'í. For this, he was imprisoned three times. He made journeys through Persia as well as to Moscow, Turkey, China, Syria and Egypt to teach the Faith. In 1901 and 1902, he was in America at the request of 'Abdu'l-Bahá to aid the American believers combat Kheiralla's Covenant-breaking. Mírzá Abu'l-Faḍl also wrote a series of books defending and explaining the Faith, including *The Brilliant Proof*, which he wrote in 1911 to refute a fanatical English cleric.[16]

Various visitors and activities

In a letter to Isabella Brittingham, Emogene Hoagg wrote about the problems facing the American believers. 'Abdu'l-Bahá said to her: 'Before leaving America I mentioned in many meetings the things that would happen. I said that after I left, the clergy would begin to cause many doubts, that the believers would be blamed and found fault with, and that they would fall into many tests, but that the ones who would remain firm would be established in the Kingdom of God.'[17]

On 14 February the Master went to the Pilgrim House near the Shrine of the Báb and sat facing the Shrine of Bahá'u'lláh at Bahjí. Looking out over Haifa and the distant 'Akká, He told those gathered:

> The view from this hospice is very beautiful, especially because it faces the tomb of the Blessed Beauty and Acca. In the future it will all be built up between Acca and Haifa. Acca and Haifa will be joined together and will take the first place in the world. Now, as I glance into the future, I see the greatest port in the world here. This semi-circular bay will be a large harbor for ships, so that the entering boats may be protected from the waves and winds of the storms. The harbor will be filled with ships of the nations. All of these regions will be decorated by buildings and lofty places. Many gardens and flower beds will be made. There will be electric lights and from here to Acca will be flooded with them. It will be a wonderful sight, especially at night, for those who come from the sea or who look from the summit of the mountains. From all of these regions, the cry of 'Ya-Baha-el-Abha!' (O Thou Glorious of the Most Glorious!) shall rise. All the souls will come in a state of supplication, imploring and chanting the communes. In every town, the melodies from the Mashrak-el-Azkar on this Mount Carmel, will be most pleasing to the ears.[18]

On 28 January, Ahmad Sohrab had a new home built for him by the Master. He called it the 'Bahá'í Nest'. It was set close to the Shrine of the Báb and the Pilgrim's House with views of both as well as the sea. His writing table was placed so as to have all these views visible. He could also see the House of the Master below.[19] When 'Abdu'l-Bahá made His first visit a few weeks later, He joked with 'Abbás-Qulí, the custodian of the Shrine of the Báb, about how 1,000 Piastres, or $40,000, had been spent fixing it up. The Master said, 'Do you hear, Abbas Goli. Get hold of Mirza Ahmad and do not leave him till he pays you the money.' Sitting on Ahmad's couch, 'Abdu'l-Bahá said, 'How charmingly quiet is this room and how varied and entrancing is the scene spread before one's view!'[20] For Ahmad, it was a place to have some peace and quiet, but it was soon to become the focus of a number of the Master's translators because of its tranquillity.

Pilgrims came from every part of the world. Some, such as Alice Beede, Mrs von Lilienthal, Mrs Wise, Mrs Sprague and Elinor Hiscox, had taken advantage of their location to also visit Damascus and Tiberias and then returned to the presence of the Master. Emogene Hoagg was living with one of 'Abdu'l-Bahá's daughters while teaching them English and learning Persian.[21] The women, except for Emogene, departed for home on 15 February.

On 9 February 1914, a young Englishman arrived in Haifa to see 'Abdu'l-Bahá. Economics was his primary interest and he asked the Master, 'When the time comes for the working people to become the partners of their employers, will they have their own representatives to consult with the company and will those who invest more capital receive more shares?' 'Abdu'l-Bahá answered by telling him that the workers would 'select their own representatives for consultation and those who have more capital will earn more money.'[22]

Two days later, Ḥájí Músá, a Bahá'í from Azerbaijan, arrived. 'Abdu'l-Bahá told him and his fellow pilgrims:

> Readiness is necessary in order to be a recipient of divine bounty. Souls who are prepared are like candles coming into contact with fire. They become illuminated. They are swayed by the wafting of a breeze. They become green and verdant from a drop of the sprinkling of the cloud of favor. They find merciful susceptibilities by hearing a word. But no fruits nor results can be obtained from the souls who are not ready. Thus the prepared souls, on hearing the divine call, respond, 'Here we are!'[23]

A large group of American ladies, who were on their way to Jerusalem, visited 'Abdu'l-Bahá on the morning of 15 February. After their visit, it was the turn of a judge and several 'statesmen' to seek the Master's views. He 'spoke to them in detail about historical matters, scientific facts, the life histories of some of the doctors and sages of the past and of the requirements for this great century, the oneness of the world of humanity and universal peace.'[24] That afternoon, Dr Howard Bliss, President of the Syrian Protestant College, came to see 'Abdu'l-Bahá to arrange a visit for his students.[25]

A group of Persian pilgrims from Khurasan arrived two days later. When they came into the presence of 'Abdu'l-Bahá the next morning, they all bowed and fell at His feet. 'Abdu'l-Bahá stopped them saying 'No, it is unlawful. It is unlawful, because, according to the blessed command, kneeling, kissing of the hands and bowing are prohibited. They are not accepted in the Cause of God. They belong to the holy tombs of Baha'o'llah, and the Bab and to the house of God.'[26]

On 18 February, 'Abdu'l-Bahá revealed 'explicit commands' for the American and English Bahá'í teachers in India, absolutely forbidding them from becoming involved in political activities, stressing that they should spend their time 'spreading the spiritual fragrances and in elevating the Cause of the affectionate Lord'. Later, that day, Abdu'l-Bahá was told that Andrew Carnegie, one of the richest Americans, had given $2,000,000 in the hope of creating unity within the various Christian sects. 'Abdu'l-Bahá replied: 'His aim is good and a service to the world of humanity. O how I wish that all of the leaders of the people would spend their energy for unity and peace among all nations and sects!'[27] The problem with feuding Christian sects was addressed again in June when a copy of the *Christian Commonwealth*, an English Christian newspaper, was read to 'Abdu'l-Bahá by Ahmad Sohrab. In one article, a minister said that 'the time had now come for us to be ashamed of receiving high salaries and to be living in such comfort and luxury while the poor are left in such misery. We must leave the thoughts of our desires and become self-sacrificing.' 'Abdu'l-Bahá then said:

> They talk of doing, but they do not act. They think it would be easy to do this. They do not understand the meaning of martyrdom or self-sacrifice. As soon as a needle pricks the hand, their cries reach the heavens. There is no comparison between these souls and the sanctity and the self-sacrifice of the disciples of His Holiness Christ. They do not even breathe alike. It is the Bahais who walk in the footsteps of Christ and his disciples. They endure such calamities,

> hardships of hunger and thirst, prison, murder, persecution and malice. They have endured all sufferings. These men of passion and desire – how can they do such things? . . . it is very easy to write and speak upon these matters, but it is hard to put them into action.[28]

'Abdu'l-Bahá wasn't just the goal of Bahá'í pilgrims, He was becoming a bit of a tourist attraction as well. There were the American women on 15 February, and on the 22nd a group of English tourists came to see Him. He told them about the basic teachings of the Faith and its history. When they left, 'their hearts [were] exceedingly touched and attracted'.[29]

One day, 'Abdu'l-Bahá was dictating Tablets when an Arab arrived, followed soon thereafter by another. These two men did not like each other at all, so the Master began to tell funny stories.

> Each of them sat there inwardly growling at his enemy. At first the Beloved spoke to them in such a manner as to make them laugh. They did not want to laugh, neither did they want to look at each other, but they could not help doing both. Thus the ice was broken. Then with His deep insight into the dispositions of these men, He said: –
>
> 'The life of man is but a few days, then death overtakes them. Is it not foolish to attach one's heart to the worldly love and hate . . . Happiness is the King of our hearts. Let us not part from it. If the candle of happiness is ignited in the chamber of the heart, all the foreboding gloom of evil suggestions will be dispelled. My home is the home of peace. My home is the home of joy and delight. My home is the home of laughter and exultation. Whosoever enters through the portals of this home, must go out with gladsome heart. This is the home of light; whosoever enters here must become illumined . . . This is the home of Love: those who come in must learn the lessons of love; thus may they know how to love each other . . .'
>
> Then He related to them story after story, making them now laugh and now serious. Finally when he observed the time had come, he got up from his seat and asked them to kiss each other and be true friends ever afterwards. 'Is it not much better to be friends than enemies?' . . . Then he went into another room and brought candy and two silk handkerchiefs for each one. 'By this token you are plighted together forever.'[30]

'Abdu'l-Bahá walked in His garden on the morning of 20 February enjoying the beautiful day. Looking at the violets and carnations in the garden, He told those with Him:

> As long as a thing is rare and scarce, it seems more attractive and has greater value. In Bagdad there were few violets in our home and they were indescribably dear and attractive to our sight. But here none look at these violets and they are lost among so many flowers. As the quantity of a thing increases, its value decreases. And so it is in the beginning of the days of the Holy Manifestations; because the souls are so few, they are counted as the essences of existence in the estimation of God. They are always mentioned and considered in the holy threshold and the sacred court and they attain to everlasting life and eternal bounty because they are detached from all conditions and have lost themselves entirely in the good pleasure of God.[31]

On 23 February, Baron Edmond de Rothschild, one of the richest people in the world, was in Haifa, but though he toured some of the area, he did not seek a meeting with 'Abdu'l-Bahá. At a talk that day, the Master spoke of the burden that riches can become for the wealthy:

> Instead of a blessing wealth becomes a great calamity to them. The supervision of their colossal fortunes and their proper financial administration becomes the sole object of their lives. Day and night, asleep and awake, they think and work to make *their* piles larger and that of others smaller till finally they become mere money machines devoid of any other feeling or of higher emotions, wild-eyed, always hungering for more. Greed and selfishness become the dominant influences of their lives. Grab, grab, grab; right and left they grab at everything. In the mad rush and struggle for more lucre, for more worldly goods they walk over the bodies of the toilers and the children. They become the embodiment of heartlessness and cruelty. Pride and haughtiness lord it over them and they become mere tools in the hands of sordid, fiendish passion . . .
>
> Wealth has a tempting and drawing quality. It bewilders the sight of its charmed victims with showy appearances and draws them on and on to the edge of yawning chasms. It makes a person self-centered, self-occupied, forgetful of God and of holy things.

> On the other hand there are souls who are the essence of existence; in their estimation wealth offers no attractions. If the doors of the heavenly blessings are opened before their faces, if they become the possessors of the riches of all the world . . . their spiritual independence will undergo no change or alteration, their faith in God will increase, their mindfulness will augment, the heat of the fire of their love for true democracy and the education of mankind will burn away all barriers of ostentation and pride. Their intense passion for God will wax greater day by day. Such rich men are in reality the light-bearing stars of the heaven of mankind, because they have been tried and tested and have come out of the crucible as pure gold . . . unalloyed and unadulterated. With all the wealth of the world at their feet they are yet mindful of God and humanity, they spend their acquired riches for the dispelling of the darkness of ignorance and employ their treasures for the alleviation of the misery of the children of God. The light of such rich men will never grow dim and the tree of their generosity will grow in size and stature, producing fruits in all seasons.[32]

On the afternoon of 1 March, Ḥájí Áqá Ḥusayn, the brother of Aḥmad Yazdí, gave a feast for all the believers and pilgrims, including the Holbachs and Emogene Hoagg. The Master entered while they were drinking tea and the group rose as one. When He was seated, 'a deep spiritual silence' fell over the gathering. 'The hearts were praying, while the eyes were turned toward him, and all attention was centered upon Him.' Then 'Abdu'l-Bahá began to speak about the martyrs:

> With what joy and transport they hastened toward the arena of martyrdom! With what attraction they gave up their lives in the Path of the Blessed Perfection! With what enkindlement they have associated with the people! They were always surrounded with danger and impending peril. They rested not for one moment. Their nights were spent with the apprehension that tomorrow would be their last day. Their days were passed with the dread that they would not see another night . . . Friends! Let us read and remember the incidents of the lives of these heroic martyrs, bring before our eyes the glorious records of their deeds, print upon the tablets of the hearts their flowing, self-convincing utterances, so that we may become inspired

with the same severance, impelled by the same detachment, release ourselves from every thought and mention and devote our time to the service of the Glorious One! . . . We must ever remind ourselves of these events, and be aware and thoughtful. If these wonderful, tragic lives are not reviewed from time to time, their significance and spiritual import will be lost sight of. We must read and ponder over the details of the lives of these martyrs . . . If we are not fortunate to run with them shoulder to shoulder toward the arena of martyrdom, we can at least be their humble followers. Thus we may discover the key to their spiritual state, to their severance, their attraction, their exhilaration and their rapture.[33]

Narayenrao Rangnath Vakíl and Muḥammad-Riḍá Shírází

In early March 1914, Narayenrao Rangnath Vakíl arrived as a pilgrim in Haifa, having come by sea from Bombay. Mr Vakíl learned of the Faith from Mírzá Muhram in Bombay. In January 1909, he declared his faith in Bahá'u'lláh to Mírzá Muhram and is believed to be the first person from a Hindu background to do so. His teacher, however, was not satisfied. 'If you want me to believe that you have intelligently accepted the station of Bahá'u'lláh, then prove it to me by leading your friends and neighbors to accept Him as you have accepted Him.' So Vakíl began his career as a Bahá'í teacher.[34]

Vakíl considered his 27-day pilgrimage to be the most important event in his life. 'Abdu'l-Bahá's praise of him was amazing:

> From India I have received many letters praising and commending you. Now I see with my own eyes, that praise be to God, these praises and commendations are not only fully manifest in you, but your character looms larger and more significant. You are greater than the picture portrayed in the letters . . . How significant that you are the first believer in that community! I hope that when you will leave this Holy Spot, you will become the cause of their guidance . . . Thou wilt go away with a new fire burning in thy heart and a new power impelling thee onward, and thou shalt be confirmed.[35]

> In the future the members of your family will honor thy faith and glorify thy name.[36]

Vakíl was betrothed to marry a Hindu woman and, now that he was a Bahá'í, that worried him. He asked 'Abdu'l-Bahá if he should go through with the wedding. The Master said he should and that He would pray that she would become a Bahá'í. In 1929, Vakíl returned with his wife, Jashodaben, who was still a Hindu, and their two daughters. While staying in the Mansion of Bahjí during the pilgrimage, Jashodaben had a dream in which Krishna came and opened a cupboard containing beautiful crowns. These He proceeded to take out and give to her. Bahá'u'lláh then came and Krishna directed her to give the crowns to Him. At that point, Krishna removed His own crown and gave it to Bahá'u'lláh, as Bahá'u'lláh gave his taj to Krishna. Then Krishna said, 'There is no difference between us. We are the same.' The next morning, she awoke as a Bahá'í.[37]

In addition to being a dedicated Bahá'í teacher, Vakíl was later elected the first chairman of the National Spiritual Assembly of the Bahá'ís of India and Burma in 1923 and remained on that body for the next two decades.[38]

On 10 March, Vakíl and other Bahá'í pilgrims including Mírzá 'Alí-Akbar Rafsanjání and Mírzá 'Alí-Akbar from Russia, had their photograph taken with 'Abdu'l-Bahá on the steps of the Master's House.[39] Mírzá 'Ali-Akbar Rafsanjání had spent almost two months teaching the Faith in Germany.

Muḥammad-Riḍá Shírází arrived on pilgrimage from India on 6 April and stayed for 21 days. 'Abdu'l-Bahá was in 'Akká at that time so Shírází hurried to the ancient city. When he arrived, he entered a room 'at the corner of which sat a most majestic figure on a sofa – wide nostrils, piercing yet pitiful eyes, commanding yet sweet voice, merciful and kind, fixed eye brows with a serene yet strongly marked forehead, white fez and turban, white flowing robes with white locks of hair and white soft beard.' 'Abdu'l-Bahá graciously welcomed him and told Shírází that He knew all about a long teaching trip he had made throughout India in 1912. Shírází had arrived with a Hindu Bahá'í friend who told the Master that according to the rules of his caste, he should be excommunicated for becoming a Bahá'í and visiting 'Abdu'l-Bahá. The Master replied, 'Your friends and relatives, nay, your father and descendants shall soon glory over this action of yours, that you have overcome such barriers and have come and lived among the disciples of Bahá'u'lláh.'[40]

'Abdu'l-Bahá soon returned to Haifa and Shirází described his schedule:

> 'Abdu'l-Bahá has always a busier time at Haifa than at Akka. Early in the morning after his return from the green meadows he sends for various pilgrims, either one by one or in numbers and receives them. Then you see him come out into his garden, move amidst flowers and dictate long tablets to his secretaries. Sometimes he sits on one of the stairs of his house and talks on various subjects with the Bahá'ís who have meanwhile gathered at his house. You can never imagine a man more simple of expression, attire, and habit, yet so wonderfully able to command and direct men towards God. Then 'Abdu'l-Bahá retires and perhaps hardly takes an hour's rest and returns to his parlour, personally peruses the tablets which have been meanwhile copied by his secretaries, corrects and signs them, dictates their answers or sometimes replies in his own hand. His only rest lies in occasionally talking to someone who is present while he does all that work. Unless someone comes to call on him, his evenings are spent in returning calls which is the etiquette of the East. His Friday noons are spent in the mosque and Sunday mornings at the home at some of his resident European friends. Thrice a week all the Bahá'ís gather in his large drawing hall and hear him talk or reply to the various questions which are put to him at his own suggestion and chant some of the tablets of Bahá'u'lláh. An English lady who was staying in his family told me that there was quite a different charm about 'Abdu'l-Bahá, when he was amidst his daughters and the members of his family. Even the little children of Haifa, and of his family pay quite a different kind of respect to 'Abdu'l-Bahá. When he returns from his walk in the evening children see him from the distance, stop their play, and inform others that the master is coming.[41]

Vakíl and Shirází energetically tried to coax 'Abdu'l-Bahá to visit India. The Master responded by saying, 'India must become prepared. A center of magnetic power must be created there in order to attract me. If such a center of attraction comes into being, I might come.' They continued their petition until they departed to India, Vakíl on 19 April and Muḥammad-Riḍá on 27 April. The Master, however, told Vakíl that since He could not go to India, he would send Vakíl back with special spiritual power.[42] Shírází later went travel-teaching in America at the request of 'Abdu'l-Bahá.[43]

Shaykhs, pilgrims, friends and students

Eight Shaykhs spent a long time with 'Abdu'l-Bahá on 30 March. Ahmad Sohrab described them as 'extremely picturesque, with their long flowing robes and black or white beards.' They were 'learned men of the Mohammedan religion' but the Master spoke to them 'with command and authority' on the Biblical passage: 'In the beginning was the Word, and the Word was with God, and the Word was God.' From the Master came a 'flood of spiritual interpretation . . . sweeping away from before them every thorn of objection and every thistle of denial' and His visitors were 'motionless, enraptured'.[44]

On 4 April, a young tourist, Mr Hill from Scotland, arrived to see the Master. Mr Hill was a friend of Scottish Bahá'ís Alexander and Jane Whyte and their son, Frederick. The Master spoke to the young man about education.[45] Two days later, the first of four groups of students from the Syrian Protestant College in Beirut, which Shoghi Effendi attended and which later became the American University, visited Haifa and 'Abdu'l-Bahá. When the Easter holiday arrived, the students thought that a good way to 'refresh the body and mind from the daily routine of life was to see the charming face of Abdul-Baha, the Center of the Covenant.' With 'Abdu'l-Bahá's approval, all 27 Bahá'í students at the college journeyed to Haifa over the 16-day Easter break. One of the students, Badi Bushrui, who was later to become one of 'Abdu'l-Bahá's secretaries and the Governor of the province around 'Akká and Haifa, wrote about the event for the *Star of the West*:

> On account of the large number of pilgrims in Haifa coming from different parts of the world, wisdom demanded that we should form four parties, each of which could stay in Haifa for four days at least. This arrangement was convenient and during the sixteen days of vacation all the students had the great blessing of seeing the Beloved Abdul-Baha. The four parties were in the process of going and coming beginning from April 6th to April 22nd, which marks the resuming of the academic work for the remainder of the year . . .

> . . . Imagine yourself on board a steamer. It is an April afternoon, the sun is just beginning to set; the beautiful rays of light shooting like arrows towards the East and being reflected from far off villages in the mountains enhanced by the beauty of the green meadows of the plain of Esdraeleon. The boat anchors and you go ashore. You see a group of people, most of whom you do not know by face, but no sooner do you set your foot on land than you find yourself embraced by them, each bidding you welcome as lovingly as a father or mother or brother. You are so much impressed by this sight that you not only lose yourself but you do not know what becomes of your baggage. One thing you observe, and that is the willingness of each individual to serve you as much as he can. Thus you start towards the house of Abdul-Baha situated at the foot of Mt. Carmel . . .
>
> You enter a house full of different kinds of flowers – nature is indeed full of joy; birds are singing and humming bees, flying from one flower to another, prepare to go to their hives for a rest. Twilight advances and all things are at peace . . .
>
> Suddenly, a voice is heard. A general hush comes over the pilgrims and 'the Master' enters. He welcomes all and bids them take their seats. He begins to talk and all are eyes and ears. His words strike the right note in each man's life and this you can easily see from the expression of their faces. After an hour or so they are dismissed and the meeting is adjourned. The pilgrims start for the pilgrim's house on the top of Mount Carmel.
>
> Here is an interesting scene: the Hindu, the Zoroastrian, the Jew, the Moslem and the atheist start singing songs of joy, praising BAHA'O'LLAH that, through His Grace, they were enabled to meet on the common-ground of Unity . . .
>
> I spent sixteen glorious days in Haifa. These days have made a deep impression on my mind and I shall never forget them.[46]

'Abdu'l-Bahá was very impressed with the American College. One day He spoke about it, saying:

> The American College at Beirut is carrying on a sacred mission of education and enlightenment and every lover of higher culture and civilization must wish it a great success . . . Years ago I went to

Beirut, and visited the College in its infancy. From that time on I have praised the liberalism of this institution whenever I found an opportunity. Some of the bigoted Mohammedans complained bitterly because the College gives or rather insists upon a religious education, and the students are asked to attend a Sunday service in the Church. They carried their complaints so far as to write articles on this subject in the daily press. I told one of these men that all these talks were based upon ignorant prejudices. I am sure the morals of the students will not be corrupted. They will be informed with the contents of the Old and New Testament. What harm is there in this? A church is house of prayer. Let them enter therein and worship God. What wrong is there in this? These students attending the services in the Church glorify God, their Maker, and not the Devil. I have no doubt that much good will be accomplished, and many misunderstandings will be removed, if the Mussulams [sic] attend the Churches of the Christians with reverence in their hearts and sincerity in their souls, and likewise the Christians may go [to] Mohammedan Mosques and magnify the Creator of The Universe. Is it not revealed in the Holy Scriptures that 'My House shall be called of all nations the House of Prayer? All the houses of different names, – Church, Mosque, Synagogue, Pagoda, Temple are no other than the House of Prayers. What is there in a name? Man must attach his heart to God and not to a building. He must love to hear the Name of God, no matter from what lips . . .[47]

Every day Ahmad Sohrab kept up his diary chronicling the happenings in Haifa and 'Akká and it had not gone unnoticed. One day when 'Abdu'l-Bahá began to speak to a group, Ahmad pulled out his notebook and began to record the talk. 'Abdu'l-Bahá looked at him and

waved his hand laughingly toward me and said: 'Don't write this!' Then he turned his face toward Haji Mirza Heydar Ali and said: 'This Mirza Ahmad has become the 'recorder of my deeds'. As soon as I open my mouth, he takes out his note book. If I make a joke, it will be spread all over Europe. If I smite the face of Abul Gasem, all America will know about it. He writes in his note book that on such and such a day and such and such an hour, Abdul Baha laughed. What can I do with him? O Haji! O Haji! Canst thou not deliver me

> out of his hands? (He laughed heartily.) But I am afraid we cannot send him away, and he will not go away himself. He has become a fixture in Haifa.[48]

Mírzá Aḥmad Sohrab and Shaykh Muḥammad Ḥusayn, both from Nayriz, hosted a feast on 16 April, a mid-day lunch at the Pilgrim House near the Shrine of the Báb. Few were given this privilege. More than 100 men were present to enjoy the pilau, roast meat and sour milk spread on the table. With so many present and only 28 able to sit at the table at one time, they had to eat in four shifts. 'Abdu'l-Bahá ate with the first group then retired to his room in the house of 'Abbás-Qulí. Later, Ahmad was surprised to see 'Abdu'l-Bahá standing on the porch of his Bahá'í Nest. He immediately understood why he'd had such a strong urge to clean up his room and decorate it with fresh flowers that morning. Taking a bundle of letters from His pocket, 'Abdu'l-Bahá then proceeded to dictate Tablets in response. With that done, He lay down on Ahmad's couch and slept for half an hour. When the Master arose, He returned to the Pilgrim House just in time for the afternoon tea, hosted by Mr and Mrs Holbach, who had filled dishes with oranges and cakes which Vakíl, Shírází, Badi Bushrui and Ahmad served.[49]

The Feast of Riḍván was celebrated at a tea at the Pilgrim House given by Mírzá 'Alí-Akbar from Russia. There was a good crowd with men in one room and women in another. A large table, decorated with roses, was covered with oranges, cakes and Persian baklava. No sooner had everyone arrived than 'the wind started its furious howling, and suddenly the sky poured down a storm of hail, making the mountain white'. The storm was torrential but brief, leaving the mountain laced with 'charming cascades of green'. Soon afterward, 'Abdu'l-Bahá arrived in his carriage, exclaiming, 'I had a wonderful ride over the Mountain. It hailed and rained and the wind blew furiously, and I enjoyed it so much!' After the Master had distributed the oranges and candies Himself, the men, together with Emogene Hoagg and Edith Sanderson as the only Westerners – and the only women – walked over to the Shrine of the Báb for prayers.[50]

Two German Bahá'ís, Oscar Niedermayer and Dr Ernest Dietz, arrived in Haifa on 27 April after travelling and teaching for almost two years in Persia. Both had become fluent in Persian and were able to converse with 'Abdu'l-Bahá without an interpreter. Oscar was a 'young man, clean-shaven, alert and most delightful', while Ernest was older with short whiskers and 'many anecdotes to relate for the enjoyment of their listeners'. After their extensive travels, the men were headed to Vienna and Munich.[51]

Hot springs and Tiberias

On 1 May 1914, 'Abdu'l-Bahá boarded the train, along with Mírzá Hádí, Khusraw and Ahmad Sohrab, and headed for the Galilee, a four-hour trip to the east. The Commander of the Army, Zakki Bey, joined the Master at His invitation and they shared a compartment. The train left at 6:05 in the morning, passing through six stations before reaching Al-Hamma (which Sohrab called Alhammeh), where the Commander left the party. The camp was close to the train station and consisted of a tent for 'Abdu'l-Bahá and shelters called *areesheh* for the rest of the party. The areesheh was a bower made of the intertwined branches of the oleander tree complete with their leaves and pink flowers. The floors were covered with Persian carpets and they were much cooler than a tent. The area was populated by Bedouins, and members of the party were warned not to walk too far afield without an escort for fear of robbery, though Ahmad thought the warning exaggerated: 'those I have seen in the camp and with whom I have conversed, are quite gentlemanly and polite. Many people are unnecessarily afraid of the Arab Bedouins; but notwithstanding all their failings, they are a simple good-hearted community.'[52]

The valley near the station contained many hot springs, but only three were used by the public and each was designated for its special cures. One, called Jarab, was for skin diseases and was hot. The second was called Magleh, and was for many other illnesses; it was very hot. The third, called Reeh, was for many illnesses and was lukewarm. Everyone bathed in the nude, but there were separate hours for men and for women. Sohrab noted that 'often one sees fifty to one hundred men enjoying the hot water, naked, unashamed, not knowing what modesty means'. Bathers paid from one to ten cents per day to use the baths.[53] The Magleh spring was surrounded by the ruins of ancient Roman baths of what today is known as Hamat Gader.

Initially, 'Abdu'l-Bahá's party at the hot springs was small and Edith Sanderson, who had arrived on the same day as the Master, was the only Westerner, but day by day more people arrived and within a few days there were as many as 30. In order to have enough milk, every morning four cows were brought into camp and milked by Bedouin women. With the larger party, guards were posted each night to ward off thieves. 'Abdu'l-Bahá would now and then get up between 2 and 5 in the morning and challenge the guards to see if they were awake.[54] Emogene Hoagg, who had joined the group, wrote:

> Only Bedouins to be seen in that section of the country – fine specimens of humanity – very picturesque, and clothed in their native garb, most fascinating. It was truly interesting to see Abdul-Baha walking among them always as a figure apart, distinct. The Bedouins are treacherous and natural thieves. Two men guarded our camp every night, and we were not permitted to walk to the baths without escort. During our stay of 16 days we heard of three robberies and murders very near us.[55]

On 8 May, Commander Zakki Bey returned on the train. When he arrived, the Master 'got hold of his hand, and embraced and kissed him before the eyes of all the wondering spectators. Hand in hand, talking and laughing, they walked toward the tent.' Ahmad Sohrab noted that the Commander was a 'dashing, tall, handsome officer, powerful enough to command and direct the movements of several Turkish regiments' while 'Abdu'l-Bahá was 'old, with white beard, but with youthful energy and power.' He said they were 'two generals, but each one is marshalling different forces.' The next morning, the Commander and the Master had an animated talk over breakfast and took a long walk together.[56]

Not long after 'Abdu'l-Bahá's arrival, the station master gave two rooms in the station building to 'Abdu'l-Bahá and Munírih Khánum. The Master spent His days in His tent, but slept in the rooms at night.[57] The camp kept expanding and soon had up to 50 people. In spite of the increase in tents and areeshehs, the Master enjoyed getting up early in the morning and listening to the melodies of the songbirds, sitting in his chair in front of his areesheh.[58]

On 16 May, 'Abdu'l-Bahá took the train to the Es Samach station, at the southern end of the lake, where He was met by a dozen Zoroastrian Bahá'ís who farmed at 'Adasiyyih, a Bahá'í farming village south of the lake along the Jordan River. 'Abdu'l-Bahá had purchased the 'Adasiyyih area in 1901 when the owners offered to sell 920 hectares.[59]

Twenty horse-riders left the station and passed through fields of barley and wheat on their way to the farms, a fifty-minute ride. 'Abdu'l-Bahá stayed overnight at the farm. The next morning, He talked with the residents, asking them many questions about crops of onions, turnips, cucumbers, beans, tomatoes and potatoes, as well as giving them much advice on how to get better crops.[60]

When the Master's group arrived back at the train station, the Commander was waiting for Him and escorted Him the short distance to the pier where they boarded the steamer *Sharyah*. Hand in hand, the Master and the Commander boarded the ship and steamed across the Sea of Galilee to Tiberias. After an hour's journey, they were in the Hotel Tiberias with all the western conveniences. 'Abdu'l-Bahá was given room 17. That afternoon, the stream of callers commenced. The Mufti of Tiberias, the Governor, a judge and many other officials came to pay their respects.[61]

'Abdu'l-Bahá stayed in Tiberias from 17 May until 15 June. Though far from his normal home, people still searched Him out. On 28 May, retired Turkish General Mostafa Ramzi Pasha, a devoted admirer of the Master, came and spent a few days in His company. The Mufti of Tiberias came every day and begged the Master to stay in his waterfront home so, on 3 June, the Master's party moved into his house.[62]

Ahmad Sohrab was called by 'Abdu'l-Bahá at 3:30 a.m. on 5 June because it was the day He had invited the government officials of Tiberias to spend the day out. Just as the sun rose, the group of 33 departed for Nagaib (Nughayb), a Bahá'í farming community on the eastern side of the Sea of Galilee, on board a motor launch and a larger boat it towed. The guests included Mohammed Ali Bey, the Governor, the Tiberias Director of Finances, a judge, the Mufti, the City Accountant, Zakki Bey and many others, including merchants and other prominent people. After an hour and a quarter, during which the Master spoke, sometimes in Arabic and sometimes in Turkish, about the deeper spiritual significances of the Holy Books, they arrived at Nagaib and were met by the famers from 'Adasiyyih who served breakfast.

'Abdu'l-Bahá spent the morning answering the questions of his guests about laws, divinity and a just society. By the time the lunch of roast meat and chicken was served, there were a hundred people ready to eat. According to custom, most of the people took a nap after lunch. Later tea was served and 'Abdu'l-Bahá regaled His guests with stories of California. After a dinner at 8 p.m., the launch was ready to take the crowd back to Tiberias. The water, unfortunately, had become quite rough and the launch had to anchor a way offshore so, to get the passengers aboard, the boatmen removed some of their clothes and carried the people in their arms. 'Abdu'l Bahá was talking with the Governor when suddenly a tall Arab picked Him up and, to His amazement, quickly waded through the water and deposited Him on the launch. Because of the rough water, it took three hours to return to Tiberias.[63]

On 8 June, Mr E. M. Newman, a well-known American lecturer, arrived in 'Akká hoping to interview the Master. Newman spent several months each year travelling to different countries to gather stories, photographs and movies which he then presented across America. Not finding 'Abdu'l-Bahá in 'Akká, Newman and his party of two men and a woman followed Him to Tiberias. When Newman asked about the purpose of the Bahá'í Faith, 'Abdu'l-Bahá told him:

> The purpose of this Cause is the investigation of Reality and the oneness of all religions. BAHA'O'LLAH accepted fifty years of banishment, persecution and imprisonment for these divine principles. Now, praise be God, His teachings have illumined the horizons of the East, delivered the souls and minds from worthless limitations, elevated the signs of guidance and united the East and the West with a spiritual power.[64]

When Newman departed three days later, 'Abdu'l-Bahá told him and his companions that 'I pray that God may aid your journeys and that you may return to America with the utmost of happiness and safety. May you be confirmed in a great service to the world of humanity. I shall think of you continually . . .'[65]

'Abdu'l-Bahá sat on the balcony of his hotel in Tiberias for two hours on 13 June talking with the mayor, a judge and other town officials. They were all 'exhilarated by his utterances'. Later, when the moon rose over the lake and was reflected from its surface, the Master told the friends about Jesus and His earliest followers:

His Holiness Christ, used to walk most of the nights when in the region of this lake. He was all alone, thinking of the illumination of the world of humanity. He did not rest for one moment. He was not at liberty for even one day. He spent his days as a wanderer, and was shelterless in these deserts and mountains. The place where he called the disciples to enter the Kingdom of God is in this region. They were engaged in fishing. His Holiness Christ, used to walk alone on the shore. When he saw the signs of acceptance in their faces, he said, 'Come, so that I may make you fishers of men,' and they at once left everything and followed that Light personified!

God be exalted! Always in the beginning of the Cause, common souls, who in the estimation of the people, were of no importance whatever, have advanced to the divine Manifestation. For example, these fishermen believed in His Holiness Christ. In the Koran it is revealed that the ignorant of the people would say to His Holiness the Messenger (Mohammed), 'None have followed thee except the most degraded of the people; the learned sages, the nobles and the high class count thee as a fool.' However, it cannot be said of this Cause, for everyone testifies that all of the learned philosophers and nobles of every nation were humble in the presence of the Blessed Beauty, and great numbers of these became believers.[66]

Later that day, Ahmad Sohrab had a dilemma. He had received a letter from Dr Rajab Ali Khan from Persia, who had been with the Master three months before. The letter announced the death of his 14-year-old daughter, which had devastated the doctor, and Ahmad was unsure how to respond. He had kept the news from the Master, but now felt the time had come to tell Him. Suddenly, the door to Ahmad's room burst open and the Master urgently asked, 'What is that letter in thy hand?' When informed of the contents, He said, 'Bring paper and pen and I will dictate something for him,' and He revealed a Tablet to make the doctor's heart rejoice. Later, 'Abdu'l-Bahá returned with many more letters saying, 'Come, come! Mirza Ahmad! Relieve me from this burden!' The Master would take each letter, look at the stamp and the writing, then open it Himself before passing it to Ahmad for translation. They spent the afternoon reading letters from many cities in America and writing replies.[67]

Archie Bell

Archie Bell, a newspaper reporter and editor from Cleveland, Ohio, who described himself as one of the 'wanderers over the face of the earth', went to the Holy Land in 1914 as a spiritual wanderer, not looking for anything in particular but having promised himself that he would not let religious prejudice 'alter what I thought was my open-mindedness'.[68] But one day, he met a man on the beach at Tiberias who strongly affected him.

> One morning as I was walking along the beach of the Sea of Galilee, just beyond Tiberias, thinking of the important events in history that had transpired on those sands, and of the fishermen who had been called from their nets to carry a new gospel to the world about two thousand years ago, I met a man whose appearance was more striking than any man I have ever seen in my life. He was a comparatively short old gentleman with long white beard. He wore a long white robe that reached to his ankles and a white turban covered the top of his head. Doubtless I stared at him in amazement; he was so different from any human being I had ever seen. He was walking slowly, his head slightly bowed, and evidently in deep thought. But he looked up, saw me looking at him, and then raised his hand to his forehead in Oriental salutation as he passed. I was alone, and, believing him to be some personage of Tiberias, I admit walking slowly behind him until we reached the city, and, as I conveniently met a dragoman, I inquired as to the identity of the old gentleman who attracted me. 'That's Abbas Effendi,' he replied, 'Abdul Baha.'
>
> . . . He is a person of tremendous magnetism. One 'feels' him when in his presence. Irrespective of his religious teachings, the wise men of the earth, who have met him, have considered him one of the wisest who lives.[69]

Archie greatly wanted to meet this magnetic person, but was told that He only spoke Persian. The language problem was solved when he encountered one of 'Abdu'l-Bahá's interpreters, 'a Persian gentleman who had been for ten years attached to the Persian legation at Washington'. Archie was immediately taken to meet the man he had begun to think of as a 'prophet'. That first visit was very brief, but he arranged for another that afternoon. Of the afternoon's visit, Archie wrote: 'Together we walked slowly along the sands and together we sat on his little balcony near sunset and I heard of that great new religion which is to reconcile the whole world.' From the Master, he learned the history of the Bahá'í Faith and its principles. From the Master's followers, he heard many things that weren't particularly accurate, such as that there were 'three and four millions [of believers] in Persia' and 'fifty thousand converts to the Bahai Movement in America'.[70]

Between his interviews, Archie had lengthy talks with Ahmad Sohrab, whom he described as 'the brilliant young Persian who is devoted to the head of the Bahaists and spends his entire life in his company' and was intent on writing down everything that 'Abdu'l-Bahá said.[71]

Archie was amazed at the stamina and energy 'Abdu'l-Bahá displayed:

> His life as a prisoner might have left him a physical wreck, but instead of that he seems to have undergone an almost superhuman recuperation. He rises early in the morning, receives visitors of all nationalities and creeds during the day, often attends the services of the Jews in the synagogues, goes to prayer with the Moslems in their mosques, and attends Christian churches. He carries on a correspondence with his followers in all parts of the world, and directs any number of momentous affairs; but his secretary tells me that after the affairs of his busy day are over he will often call him, assure him that he is not weary, and will either read, dictate or talk until far into the hours of the night. He knows not fatigue, but attendance upon him often wearies the younger men, who carefully record his sayings and habits, day and night.[72]

Visiting 'Abdu'l-Bahá in His house overlooking the Sea of Galilee, Archie was greeted with a cup of tea. Knowing that Archie was an American and probably more a coffee drinker, 'Abdu'l-Bahá asked: '"Perhaps you do not like tea," he said, "but this is Persian tea and there is a difference. I assure you that this is worth drinking."' Then:

> 'Why,' he asked, 'why is it that you come to see me? You say you write for American readers. People of the world care to hear more about the successful and beloved men of the world, so why do you

not speak to them? I am an outcast among men, for I have been until now a political prisoner - and I am the son of a prisoner.'[73]

'Abdu'l-Bahá then explained the unity of all religions:

> There may be a light in a room, but it merely sheds light in that room . . . There may be many lights, with coloured bulbs of various hues and shades. But the source of all those lights is the same – and there must be sources; it is the dynamo that is hidden from sight. So it is with all the religions. They sparkle here and there in various colours – but there is but one source for them all, just one Light, and that is God. Self-seeking preachers and teachers have wandered far from that Real Light. And it is the Light that we now seek in the real truth. Men have wandered far from the teachings of Christ, Buddha, the Jewish prophets and all of the others. Ours is not a new religion. It is the very old one; we desire to unite all forms in their original purity.[74]

After his last visit, Archie summarized his understandings:

> And that, in a nutshell, was what I gained from my interviews with Abbas Effendi himself. He believes that Christ taught 'love thy neighbour as thyself'. He believes that Mohammedans, Jews, Buddhists and Zoroastrians were taught the same thing, and that not one of them is doing as they were taught. Thus he would become the great 'renovator' or conciliator. He would bring all men together in a spirit of brotherly love – and he would raise the status of women – particularly in the East, so that they might have an equal standing with males. And as Queen Victoria wrote to his father in 1869, 'If this is of God, it will stand; and if not, there is no harm done.[75]

Return to Haifa

On 15 June, after six weeks away, 'Abdu'l-Bahá returned to Haifa. At noon, He waved goodbye to many of Tiberias's prominent citizens as He boarded the steamer that would carry Him to the train station at the south end of the lake. On the train, there were several military officers in His stateroom and, when they learned with whom they were travelling, 'they showed him the greatest consideration all the way through'.[76] The travellers were met in Haifa by three of the Master's sons-in-law and Isfandíyár, His carriage driver. Back in His own home, 'Abdu'l-Bahá said,

> I went to Tiberias, but I stayed there longer than I expected. Tiberias is situated in an out-of-the-way place. It is a place of seclusion and contemplation. There is no noise of men or the uproar of industry. It is as though one lived in a remote desert, far away from the haunts of men. It is a spot hallowed with the presence of His Holiness Christ . . . Often he walked around the shore of the Sea of Galilee, and as He walked, taught His disciples. As I walked on the shore, those immortal deeds were brought back to my memory.[77]

1914: JULY–DECEMBER

Start of the War

On 28 June, Archduke Franz Ferdinand and his wife, of Austria, were assassinated in Sarajevo. Though the World War didn't officially start until a month later when Austro-Hungarian troops invaded Serbia and Germany declared war on Russia, 'Abdu'l-Bahá sent all the pilgrims home on the 29th. An article in *Star of the West*, entitled 'Abdul-Bahá dismisses all pilgrims', said:

> The 29th day of June, 1914, was a day of great sorrow in Haifa because Abdul-Baha dismissed all of the pilgrims and bade them return to their countries. In the morning he spoke to the visitors from Ishkabad, Turkestan, Russia: 'Ishkabad is now a good center. In the past, Merv was the center of Khorassan, which is such a vast country including the provinces of Afghanistan, Sistan and Belkh. Ishkabad also is near Merv. The Blessed Beauty often spoke of Khorassan in the tablets, saying that from this country would arise the first mention of God, which amazed the people. When Ishkabad came into existence and the Mashrekol-azkar was built, the hope of the Blessed Beauty became manifest and this, the first temple of the Bahai world, has become a shelter and refuge to the friends of God. They are drawn hither from all directions and when in difficulties they go to Ishkabad. The friends made a tremendous effort to build this great edifice, they strove with heart and soul. At first it seemed impossible of accomplishment, but, thanks be to God, they were confirmed and assisted. Now, through this inspiration, the friends in all places are planning to build likewise, when it is possible. By founding the Mashrekol-azkar in the world the wonderful signs of God become manifest and evident. One must be built in every place, even though it be only a house or one rented room, if necessary, under the earth . . .'
>
> In the afternoon, Abdul-Baha gave the following talk:
>
> 'This is the day of farewell and the time of leave-taking is very

> hard. The Arabian poet says, "The days of my union with the beloved were so few that the greeting was the farewell." Indeed, I am deeply grieved, but I do not say good-bye to you because there is a complete connection among the hearts, and among the souls there is unity and agreement. We never have a separation from one another. This nearness and remoteness concerns the world of bodies. In the world of spirits and souls there is union, never separation. The heart feels the union. The eye sees and carries the sight to the heart which becomes affected. When the heart is engaged with the friends there is no separation, especially if you go in service to the Cause of God.'[1]

Pilgrims were not the only ones leaving; some of the resident Bahá'ís also had to depart. 'Abdu'l-Bahá sent Mírzá 'Alí-Akbar-i-Nakhjavání and Mírzá Maḥmúd-i-Zarqání, who had travelled with Him on His tour of America, to the Caucasus and India, respectively. Emogene Hoagg was directed to Italy.[2]

On 28 June, the German battleship *Goeben* arrived at Haifa for a short stop. The following day, Admiral Wilhelm Souchon[3] and his officers were entertained by the Persian Consul at dinner in the village of Nahr. After eating, the Consul, along with the mayor of 'Akká and a group of Turkish officers and politicians, went to Bahjí at 'Abdu'l-Bahá's invitation for tea. Afterwards, the Admiral and 40 of his officers visited the Shrine of Bahá'u'lláh, which was the primary reason the Admiral had come ashore. They approached the Holy Threshold with 'the utmost respect' and prayed. Afterwards, the Admiral said that he 'had been in many sacred places, but had never encountered one so filled with spirituality, or that had such a wonderfully beautiful site.' Before they left Bahjí, they were served tea and cake, then visited the Garden of Riḍván, where a military band played for them. Leaving the Garden, they sailed that night.[4]

A walker is surprised

Though the Bahá'ís and pilgrims quickly departed, others continued to come. On 30 June, a young German from Stuttgart, Hans Springer, arrived. The 23-year-old was walking around the world promoting the Esperanto language and had already walked 35,000 kilometres. He liked to adopt the clothing of whatever country he was in and Ahmad Sohrab wrote that he was 'today an Arabian gentleman, but his blue eyes, white skin and brown vandyke beard heralded from afar off his European origin. He spoke German, Italian and Esperanto but I could not speak with him in any of those languages. Finding that he understood a little French, we struck on that.' Ahmad recorded the conversation between 'Abdu'l Bahá and His visitor:

A.B. 'What is the object of thy world tour?'

H.S. 'First to spread the knowledge of Esperanto because I believe it will help to unify mankind. Second, to see the world . . .'

A.B. 'Dost thou travel always on the surface of the earth? Would it not be excellent if thou couldst take a trip toward heaven?'

H.S. 'Heaven! I have never heard of anyone going to heaven. This is impossible.'

A.B. (smiling). 'Why impossible? Did not Elijah go to heaven, and did not Christ ascend to heaven after his crucifixion and burial?'

H.S. (puzzled). 'I am neither Elijah nor Christ. I have not two wings to fly with. It seems to me there must needs be a pair of wings.'

A.B. 'Everything is possible. Christ says: "Be ye therefore perfect even as your Father which is in heaven is perfect." Thou canst have the pair of wings. One is the love of God and the other is renunciation of aught else save him'.

H.S. 'Then you do not mean this phenomenal heaven?'

A.B. 'I mean the heaven from which Christ descended – the heaven of the divine will, the heaven of spirituality.'

H.S. 'How can one ascend to that heaven? Is it not most difficult?'

A.B. 'It is no more difficult than touring the world on foot. When the spirit of the teachings of Christ takes possession of the heart and suffers man to become a servant of the world of humanity, then it will be very easy for him to ascend to heaven.'

H.S. 'But in this age the Christians have forgotten the commandments of Christ.'

A.B. 'What has thou to do with others? Live thou according to the teachings of Christ.'

H.S. 'You are right. I will do my best.'

A.B. 'Whom dost thou think Christ was?'

H.S. 'I believe he was a great philosopher.'

A.B. 'Oh no! He was much greater than a philosopher. He was the Word of God, the Spirit of God.'

H.S. 'Whew! There are too many scholars in Europe who do not believe that there was ever such a person as Christ. On the other hand there is an increasing host of people whose faith in Christianity is shaken because the ministers of the Gospel do not live in accord with the behests of their Master. They have become worldlings wrapped up in traditions and dogmas. When I was in Jerusalem, I observed that the Christians have divided the Church of the Resurrection into many sections, like a bazaar, and they are always engaged in acrimonious controversies and factional fights, while they claim Christ brought peace and salvation. Where can one find peace, and how can one be saved? Through their religious hatred for each other they have shut the door of salvation.'

A.B. 'What thou sayest is true. But we are not looking at the present conditions. Let us look at the glorious life of Christ and those sanctified souls who came after him. Did they not embody in their deeds the ideals of their words? There have appeared many philosophers in the world, but they are all forgotten. But because Christ was the Spirit and Word of God, he and his disciples through him, became the fountains of the water of life. Now I hope that like unto them thou wilt be the means of the illumination of the world of humanity and serve God.'

H.S. 'Serve God? There is no one in this world who can serve God, because we are not able to see Him. He is above our human ken. In my mind the only way we can serve Him is to serve mankind and try to alleviate the sorrows and sufferings of the people.'

A.B. 'Christ served God and his apostles served God. Their service was to humanity, which was a reflection of their service to God.'

H.S. 'What are you doing?'

A.B. 'I am serving God. I am the servant of God. I give sight to the blind, hearing to the deaf, the power of speech to the mute, and knowledge to the ignorant. I raise the dead, deliver those who are in darkness and guide them into the realm of light. I make the poor rich, and the weak powerful. I satisfy the hungry ones with the Bread of Life and allay the thirst of the thirsty ones with the pure water of Immortality. This is my work.'

H.S. 'When I was in Stuttgart I attended an Esperanto meeting addressed by Abdul-Baha. Does Abbas Effendi know him? He is a wise man and is in great sympathy with the Esperanto language. He had many followers in Stuttgart. His religion is called Bahai.'

(The translator here informed Hans Springer that he is speaking with Abdul-Baha; that he is in his presence. Immediately he became more respectful and expressed great joy and happiness.)

H.S. 'Is it possible that I am in the presence of Abdul-Baha?'

(Taking in his hand the last book of tablets to correct, Abdul-Baha became silent. After a few minutes, conversation started again.)

A.B. 'Even a bird can fly around the world. It is not a difficult accomplishment. Therefore, become thou a royal bird of the kingdom, and like unto an angel soar toward the heavenly worlds. I can assure thee that the experiences will be more than marvelous.'

H.S. 'I hope to get a pair of strong wings to accomplish this difficult task.'

A.B. 'I pray that when thou goest to Nazareth, the place of Christ's nativity, the Spirit of God may descend upon thee and wings of light be granted thee, so that thou mayest soar in the immensity of God's space and behold the wonders of His creation.'

H.S. 'I will also pray for this.'[5]

With the interview concluded, 'Abdu'l-Bahá shared tea and cake with His visitor. Then He shelled a bowl of pistachios and gave them to Springer. When Springer left, the Master gave him a coin, and wished him success in his adventure. The leftover cake and the pistachios were put in a bag and given to him for his lunch.

On 5 July, Ahmad Sohrab found himself trapped by the customs of the day. 'Abdu'l-Bahá had ordered him to come to 'Akká in His carriage, which Ahmad thought to be a wonderful privilege. But when he boarded, he found himself sitting across from the Greatest Holy Leaf and the Holy Mother (Munírih Khánum) – and he had never before shared a carriage with any Persian women, much less these two illustrious souls. In normal circumstances, he would have debarked and taken the train, but that was not possible so he awkwardly sat beside Mírzá Munír. After a while, Ahmad very much wished to ask the ladies about their early time in 'Akká, but protocol dictated that he could not speak directly to them. To solve this dilemma, he whispered his question to Mírzá Munír who, as a member of the family, could speak directly to the women. Thus Ahmad had his wish fulfilled.[6]

A theologian

Very few people, enemies included, failed to be impressed when they met 'Abdu'l-Bahá, but not all were convinced by His arguments. Dr Joseph Kruszynski called on 'Abdu'l-Bahá on 14 July. Years later, in 1934, when he was interviewed by Martha Root, Dr Kruszynski was the President of the Roman Catholic Theological University at Lublin

University in Poland. A Russian doctor had told him about 'Abdu'l-Bahá so he decided to see who this 'world-renowned spiritual teacher' was.

> 'I went at eleven o'clock in the morning to visit him . . . He received me so courteously and with such friendliness. He led me to His drawing room and had me sit at His right beside Him on the divan . . .'
>
> The President explained to me [Martha Root] that with them, that morning, was a secretary who was also an interpreter, but they did not have him interpret as both the Catholic and 'Abdu'l-Bahá knew Arabic. 'And 'Abdu'l-Bahá knew Persian and Arabic extremely well; I was impressed by His command of these languages,' said the President, 'and He always used the intimate word "thou" in addressing me, it was very pleasant.'
>
> First they spoke of Poland and Polish writers, and the Catholic said He was astonished that this Persian scholar knew so much about the history and sufferings of the Poles and that He had read their literature . . .
>
> Dr. Kruszynski asked 'Abdu'l-Bahá what He thought of the condition in Europe and the latter replied: 'There will be a great war in all Europe and after the war, Poland, thy Fatherland shall be free!'
>
> These remarks about political, national affairs and about writers only were the introduction to the real topic of the visit which was religion. 'I asked 'Abdu'l-Bahá', said Dr. Kruszynski, 'what is Baháism? And He told me that it is a religion of brotherhood. He explained to me about a Mashriqu'l-Adhkár, a great Bahá'í temple which is being built near Chicago, and He gave me a picture of it . . .'
>
> The President told me how 'Abdu'l-Bahá served them Persian tea and then . . . they visited His beautiful garden, and later they went to 'Akká to see the Prison where Bahá'u'lláh, His Father, had been incarcerated, and they went last to Bahjí, just out from 'Akká to visit the Tomb of Bahá'u'lláh . . .
>
> We spoke of religion, of Roman Catholicism and the Bahá'í Movement. 'What do you, a Roman Catholic scholar, think of the Teachings of Bahá'u'lláh?', I [Martha] asked, and he replied: 'Bahá'u'lláh as a reformer of religion and as a philosopher is very

great. From my viewpoint as a Catholic, I can say that I like this Bahá'í concept of religion because it is a religion of brotherhood . . .'

'I asked 'Abdu'l-Bahá, "who is Christ?" and He answered that Christ was only one of the great Prophets, World Teachers, that Moses was a great Prophet but that Jesus Christ was greater than Moses and came to make the world better than it was at the time of the Jews. He said that Muhammad came to make the people better and now in our time all these religions are not sufficient, and Bahá'u'lláh came . . . to make better the Muhammadan religion, the Christian religion, the Jewish religion, all the religions. 'Abdu'l-Bahá also said that Bahá'u'lláh's religion was better for this epoch than Christianity and Muhammadism.'

'I told Him', continued Dr. Kruszynski, 'that the correction of His Father is very great, but only for the Muhammadan religion, because the Muhammadan religion is an exclusive one, but His Father had made religion less exclusive and more a religion of brotherhood. However, in the Christian religion, we believe in a revealed religion; we believe the Bible is a Revelation direct from God and that Jesus Christ is God and man in one, and this cannot be changed. I know that among the Christian believers are abuses, faults, but the idea of our religion is correct. And 'Abdu'l-Bahá considered that the religion of His Father, Bahá'u'lláh, is the last and best religion.' 'So between our viewpoints,' the President concluded, 'there was just this difference, that I cannot think that Bahaism is the last and best religion . . . The relation of Bahá'u'lláh to Moses and Muhammad I think is correct, but the relation to Christ is not correct.'

Again Dr. Kruszynski said: 'I believe the Teachings of Bahá'u'lláh are the Teachings of a very great philosopher. I consider that Bahá'u'lláh has been the greatest philosopher in our times. He has given the world a system uniting religious beliefs with social foundations. I remember one sentence I said to 'Abdu'l-Bahá, I believe your reformation is very great, very good for Muhammadans because they are intolerant, very exclusive, they will not participate in or associate with other religionists; Christians are more tolerant . . .'[7]

Even though visitors still came, the war was always in the forefront. In late July, 'Abdu'l-Bahá met with the German Consul and other

Germans. They were adamant that the war was a necessary thing. The Master talked of the power of love and peace, but the men, though silenced in their arguments, remained unconvinced and strongly in favour of the coming conflict.[8]

Ameen Fareed openly shows his defiance

By July, Dr Ameen Fareed, who had been with ‘Abdu’l-Bahá in Europe and America, was travelling through Europe in open defiance of ‘Abdu’l-Bahá’s orders not to. Fareed was contacting Bahá’í communities and having them set up meetings at which he could speak. During the meetings, he would solicit funds, ostensibly for the Faith, but actually for himself. The hall in London where ‘Abdu’l-Bahá had spoken the previous year, had been booked for Fareed, but Dr Lotfu’lláh Hakím managed to prevent him from speaking there. ‘Abdu’l-Bahá described Fareed’s nefarious activities:

> One of the things that Dr Fareed has circulated in London is that I have grown old and weak, and that my physical forces are on the wane, consequently some people have gained ascendancy over my mind and caused me to issue ‘these commands.’ My Power consists of the Bestowals of the Blessed Beauty. They are all spiritual Favors given to me by Bahá’u’lláh. From early morning until now (4⁰⁰ P.M.) I have been reading and writing and I am feeling exceedingly well. Young people like you can only work three or four hours without ceasing.[9]

Ḥájí Mírzá Ḥaydar-‘Alí, upon hearing of Covenant-breaking activity in London, had thrown himself at the Master’s feet and begged to be sent there in spite of his 88 years.[10] Instead, ‘Abdu’l-Bahá sent Emogene Hoagg, along with a brother of Munírih Khánum, to Britain:

> They were to explain to the English friends that Dr. Aminu’llah Farid [Ameen Fareed] had been cut off from the Faith and was not to be allowed to hold further meetings. This man, who had been in the entourage all through the American tour as translator, had displayed ‘erratic and damaging behavior . . . soliciting of money’ against ‘Abdu’l-Bahá’s commands, estranging seekers and believers

> alike from the Cause. Now, he had gone to London without permission to become a leader there.[11]

'Abdu'l-Bahá also sent Americans Mason Remey and George Latimer to teach the Faith and to counter Fareed's activities. In addition, He sent Dr Habíb Mu'ayyad (Habíbu'lláh Khudábakhsh) and 'Azízu'lláh Bahádur to Europe to assist them. Dr Mu'ayyad had only just finished his studies at the American University in Beirut a few weeks before and 'Azízu'lláh Bahádur still had a year of studies to go.[12]

On 31 July, writing from Leipzig, Mason Remey shared a Tablet from the Master to Alma Knobloch: 'Doctor Fareed, his mother and his relatives intend to make a journey to those parts. These people are violators of the Covenant and in the utmost rebellion. Beware, beware lest anyone associates with them. Association with them is poison. Warn all the friends.'[13] A few days later in another letter from Stuttgart, Mason wrote:

> we learned of the presence in the city of Dr. Habilbollah [sic] and Mirza Azizollah Bahadur – Persian Bahá'ís whom Abdul Baha had sent to Europe on a spiritual mission . . . here in Stuttgart on their way to London in order to strengthen the English friends against the present activities of the violators of the Covenant and the enemies of the Cause of God. Abdul Baha also has sent to London Mirza Assad'o'llah, the father of Fareed, and also Mirza Yahah – the maternal uncle of Fareed, to argue with him and to strengthen the friends against his pernicious influence. The instructions given to the two brothers here was to remain in Stuttgart for one week, but now they are obliged to remain indefinitely as all foreign travel is cut off.[14]

It is quite ironic that Mason Remey was so strongly warning people against Covenant-breakers when his own path, much later, would lie in the same direction.

Dr Ḥabíb Mu'ayyad and 'Azízu'lláh Bahádur were still in Stuttgart when the war started and 'Abdu'l-Bahá told all four men to come to Haifa,[15] which they reached after 'six months of exciting travel'.[16]

Edward and Lua Getsinger

The war affected people in many places, including the Germans in Haifa and the Getsingers in India. Lua and Edward Getsinger had been teaching the Faith in India for a year. When Lua became very ill in Bombay, the American Consul recommended that they leave India because of the German origin of their name – Getsinger. Edward left first and returned to America with a short stopover in Haifa.[17] He arrived in Haifa on 3 August 1914 and was strongly affected by the oppression of the Turkish authorities. In an article he wrote afterwards, he reported that there was general conscription to the army and that there was no compensation to families who were left without a bread-winner. This meant that shops and farms were devoid of men. With no men on the farms and the government confiscating 80% of all food-stuffs, food prices had doubled. Thousands of sheep were taken and the owners paid nothing.[18] Horses and wagons were also confiscated, though 'Abdu'l-Bahá kept his beautiful Arabian horse.[19] Edward noted that when one merchant complained to the commanding officer that soldiers had taken 300 bags of rice from his shop, the officer threw the merchant into prison. Edward continued his journey to America on 24 August.

The day Edward arrived in Haifa, the Turkish government had issued an imperial 'Irade' (decree) stating that all Turkish male citizens between 18 and 45 had to register for the army. This threw the area into a panic because there was no escape unless someone was a Christian or a Jew; these were able to buy their way out of the army for $250. In reality, since almost no one could afford such a price, all were liable to be drafted. The towns and villages were virtually deserted and that led to an increase in Bedouin banditry. 'Akká, however, swarmed with thousands of new soldiers who had to be fed, and everyone was expected to contribute food or money for their care.

'Abdu'l-Bahá addressed this chaos:

> The world is topsy-turvy! The wrong side of human character is up! A tremendous conflict is at hand. The world is at the threshold of a most tragic struggle . . .
>
> While in America I spoke before many Peace Societies, Churches and Conventions, and foretold the fearful consequences of armed

peace in Europe. I said 'Europe is like unto an Arsenal and one tiny spark will cause a universal combustion. O Men! Come ye together and as far as possible try to extinguish this world-raging fire' . . . I found no one to listen to my advice . . .

If we reflect carefully we observe that, since history has been written and the deeds of mankind recorded and preserved, no one can point out a single instance that Peace, Love and Amity have been ruinous and harmful in their result. They have filled the world with joy and radiance and happiness . . .[20]

While the soldiers trained and the Ottoman government stole everything it could from its own citizens, 'Abdu'l-Bahá continued to deal with the problems of people in every part of the world. Ahmad Sorab described the flood of letters the Master received:

Touching the human plane, the range of personal wishes and individual aspirations is as infinite as the mind of man is able to conceive! Aside from the more legitimate desires of men for happiness, comfort, success, usefulness in life, etc. with which the letters teem eloquently, now and then comes the record of the most interesting desires. Here is a letter from an expectant mother. She asks for a name for her yet unborn child; another person desires to move from her present apartment, and she would like to know whether Abdul Baha approves of it; a young man has quarrelled with his sweetheart, and he wonders whether the Master's spiritual power is strong enough to bring about the much-longed-for reconciliation; unexpected events have estranged a man and wife, and false pride has separated them; he is repining, in loneliness. Will not the Beloved bring back into their lives the sweet harmony of the first few months of their ideal courtship and the first few years of their blissful, happy married life? A man has invented a transatlantic airship; will not Abdul Baha inspire the heart of a capitalist to assist him financially in the construction of this air-craft, and thus demonstrate to the world that the science of aviation has been made practical. Another person desires to build a house; will not the Master introduce him to a rich somebody? A woman has been ridiculed and abused by her enemies; should she not carry the case to the Court? A man is tormented by the animal magnetism of his foes; will Abdul Baha be kind enough to stop them from this fiendish work? A woman cables whether she should be operated upon; will the Master advise her what to do? . . . Amongst other interesting things are the children's letters, so full of affectionate simplicity, sweetness, directness and beautiful trust.[21]

Mason Remey and George Latimer

When 'Abdu'l-Bahá recalled Mason Remey and George Latimer from their efforts to educate European Bahá'ís about Dr Fareed, it wasn't easy for them to return to Haifa. Both the United States consular agent and their travel agent tried to discourage them from going into Turkish territory, but 'Abdu'l-Bahá had told them to come, so they took the first available steamer. Mason and George were travelling with Dr Habíb Mu'ayyad and 'Azízu'lláh Bahádur, so they attracted quite a bit of attention. The British were also worried that Westerners might be trying to stir up trouble with the local people, so the group were carefully watched by a pair of British officers.[22]

They reached Haifa on 4 October. George described their arrival:

> . . . as we rounded the reef we beheld the Blessed Tomb of the Báb. At this moment the Sun broke through the clouds, just before setting, and its rays fell upon the Great Prison across the bay, lighting up that wonderful place in a dazzling manner, just as when the rays of the sun strike upon a mirror. Shortly afterwards the moon, in all its splendor and fullness, arose directly over the city of Acca . . . And wonder upon wonders our ship headed straight for the spot and dropped anchor at Acca, something unheard of in these days . . . the boatmen who arrived at the ship told us that 'Effendi' (the Master) was in Acca.[23]

Mason described their arrival differently: 'Upon our arrival in Haifa we found that the troubled condition of the land had not been exaggerated. The mobilizations of the army had been on for some time. All the foreign post offices were closed; the banks were also shut; consequently business was almost at a standstill, and the mass of the people were under the spell of war panic.'[24]

This panic was widespread, as was shown on 18 October when a group of Muslims and the Spanish Consul and his family wanted to meet 'Abdu'l-Bahá to ask for advice. The Master sent His carriage for the Muslim group, but they were so long in coming that He had to rent another carriage for the Spanish Consul. Afterwards, He said:

> These people who called on us today were in a state of fright. They are expecting daily the bombardment of Haifa by foreign warships. As soon as they see a little moving speck in the horizon of the sea, they look through their glasses, anxiously scanning to see whether these are the expected cruisers. Their hearts are in a state of anxiety. They are terror-stricken. They have no peace of mind. This is one of the signs of absence of faith. It is stated in the Koran: 'They imagine every cry raised is an enemy unto them.' For example, when a thief enters a house, the least noise causes his flight. He trembles and quakes.[25]

The awaited bombardment and destruction of Haifa never happened, though a ship did fire a few rounds at the railway bridges between Haifa and 'Akká the next year. On 24 August, two British warships sailed into the harbour and anchored. This further spooked the populace into believing that the feared bombardment was about to start. But the captains of the ships only spent an hour in conversation with the British Consul, then sailed away.[26]

Mason wrote that 'In the midst of all the unrest and confusion we found Abdul-Baha serene, calm and peaceful.' And because 'Abdu'l-Bahá was calm, His followers and those closely associated with Him were calm, at least relatively so. 'Abdu'l-Bahá had sent many of the Bahá'í families up into the mountains east of Bahjí for safety and was there seeing to their needs when the two Americans landed in Haifa so they had to wait for His return.[27]

Arriving in Haifa, Mason and George went to the house of the Master where they were served 'our first Persian tea' by Bashír, 'Abdu'l-Bahá's dedicated gardener. Refreshed, they continued up the hill, pausing at the Bahá'í Traveller's house (the Eastern Pilgrim House) for another cup of tea with Ḥájí Mírzá Ḥaydar-'Alí, and then went on to the Tomb of the Báb where they encountered twenty Bahá'í students from Beirut, who made them more tea.[28] They were enchanted by the great panorama spread out below them.

> The Tomb about half way up on the side of Mt. Carmel commands a magnificent view of the town of Haifa, the bay, and the Prison of Acca across in the distance. The front of the Tomb is on an axis with the main street of the German Colony, many feet below. The white houses, with their red roofs, the tall and stately cypress trees, the blue bay, dotted with sail boats, with the Valley of Sharon and the Lebanon foothills in the distance, forms a setting well qualified for the great and powerful drama of God . . .[29]

When Mason and George arrived in Haifa, 'Abdu'l-Bahá was away and it wasn't until 6 October that He returned. He then spent most of the next two weeks living with 'Abbás-Qulí in his house near the Shrine of the Báb. George and Mason were at the Shrine with the students when 'Abdu'l-Bahá returned. 'Suddenly, shortly after ten o'clock, someone cried out: "The Master has come" and we all rushed to the edge of the walk and far down below we saw a carriage drive up to the door of the Master's House and the figure of the Beloved became discernible, without use of field-glass, as He alighted and walked slowly through the garden and up the steps to the door.' The students became very excited and began singing 'Joy to the world, the Lord has come.'[30]

Soon word came for George and Mason to come to the Master's house. They arrived to find the students already lined up on both sides of the garden walk as they were ushered into the house. The Master greeted them warmly, saying how young Mason looked, then spoke of the war they had barely escaped, saying 'how the Bahá'ís in Germany were at peace with the Bahá'ís in France while their brothers were fighting against each other.' Mason then presented 'Abdu'l-Bahá with copies of a new edition of Mírzá Abu'l-Faḍl's *Bahá'í Proofs* and a bound volume of *Star of the West*. Upon opening the former and seeing Mírzá Abu'l-Faḍl's photograph, He gazed at it a long time and said, 'If you had brought me the whole world, you could not have brought me a better gift than this.'[31] Mírzá Abu'l-Faḍl had passed into the Abhá Kingdom less than nine months before.

On 7 October, George watched with fascination as 'Abdu'l-Bahá went about His normal life. The Master was sitting in the 'shade near the gate correcting Tablets . . . A man came to sell Him fish, others had questions, the keeper of the Pilgrim House, Aga Mohammed Hasan, rode down on his donkey and stopped to ask the Master some questions about the daily marketing.' At one point, 'Abdu'l-Bahá walked through His garden and brought Mason a flower saying in English, 'Yellow', then He gave George a lily. George wrote that it was a 'wonderful, heavenly picture to see Him walking thru His garden, stopping here and there to pluck out some weed or to straighten some branch.'[32]

'Abdu'l-Bahá's sense of humour was always present. One day, George tried to sneak a few photos of the Master, whereupon 'Abdu'l-Bahá marched up to him and pulling his ear and slapping him gently twice on the cheek, said 'You want to steal my picture.'[33]

On the night of 7/8 October, 'Abdu'l-Bahá's gardener Bashír was shot in the leg. With the war, Haifa was not a safe town, so there were always two guards at the Master's house at night. Apparently, Bashír had approached the house about midnight and didn't respond to the guard's challenge. The guard, thinking him to be a thief, fired. Bashír passed away the next night in the Master's house. Shortly before his death, 'Abdu'l-Bahá had gone to see him and, finding him unconscious, opened his eyelids for several minutes until Bashír awoke and said 'Alláh-u-Abhá.' The Master responded with the same and after looking at him for some time left and said, 'It is God's Will.' Bashír had been part of the Master's household since he had been a child.[34]

'Abdu'l-Bahá took the opportunity to talk about life and death:

> The length or shortness of life is not considered important. Whether a man lives a few years or a hundred years, the purpose of his life is to achieve some definite results. If the tree of his life does not yield those luscious fruits, the purpose of his existence has not been accomplished, even if he has lived many, many years. But if he has lived only a few years and the tree of his life has attained to fruition, he has obtained spiritual success. Consequently the duration of life is a conditional matter, subject to the Will of God.[35]

On 14 October, George commented to 'Abdu'l-Bahá about how beautiful His garden was. 'Of course it is beautiful,' replied the Master. 'Carmel is a derivative of two words, "Carm" and "El." Carm means garden and El means God. Therefore it is the Garden of God.'[36]

Two days later, George and Mason went up to Ahmad Sohrab's little house, his 'Bahá'í Nest', near the Shrine, where several secretaries were translating letters and Tablets. George wryly commented, 'The chief occupation of the morning was the starting of a garden in front of the Nest, in which everyone offered their services as overseer and consequently little was done. About eleven the Master rode by on his donkey on his way to the mosque.'[37]

Shoghi Effendi, who had spent a lot of time with the Americans, came up to the Bahá'í Nest on 17 October and presented each of them with a silk handkerchief from the Greatest Holy Leaf and a small photograph of the Master. Shoghi Effendi was to leave that day to return to Beirut, but before he left, the group had a large feast on the veranda of the Bahá'í Nest. Present were George, Mason, Shoghi Effendi, Ḥájí Mírzá Ḥaydar-'Alí, Ḥasan Effendi, Ḥusayn Afnán, Badi Bushrui, Habíbu'lláh Mu'ayyad (Khudábakhsh), and Ahmad Sohrab. George wrote: 'We sat down, some in Persian fashion, some in Turkish fashion and some in any old fashion . . . [to] a Turkish dish called U-Moustali, round loaves of bread twice as large as a plate and large Damascus grapes' while looking over the view of Haifa and the bay. Later that day, when 'Abdu'l-Bahá was with Ahmad Sohrab, the Master asked him with a 'mischievous smile': 'I have heard that you have had a feast today. Why did you not invite me? I shall bring a suit against you in the court.'[38]

George and Mason were ushered into the Master's presence on the evening of 18 October. George wrote:

> He was seated in one corner of the room on a chair. There was a lamp burning on the table and the couch was covered with Tablets and manuscripts. He greeted us most heartily, with that wonderful smile that fills one with new life and energy. After greeting us with 'Marhaba, How are you? Are you well? Are you happy?' He said to me: 'You are always smiling.' I replied that people said that it was my best asset and He replied: 'It is a good asset.'[39]

Then He 'gave us an inspiring talk' and said, 'Now I desire to send you back to the United States . . . May you be confirmed and assisted and may you raise such a melody and sing such a song as to stir and move the hearts of the American people. I anticipate to receive glad-news from you.' The two descended the mountain that night with mixed feelings of sadness and happiness. Sadness because their pilgrimage was about to end, but 'joy and eagerness to be off on our new mission'.[40]

Their last day was 19 October and they walked up to the Bahá'í Nest where they found Ahmad Sohrab 'hard at work – physical work in his future garden pruning some of his surplus avoirdupois. Badi was busy transcribing Tablets and only Dr Habíbu'lláh was leading the life of a dervish – the life of ease and indolence, presumably acquired from his sojourn in Europe.' The two Americans had their last interview with 'Abdu'l-Bahá at 3:45. They found Him 'sitting in one corner of the room busily engaged in writing Tablets. He wore glasses and his whole aspect was that of an active and wealthy man of affairs.'[41] Then the Master addressed to them His parting words:

> You have undertaken much trouble in coming here. You must be very happy; you must be very rejoiced because you have come to this Sacred Spot and worshipped at the Holy Tomb of the Bab. For many days you have associated with Me and I have enjoyed your visit and I hope that good results will issue therefrom. Today whosoever is a herald of the Covenant is the light of the Regions . . . Be ye full of clamour and acclamation like unto a cup which is overflowing to the brim.[42]

Earlier, He had given them a warning about people like Dr Fareed to take home.

> When you return to America say to all the believers in my behalf that whenever a person comes to that country, no matter to what nationality he may belong, and tries to collect money in my name, know that it has no connection with me. I am free from it. Whosoever asks for money for me, does so of his own volition.[43]

Then George and Mason went to their ship, the *Perseo*, paid the Turkish war tax and bade goodbye to those who had come to see them off. Their last view of Mount Carmel was of a bonfire Ahmad Sohrab had set ablaze near the Bahá'í Nest.[44]

Mason wrote:

> Because of the condition of unrest in the country, there were but few people coming to see Abdul-Baha. He spent much time alone in his room writing Tablets. We often saw him apparently lost in

> meditation, and we felt he must have been sending his spirit out to the people in all parts who were suffering so intensely for that which he had to give . . .
>
> During those fourteen days in that Holy Spot a real inner awakening came upon us. It was a greater realization of the spirit of The New Day – the spirit of The Covenant of God – the spirit of BAHA'O'LLAH which is radiating so fragrantly from His Branch, Abdul-Baha.
>
> During our visit we had several personal interviews with Abdul-Baha and many times we heard him give short, informal, general talks, but the greatest blessing which was ours seemed to come to us from within our hearts as we responded to the spirit of Abdul-Baha – that spirit – impossible to describe in words – the spirit in which he does all things, and which, coming from him, penetrates to the hearts of all who in soul contact with him [sic], taking with it joy, love, peace and the life of the Covenant.[45]

At the conclusion of their visit, George wrote, 'After a heavenly stay of two weeks on the Mountain of God, Mount Carmel, Abdul-Baha has sent us back to America to make a tour of the States immediately. He has also revealed a Tablet for the American Bahais . . . This has been an interesting trip and we shall be glad to get back to a *peaceful* country.'[46] George spent the last 13 years of his life to 1948 as a member of the National Spiritual Assembly of the United States and Canada.

Abú-Sinán

When Mason and George had arrived in Haifa to find 'Abdu'l-Bahá away, He was in a village called Abú-Sinán, eight kilometres (five miles) northeast of Bahjí. With the outbreak of the war, the Master had decided to move the Bahá'ís away from the panic of the populace and the town officials, and settle them for a time in a quieter area. Merchants in both Haifa and 'Akká were in great difficulties because many of their customers fled away from the coast and many of their wares were confiscated by the government. In spite of 'Abdu'l-Bahá's calmness, even the Bahá'ís were affected by the hysteria. The children, in particular, were affected by the many 'terrible stories which were being told everywhere', and were becoming very nervous and ill.[47]

Habíb Mu'ayyad, a recently graduated doctor, joined the Master in October and wrote that

> Power rested in the hands of a number of ruthless military men who did not consider themselves accountable to anyone. It was a time of mayhem and plunder . . . The government was under the control of a number of faithless, bloodthirsty and cruel men . . . Gallows were active in every town . . . Jamal Pasha . . . had assembled an enormous force to attack and reduce Egypt and [capture] the Suez Canal. Tens of thousands of camels were arrayed solely for the transportation of the army's water rations. His agents had confiscated whatever food clothing, weapons, money, surplus and stored grains they could find . . . If anyone protested, hanging was the immediate response . . .
>
> Taking advantage of this most perilous situation, each passing day the spiteful Covenant-breakers came up with a new way to provoke Jamal Pasha against the Faith and further agitate him in this regard. Sometimes they went to Damascus and provoked the enemies of the Cause [into action]. On other occasions they sought the help of Jerusalem, presenting such extravagant gifts as the tent of the Blessed Beauty . . . In addition, they offered such sacred [Persian] carpets as remained from his time. When giving these gifts, they always registered a complaint against 'Abdu'l-Bahá, representing themselves as the wronged and the victimized. At times, they depicted 'Abdu'l-Bahá as a political mischief-maker and a religious rabble-rouser, thereby sowing seeds of sedition. At other times, they accused the Master of having designs to inaugurate a new monarchy and described his communications with the East and the West as a means for inciting political chaos; or they accused him of being a foreign agent.[48]

The Druze chief of Abú-Sinán, Shaykh Sálih, invited 'Abdu'l-Bahá to his village and put his own house at the Master's disposal. By September, about 140 Bahá'ís, with as many children, had moved to the village and were taken into peoples' homes throughout the village. The Greatest Holy Leaf, Munírih Khánum, Lua Getsinger who had arrived from India in December, Edith Sanderson, and the daughters of the Master and their families all stayed in the Shaykh's house. 'Abdu'l-Bahá told Badi Bushrui to establish a school and there were soon 25 students, mainly children of 'Abdu'l-Bahá's household, other Bahá'ís and the village chiefs. He also asked Dr Mu'ayyad to set up a dispensary, since most of the area doctors had been sent to the battle front. Lua Getsinger aided by serving as the doctor's anaesthetic technician. The Master mostly stayed in Haifa and 'Akká, coming to the village every few days and staying for one or two nights. Other than 'Abdu'l-Bahá, the only Bahá'í who remained in Haifa was Ḥájí Mírzá Ḥaydar-'Alí, who was too old and infirm to travel to the mountain village.[49]

Between 30 October and 1 November, 'Abdu'l-Bahá stayed at Bahjí with several Bahá'ís. In the mornings and evenings, He took His companions into the Shrine and chanted the Tablet of Visitation. Each day, he also spent twenty minutes pumping water for the gardens. On 1 November, 'Abdu'l-Bahá and the other Bahá'ís boarded His carriage and left for Abú-Sinán. Three days later, He returned to Haifa and sent up a box containing Tablets and holy relics for safe keeping. These items later became the beginning of the International Bahá'í Archives.[50]

On 11 November, 'Abdu'l-Bahá, Habíb Mu'ayyad and a few other Bahá'ís went to the House of 'Abdu'lláh Páshá, meeting a beggar on the way. The Master 'caressed his face and beard and spoke many words of encouragement and humor to him', then, turning to Habíb, indicated the beggar and said:

> When it is revealed, 'Consort with all the religions', the intention is association with such people. Although there is no connection between us, I have served him for twenty years. [The intention of Bahá'u'lláh's exhortation] is not to associate with a Covenant-breaker or those who curse the Blessed Beauty . . .
>
> The intention is to consort with such people as are not antagonistic, or two-faced, or conniving, or hypocritical. Such people [as this poor Arab] are not believers, and there is no harm in that; let him believe in his own convictions.[51]

The group then walked by the cemetery where some of the early Bahá'ís were buried. After stopping briefly for prayers, they continued to the train station where 'Abdu'l-Bahá sat down and asked Dr Mu'ayyad: 'Now that you have become a physician, come and take my pulse.' When Habíb did so, he was surprised that it was only 45 beats per minute. 'Abdu'l-Bahá indicated that that was normal, though He added that 'If I have a fever, it goes up to 50.'[52]

The last day of November was sunny and the Mediterranean was unusually calm. Because the water was so smooth, the people in 'Akká could see the normally wave-covered Zeeb rocks offshore. The population of 'Akká, already highly nervous, thought that the rocks were warships because the Mutisarrif had cabled that four enemy warships were fast approaching the city. Virtually the whole population of 'Akká fled, leaving doors and windows open and abandoning those handicapped people who couldn't flee on their own.[53]

'Abdu'l-Bahá had known that war had been coming for a long time and even before returning from America had set preparations in motion. He had purchased a number of tracts of land near Haifa and along the Jordan River. He put groups of Bahá'ís on the land to grow the crops needed at Abú-Sinán. During these semi-lawless years, bandits would sometimes raid the farms, taking everything they could carry. At least once, the Master was able to have the culprits arrested and forced to pay restitution. 'Abdu'l-Bahá had those tilling the fields hide the corn and wheat in special corn pits after harvesting. This supported many people during the famine years of 1914–1918.[54]

1915

Edward Getsinger returns

Edward Getsinger was back in Port Said in early January 1915 after having raised funds to help 'Abdu'l-Bahá and the Bahá'ís in the Holy Land. He found that no mail had gotten to 'Abdu'l-Bahá in two months. Aḥmad Yazdí finally selected an elderly Bahá'í who, because his age, was above suspicion as well as free from military requirements. The man made a trial run to Haifa in January, then returned to Port Said.[1] On his second trip, the man 'took what mail he could pad himself with' and arrived in Haifa on 19 January.[2] Edward padded his clothes, too, with mail for 'Abdu'l-Bahá and arrived safely on 26 January. He also carried several hundred pounds Sterling of gold in a belt around his waist. The gold came from Bahá'ís in America who had decided that 'Abdu'l-Bahá needed gold more than food. Edward objected, but ended up smuggling it to Haifa. The Master, however, refused to accept it.[3]

Edward recorded one of 'Abdu'l-Bahá's talks while he was there:

> No obstacle should be placed before any soul which might prevent it from finding the truth. Baha'o'llah revealed his directions, teachings, and laws, so that souls might know God, and not that any utterance might become an obstacle in their way.
>
> Holding to the letter of the law is many times an indication of a desire for leadership. One who assumes to be the enforcer of the law shows an intellectual understanding of the Cause, but that spiritual guidance in them is not yet established . . .
>
> Several times tablets have been written to some friends regarding a small detail in the work of the Cause, which they might attend to, such as reporting about Ezelies, nakazeen, et al., and now we hear that such tablets are used as a proof of their authority over the friends in those regions. Although the books and writings of Abul Fazl are used in many countries as text books, never did he even give a sign that he was an authority on any subject, consequently the gifts of God ever increased upon him, since he bore all honors in humility . . .

The ones in real authority are known by their humility and self-sacrifice and show no attitude of superiority over the friends.

Some time ago a tablet was written stating that none are appointed to any authority to do anything but to serve the Cause as true servants of the friends – and for this no tablet is necessary; such service when true and unselfish, requires no announcement, nor following, nor written document.

Let the servant be known by his deeds, by his life!

To be approved of God alone should be one's aim.

When God calls a soul to a high station, it is because that soul has capacity for that station as a gift of God, and because that soul has supplicated to be taken into His service. No envies, jealousies, calumnies, slanders, plots, nor schemes, will ever move God to remove a soul from its intended place, for by the grace of God, such actions on the part of the people are the test of the servant, testing his strength, forbearance, endurance and sincerity under adversity. At the same time those who show forth envies, jealousies, etc., toward a servant, are depriving themselves of their own stations, and not another of his, for they prove by their own acts that they are not only unworthy of being called to any station awaiting them, but also prove that they cannot withstand the very first test – that of rejoicing over the success of their neighbour, at which God rejoices. Only by such a sincere joy can the gift of God descend unto a pure heart.

Envy closes the door of Bounty, and jealousy prevents one from ever attaining to the Kingdom of Abha.

No! Before God! No one can deprive another of his rightful station, that can only be lost by one's unwillingness or failure to do the will of God, or by seeking to use the Cause of God for one's own gratification or ambition.[4]

Edward left Haifa for America on 5 February.

'Abdu'l-Bahá was in Abú-Sinán on 10 January when Shaykh Salmán asked about educating children. The Master replied, with an eye both to children and Covenant-breakers:

It is universally recognized that evil is stronger than good. Evil has a rapid effect, whereas good is slow in its impact. If a trustworthy person and a thief were together, the thief would never become righteous, but the converse might occur. Because of their association, a truthful person may become a liar, but it is rare for the perjurer to become truthful, or for the parsimonious to become generous by reason of his association with the charitable, or for the wicked to become virtuous, and so forth. This is because evil is stronger and its influence is more penetrating. This issue does not require proof, it is as evident as the noon-time sun. If there were a thousand healthy men, but one among them had a contagious disease, the thousand would have no effect on the ill, but the illness of that one would spread to the remaining thousand. For instance, if a person is afflicted with smallpox and comes into contact with many healthy children, all will be infected, while it is not possible for the healthy to influence the sick. It is similar with the black plague or leprosy, where the healthy may be affected but the converse would not hold.

Consider how much time it takes to raise a building, but dynamite can destroy it in the blink of an eye. It takes five years to build an armored ship, but only a minute for a torpedo to sink it to the bottom of the ocean. It takes twenty years to raise a person to maturity, but he perishes in an instant by the assassin's bullet.

Therefore, if you desire for your children to be raised properly and remain protected, they must be cared for adequately. You must ensure that they do not meet or associate with ill-mannered persons.[5]

Panic, spies and a calm 'Abdu'l-Bahá

Lua Getsinger lived with the family of 'Abdu'l-Bahá at Abú-Sinán. In a letter to Elizabeth Nourse on 11 January 1915, she wrote 'Here I am safe & sound in the Highlands of Galilee with the Master and family who are all well and happy. The Master spends most of His time in Acca comforting and caring for the poor and hopeless. He is so wonderful and inspiring these days! So far all is quiet here.'[6] Lua spent part of her time in Abú-Sinán assisting the young physician Dr Mu'ayyad in performing several operations.[7]

'Abdu'l-Bahá decided that all Westerners still in the area, which included Edith Sanderson, who had been there since 6 April 1914,[8] but not Lua, should leave on 12 January. They left on the last steamer that departed Haifa for Alexandria.[9]

The Covenant-breakers threw all their resources into the effort to create havoc for 'Abdu'l-Bahá. On 30 January, a group of 'notable and affluent citizens' visited Abú-Sinán, including Namzy Bey Bashi, who was the ranking officer. At a dinner held by the villagers that night, to which Habíb Mu'ayyad and another Bahá'í were invited, Namzy Bey Bashi told them about a feast given earlier that day in 'Akká by Mírzá Badí'u'lláh, the Covenant-breaking half-brother of 'Abdu'l-Bahá. He

> had invited the military commanders of the region, the guest of honor being Haydar Bey, the chief of gendarmes. The guests were entertained with great quantities of food and alcoholic drinks and by Sadhijih, Mírzá Badí'u'lláh's daughter. She had planned to provoke Haydar Bey, who had complete authority over the region's military, into imprisoning, exiling or murdering 'Abdu'l-Bahá. This scheme had backfired however, and a huge uproar against Mírzá Badí'u'lláh had ensued in 'Akká.[10]

While the Covenant-breakers spent their resources trying to bribe or influence the military authorities, 'Abdu'l-Bahá continued His generosity to the poor. On 7 February, He had Isfandíyár take him and Habíb Mu'ayyad to the Cave of Elijah, where they found 200 poor women and children. The Master instructed his driver to give each a sum of money.[11]

The next day, 'Abdu'l-Bahá led a group of Bahá'ís up the road to the Shrine of the Báb. It was a slow walk for the Master and he stopped twice. Reaching a bend in the road, 'Abdu'l-Bahá talked about the benefits of paved roads, saying, 'This is indeed an amazing mountain and now it has good roads as well.' By this, He didn't mean that the road was actually paved, but that the large boulders had been removed. Ḥájí Siyyid Javád asked Him if electricity would someday be available on the mountain?' 'Without a doubt!' 'Abdu'l-Bahá replied, 'But not so soon. Eventually this mountain will be filled with light.' Half-way to the Shrine, 'Abdu'l-Bahá's carriage arrived and He rode the rest of the way to the Shrine.[12]

On 9 February, Mr Rothschild, a German artist who had drawn a portrait of the Master, visited and showed 'Abdu'l-Bahá his work. He then asked 'Abdu'l-Bahá if He would write a few words of wisdom to adorn it. The Master wrote:

> Humanity is created in the image of the Merciful [God], that is to say with Divine attributes. And so, the physical form will perish, but the heavenly character will endure. The soul is an effulgence of the divine, while the human body is composed of earthly elements. Therefore may a heavenly form be thine. 'Abdu'l-Bahá 'Abbas[13]

Ḥájí Mírzá Ḥaydar-'Alí, who was 85, fell ill with a severe fever and cough on 15 February. Habíb Mu'ayyad came down to Haifa from Abú-Sinán to treat him and after five days, he was well enough to bathe.

'Abdu'l-Bahá was back in Abú-Sinán on 28 February, arriving with a group of military officers, including Namzy Bey Bashi and Dr Finkelstein, who was in charge of the German Polytechnic in Haifa. When the people in Abú-Sinán saw 'Abdu'l-Bahá's carriage, they rushed out with four horses for the guests to ride. Namzy Bey Bashi, 'out of deference to 'Abdu'l-Bahá and with his permission', continued to walk alongside the Master's carriage. However, since the road was uphill and the carriage was uncomfortable for 'Abdu'l-Bahá, the Master 'mounted a donkey and slowly came from behind, ordering all the others to accompany' Namzy Bey Bashi. That evening, 'Abdu'l-Bahá and Dr Finkelstein talked about how happy they were to be together. The Master told His visitor that only because of God's benevolence were they able to meet. He went on to praise the German people: 'I am well pleased with the Germans. The spiritual future of Germany is very glorious. The word "German" in Persian means "Our kinsmen". I was happier in Germany than anywhere else.'[14]

The only naval bombardment of the war took place in June when a ship fired shells at the railway bridges between Haifa and 'Akká.[15] Lua Getsinger wrote that 'the bombardment was confined to a certain locality and therefore the destruction was limited. One person only, killed and thank God no wounded. It was terrifying while it lasted.'[16] One shell landed in the Garden of Riḍván but failed to explode.[17]

Henrietta Wagner was in Haifa on 16 February. She later reported that the Turkish government had sent spies throughout the area and that this had created much suspicion and mistrust and these were even infecting the Bahá'í community. 'Abdu'l-Bahá spoke sharply of suspicion:

> Suspicion, like unto the hot blast of mid-summer, withers the roots of the sweet and delicate flowers of trust and confidence.

It extinguishes the light of love and spreads the darkness of surmise and doubts. It blights the immortal plants of faith and reliance, and increases the germs of destruction and ruin.

It is worse than the venom of the serpent and more harmful than the armies of locusts.

The poison of the adder kills the body, but the virus of suspicion destroys the spirit.

It has been demonstrated by eminent biologists that a single bacterium, after twenty-four hours of self-production and generation, would reach the total number of 16,776,216 bacteria. This is true in a higher degree of the germ of suspicion, for the generative energy is most marked and its power of fecundity well pronounced. The numerous colony of our bacteria had at least one bacterium for their primal ancestor, but suspicion cannot even claim as much. It is always of uncertain origin; it sulks in the darkness. It cannot show its genealogical tree; its genesis is never established. It jumps into the midst of a company, nobody knows from where, and immediately it starts flying around in the dust of doubt and hesitation.

The individual members of the company feel a strange and unexplainable sensation creeping over their souls and benumbing their finer spiritual sensibilities.

They look at each other with different eyes; they begin to suspect one another and shun each other's association.[18]

Jamál Pá<u>sh</u>á and threats to 'Abdu'l-Bahá

In early 1915, Jamál Pá<u>sh</u>á took control of Palestine and began a reign of terror, executing anyone who might have opposed him. Mírzá Muḥammad-'Alí leaped forward to tell the new commander that 'Abdu'l-Bahá opposed him. The Covenant-breakers went so far as to steal the tent 'Abdu'l-Bahá used to meet visitors and gave it to Jamál Pá<u>sh</u>á. They also began rumours that 'Abdu'l-Bahá had been banished to Damascus. When Jamál Pá<u>sh</u>á came to 'Akká, he decided that he must see this trouble-maker, 'Abdu'l-Bahá. The Master rode His donkey to meet him and was received courteously enough, but then Jamál Pá<u>sh</u>á told 'Abdu'l-Bahá that he considered Him to be a religious mischief-maker. The proof was His previous incarcerations in 'Akká. 'Abdu'l-Bahá told the commander that there were two kinds of mischief-making: political and religious. Pointing at Jamál Pá<u>sh</u>á, He said that the political mischief-maker so far had not caused any damage and He hoped that the religious one would not do so either.[19]

'Abdu'l-Bahá told the story of going out with Jamál Pá<u>sh</u>á in his carriage. The Turk had his five hunting dogs with him and when a gazelle was sighted, the dogs leaped in pursuit, but to no avail. An Arab Bahá'í with a small dog had also come along and the small dog did what the Pá<u>sh</u>á's could not and caught the gazelle. This made Jamál Pá<u>sh</u>á ashamed and he began to beat his dogs saying, 'What can I do, the Bahais are assisted.'[20]

The result of all the conniving of Mírzá Muḥammad-'Alí and his cohorts was that Jamál Pá<u>sh</u>á declared that he would crucify 'Abdu'l-Bahá when he returned from his campaign to destroy the British in Egypt in February 1915. 'Abdu'l-Bahá Himself told of this:

> When Jemal Pasha came to Jerusalem he made some remarks about me. He said: 'I will go and conquer Egypt. I will drive England out of Egypt. I will conquer all the Suez Canal. Victorious I shall return. My first command will be this, that I will hang him ['Abdu'l-Bahá] at the gate of Acca!' The German Consul was in that meeting. He was an acquaintance of mine. He came and told me that Jemal Pasha had said this . . . I said 'Let Jemal Pasha go and conquer Egypt. Then I will give myself up. Let him conquer Egypt and I am ready.' Jemal Pasha went. One day in the morning, the German Consul came to me. He said 'some strange thing has happened.' He said: 'Jemal Pasha attacked two days ago. Today a telegram has come from Bersheba.' This is clear. As soon as the battle began he fled. He rode in his automobile and fled . . .
>
> Two or three days later the German Consul came and said: 'He (Jemal Pasha) is defeated.' Jemal Pasha returned here. He began to twist his moustache, and said: 'This was a reconnoitring attack. I wanted to test the strength of the enemy.' But I understood.[21]

The battle Jamál Pá<u>sh</u>á lost at Beersheba was a momentous event for one Turkish soldier who was also a Bahá'í, Majdu'd-Din Ínán. He had been conscripted into the army from college and sent to Palestine with Jamál Pá<u>sh</u>á. Being so close, he requested permission to visit Haifa. His request was granted and he was able to meet 'Abdu'l-Bahá. While this pilgrim was with Him, the Master prayed, 'God willing, they will not send you to Beersheba.' The battle at Beersheba occurred while he was in Haifa. The rest of his unit, however, was sent into battle there and all perished.[22]

Locust invasion and famine

Near the end of March, locusts invaded Palestine, devouring plants, trees, everything. One witness stated that they arrived 'in such density that they eclipsed the sun . . . Nothing we did prevented the locusts from coming down and devouring everything green, even the bark of trees, in a matter of minutes.' This was a disaster because food was already scarce due to the British and French blockade of Palestine, as well as the Ottoman army's rapacious taking of any and all food they could find. Another witness wrote that 'Our lives are threatened from all sides: a European war and an Ottoman war, prices are skyrocketing, a financial crisis, and the locusts are attacking the country north and south. On top of all this, now infectious diseases are spreading throughout the Ottoman lands.'[23] Between 100,000 and 200,000 people starved to death or died of starvation-related illnesses during this time.[24]

Lua Getsinger experienced the insect invasion and wrote about the Master's actions:

> What has he not done for Syria! 'The army of God,' as Abdul-Baha named the locusts – which came in such clouds as to darken the sun – completed the difficulties by way of misery, starvation and death. Such suffering as was manifest on all sides can scarcely be believed. He became the sole comfort and hope of the people whether they are believers or unbelievers!'[25]

In a letter to the *Christian Commonwealth* and sent also to *Star of the West*, Ahmad Sohrab wrote about 'Abdu'l-Bahá's efforts to alleviate the suffering:

> For three years, he spent months in Tiberias and Adassieh, supervising extensive works of agriculture and raising wheat, corn and other foodstuffs for the maintenance of all of us, and more to distribute among the many starving Mohammedan and Christian families, many of whom gave eloquent testimony to his all-inclusive charity

and philanthropy. I assure you that were it not for his provision and ceaseless attention to the works of agriculture, none of us would have survived the war, for with an awful famine raging in all cities and towns, one could not find bread and even in case a loaf of black, coarse barley was found, such a high price was asked for it that one could not find enough money to buy it.

Aside from the scarcity of food and famine, for two years all the harvests were eaten by the innumerable armies of locusts, the like of which were never witnessed by the old men of the community. At times like unto the dark clouds they covered the face of the sky for hours.

This condition, coupled with the unprecedented extortions and looting by the Turkish officers and the extensive buying of foodstuffs by the Germans to be shipped to the 'Fatherland' brought about an awful famine. In Lebanon alone more than 100,000 people died from starvation.[26]

Poor communications, and threats

Communication between 'Abdu'l-Bahá and the outside world was hindered by many difficulties during this time and the threats of Jamál Pá<u>sh</u>á greatly worried the Bahá'ís elsewhere in the world. On 13 May, Elinor Hiscox wrote from Cairo that they finally had news of 'Abdu'l-Bahá. Two Bahá'ís, one a resident of Cairo and the other of Haifa, were able to board a ship at Haifa and sail to Egypt. The two men knew they would be searched as they boarded so they were not able to bring out any letters. They reported that 'Abdu'l-Bahá was in good health and 'he laughs much and is in excellent spirits. He is happier than at any time since the war began.' The Bahá'ís in Abú-Sinán had moved back to Haifa on 5 May, and 'they have enough to eat as supplies are brought in from the country villages – vegetables, fruits, grains, eggs, meat, etc. The holy family and Lua Getsinger have been staying in a village two hours inland from Acca, but now they are returning to Haifa, as Abdul-Baha considers it safe for them all to remain in their homes in Haifa.'[27]

As happy as He seemed, the threats were very real. On 18 May, 'Abdu'l Bahá called for Ahmad Sohrab. After dictating a series of Tablets, the Master closed His eyes and was silent for five minutes. Suddenly, He stood and began to walk. Then He removed His turban. Ahmad wrote that 'His white locks fell on His shoulders, adding a mystic beauty to His appearance, while His snow-white patriarchal beard, gave a Divine Majesty to His whole being.' Then:

> His former tranquil and composed Face was now completely changed and the signs of the gathering of a storm of divine emotions and sentiments, became visible . . .
>
> I have sent for thee, this morning, to speak on a confidential matter. The enemies of the Cause have again resorted to another device, whereby they may terminate my life.'[28]

The Master wanted someone to know about the dangers he faced and to be prepared to convey His wishes to the rest of the believers should the worst happen. A new and long list of accusations had been sent to Jamál Pá<u>sh</u>á charging Him with, among other things, the corruption of the morals of the youth and undermining the religion of their ancestors. Jamál Pá<u>sh</u>á in a public meeting responded by threatening to hang 'Abdu'l Bahá on a pillory if He was indeed 'disseminating such pernicious doctrines'. The Ottoman leader did not realize that one of the Master's greatest wishes was martyrdom. After telling Sohrab all this, 'Abdu'l Bahá said He was 'encircled with an impending danger', and that if anything should happen to Him, 'thou mayest convey My message to all the believers of God, and it is this':

> The friends of God must not be shaken by any test.
>
> As the lofty mountains you must stand firm in the Cause of God.
>
> As the tempestuous sea you must never become calm and still.
>
> As the brilliant stars you must ever shine and gleam.
>
> As the sweet flowers you must always diffuse the fragrances of divine civilization.
>
> As the cool warbling nightingales, sing ye throughout all the seasons.
>
> As the cool fountains gush ye forth, with the waters of spiritual explanations.
>
> As the verdant meadow be ye not scorched by the blowing of the hot winds of opposition.
>
> As the sun wander ye through your course and be not wearied of well doing.

As the real guides of humanity, illumine the ignorant with the light of wisdom, raise the lowly, inspire with noble ideals the despondent, and lead the erring ones into the Path of Truth.

Live ye in accord with the Good-Pleasure of God.

Arise ye, with an irresistible force in the promotion of the teachings.

Like unto the sanctified apostles of Christ, summon ye the people to the Kingdom of God, and invite them to walk in the road of Heavenly Prosperity and Success.

Let not any hindrance or obstacle dampen your enthusiasm.

Set aglow the hearts, with the fire of joy and exhilaration.

Adorn the temple of the world with the garment of the new creation.

I have trained you and educated you for this, your reserve powers are needed for such a Day.

Beware! Beware! lest lukewarmness overtake you, indifference master you, negligence take hold of you, and listlessness overwhelm you.

You must nurse and water and take care of the Blessed Tree of the Cause of God, so that it may grow and develop, its branches giving shade to people of the East and the West, and its luscious fruits satisfying the hunger of mankind.

Seek ye no other pleasure! Long ye for no other delight! Be ye filled to overflowing with the love of Baha'Ullah; promulgate ye the traces of His Grandeur and Dominion.

Advance ye towards His beauty, be ye attached to His Cause and receive Divine Bounty from His Inexhaustible Storehouse!

The Tree of the Cause must be watered by you, so that it may bring forth leaves, blossoms and fruit.

If you do not arise, in the accomplishment of this service, who will then arise? To whom should I look forward?

Whom can I trust with this Pearl of great price?

Who will uphold the Name of Baha'Ullah? Who will make me happy in the Kingdom of my Father? Who will give up his rest and comfort for the promotion of the Cause? Who will carry this ball from the field of self-sacrifice?

Who will raise the voice of Ya Baha El Abha! In the vast congregations of humanity?

Ah me! Who? Who will turn his face toward heaven and pray,
'Thy Kingdom come, Thy Will be done and not mine'?[29]

Ḥájí Mírzá Haydar-'Alí

One day a western woman was in 'Akká and, unusually, was telling 'Abdu'l-Bahá all her troubles.

> This was a strange thing for usually people when they enter the presence of Abdul-Baha are so filled with the contagion of his radiant love that they think only of their blessings. Abdul-Baha with great kindness listened for a half hour to the western woman's troubles. At last he arose, and said he had another engagement and must be going. 'But there,' he said, pointing out of the window, 'goes a man whom I will bring in to see you. His name is Mirza Haider Ali. We call him the "Angel of Mount Carmel." He walks on earth but he lives in heaven. He has had many troubles and he will tell you about them.' Abdul-Baha went out, but quickly returned with Mirza Haider Ali whom he presented to the woman, and then departed.
>
> The 'Angel of Mount Carmel' with great humility and sweetness of manner began to talk with the woman of the luminous century in which we live and the divine age that is to be. She listened for a while, impatiently, and at last broke in with, 'But Abdul-Baha said you would tell me about your troubles.' Mirza Haider Ali looked up in amazement.
>
> 'Troubles?' he replied, 'why madam, I never had any troubles. I don't know what troubles are.'[30]

Ḥájí Mírzá Haydar- 'Alí was known as the 'Angel of Carmel' because of his calm and happy acceptance of a life in service to Bahá'u'lláh, despite all the persecution he had suffered. Bahá'u'lláh had asked him to go to Egypt and said that he would suffer many ordeals there. It came to pass as Bahá'u'lláh said. Mírzá Haydar- 'Alí was arrested, put in chains with his feet in stocks. He and his fellow prisoners went for 45 days subsisting on a single slice of bread and a cup of water a day. Afterwards, he wrote: 'During the forty-five days we spent in the home of the Consul we suffered as in hell because of his staff and servants, but the soul was in the utmost joy beyond description.' Next, he and other Bahá'ís had huge iron collars put on their feet and a heavy wooden stock on their hands and were transported for five months in that condition. Then, after a short respite at the direction of Ja’far Pá<u>sh</u>á, Haydar-‘Alí and a companion had their hands and feet bound after which they were suspended on a camel’s back, one hanging down each side. Haydar-‘Alí was kept imprisoned in Khartoum for nine months before his spiritual nature caused his release. In 1877, he was allowed to leave and he immediately set out for ‘Akká, where he attained the presence of Bahá’u’lláh. Haydar-‘Alí made two pilgrimages and spent many years travel teaching in Persia before finally returning to ‘Akká to spend his final years with ‘Abdu’l-Bahá. He recognized the greatness of the station of ‘Abdu’l-Bahá as early as Adrianople. He passed away in December 1920 in Haifa.[31]

Communications with the world cut

Communication between ‘Abdu’l-Bahá and the rest of the world ended completely in July 1915, though it had been difficult for months. Ahmad Sohrab continued to write letters that couldn’t be sent, and on 1 July wrote to Corinne True:

> For the last ten months we have received not one letter from America nor under the present circumstances have I been able to mail to the Bahai world the spiritual words and advice as well as the description of the selfless deeds and divine actions of the Beloved . . .
>
> You must know by this time that none of the letters mailed to Port Said during the past many months were received by us . . .
>
> Praise be to God! That Abdul-Baha is quite well. After many months of stay in Abou Senan the holy family and the friends are back in Haifa and the Beloved at the present time is passing quite peaceful days with them. There are no tablets to be written, no pilgrims to meet and talk to and no strenuous outward activities. Our days are like a calm, limpid stream, flowing smoothly . . . We are happy to be in his neighborhood during these crucial months of the history of mankind and watch daily his acts of charity and hear his words of loving kindness. He is always doing some good and is ever ready to go to the help of the needy and those who are in want. He often remembers his many trips to and through Chicago and

reviews for the benefit of the friends the many meetings held in your house and other places.[32]

Three weeks later Sohrab wrote to Howard and Edward Struven saying that 'Abdu'l-Bahá was living in Haifa. The resident Bahá'ís were able to meet him two or three times a day and listen to the 'grandeur and beauty of his moral and spiritual discourses.' There were no pilgrims, though Lua was still there.[33] A month later, he wrote to Louis Gregory from 'Abdu'l-Bahá's garden. 'Abdu'l-Bahá was at that moment 'walking amidst the beds of roses and talking with a number of friends on the corruptibility of nature and the sacredness of the Word of God.'[34]

Lua Getsinger's passing

Lua was very happy living with the Holy Family, but the war situation worsened and that put 'Abdu'l-Bahá in danger. In July, He told Lua it was time to go and she finally departed from His presence for the last time on 30 August aboard the American cruiser *Des Moines*. When she reached Egypt, Lua wrote:

> I arrived here [Port Said, Egypt] a week ago from the island of Crete, having left Haifa on our American cruiser, *Des Moines*, which brought away two hundred and ninety refugees and myself. I was ready to leave the middle of June on the U.S.S. *Tennessee*, but as some of the students in Beyrouth succeeded in getting away, Abdul-Baha decided that I should stay until later. When the news filtered through of the possibility of America declaring war, and our gunboat came to the very port of Haifa, he said: 'Now is the time for you to go and give news to the friends in Egypt, Europe and America. It is a long time that they are without any word, and I desire to send you to them, after which you are to go and teach'. . .
>
> Abdul-Baha was well, though surrounded with the greatest dangers and difficulties when I left. He left Haifa for Nazareth at noon, August 29th, and I sailed the next morning, August 30th . . .[35]

On 20 September, Lua wrote to Zeenat Bagdadi from Port Said describing the locust plague that had struck Palestine:

> I promised your brother, who came to see me on board the American cruiser, *Des Moines*, August 30th, which took me and many hundreds of refugees from Haifa, that I would write you as soon as possible after reaching some destination from which it would be possible to get mail through to you. I arrived in Port Said, September 14th, so tired and exhausted that I could do nothing but talk to the friends who have been so long without news of Abdul-Baha! Praise be to God! When I left he was in good health though surrounded by difficulties and dangers which I am powerless to describe . . .
>
> I am enclosing a photograph of a tablet to the American Bahais which was revealed August 27th, and which I got through the customs house with the assistance of the American consul at Haifa. Please ask Dr. Zia to translate it to Mrs. True and then give it to the STAR OF THE WEST. I do not just yet know when I shall reach America as I have some work to do in France first. I am writing an account of my last months with Abdul-Baha and family to Mr. Hannen . . .
>
> I am sent forth again 'to herald The Covenant' by its *holy Center*, and I shall do it with his divine assistance better and more powerfully than I have ever done . . .[36]

But after arriving in Cairo, Lua was too ill to continue on to America. Though ill, she continued teaching until felled by a fatal heart attack on 1 May 1916.

The Master writes

With Haifa's streets empty of pilgrims, 'Abdu'l-Bahá began a writing project. Over the last half of 1915, He wrote *Memorials of the Faithful*, described by its translator, Marzieh Gail, as 'a book about people who were trying to get into prison rather than escape from it'. The book is about the early followers of Bahá'u'lláh, and Gail further notes that 'These are short and simple accounts, but they constitute a manual of how to live, and how to die'.[37]

On 24 December, 'Azízu'lláh Bahádur managed to reach Haifa and the presence of 'Abdu'l-Bahá with mail. He had been in contact with some of the German Bahá'ís, many of whom had been forced to serve in the military. These included Consul Albert Schwarz who had attained the Master's presence in Stuttgart and been His host at his health spa in Bad Mergentheim in 1913. Consul Schwarz was an officer in the military, but that hadn't stopped him teaching the Faith to his brother officers.[38]

1916–1918

In early 1916, 'Abdu'l-Bahá again encountered Jamál Páshá, but this time it was His wish to do so. The Master travelled to Nazareth with Mírzá Jalál and Khusraw, determined to meet the Commander-in-chief of Palestine. The day after His arrival in Nazareth, 'Abdu'l-Bahá was invited to lunch at the house of an important resident of the town. Also there were Jamál Páshá and 200 of his war leaders. For three hours, 'Abdu'l-Bahá spoke in Turkish on philosophical and scientific subjects, and on heavenly teachings. So intense was His utterance that all stopped eating while they listened to His blessed words.

> . . . Jamál Páshá, who had been His great enemy because of false accusations, had not paid the proper respect to 'Abdu'l-Bahá when He had first arrived. Now, however, having heard the Master speak so learnedly and wisely, he was most deferential and full of all kinds of politeness. When the time came for the Master to rise, Jamál Páshá most courteously held the Beloved's arm to assist Him to leave the table, and himself led the way to the reception room, and seated the Master comfortably.
>
> Finally, after answering more questions, and giving wondrous light on many subjects, the Master arose to bid farewell to His host. Jamál Páshá accompanied Him out of the house, and to the bottom of the steps, and would have gone further with the Master, but was thanked with great kindness and urged by 'Abdu'l-Bahá to return.[1]

Tablets of the Divine Plan

In 1916 'Abdu'l-Bahá began writing the series of Tablets to the North American believers that have become known as the Tablets of the Divine Plan. In March and April 1916, while at Bahjí, He wrote eight Tablets, and another six in February and March of 1917. Three of the latter Tablets were revealed in Haifa in the room of His gardener, Ismá'il-Áqá, and three in the room of Bahá'u'lláh at the House of 'Abbúd. The first five Tablets reached the American believers in 1916 before the final connection between East and West was severed because of the war, and were published in the 8 September 1916 issue of *Star of the West.* In spite of famine and danger, 'Abdu'l-Bahá was thinking of the future. Shoghi Effendi has written:

> The Divine Plan, thus set in operation, may be said to have derived its inspiration from, and been dimly foreshadowed in, the injunction so significantly addressed by Bahá'u'lláh to the Chief Magistrates of the American continent. It was prompted by the contact established by 'Abdu'l-Baha Himself, in the course of His historic journey, with the entire body of His followers throughout the United States and Canada. It was conceived, soon after that contact was established, in the midst of what was then held to be one of the most devastating crises in human history. It underwent a period of incubation, after His ascension, while the machinery of a divinely appointed Administrative Order was being laboriously devised and its processes set in motion.[2]

> The seeds which 'Abdu'l-Baha's ceaseless activities so lavishly scattered had endowed the United States and Canada, nay the entire continent, with potentialities such as it had never known in its history. On the small band of His trained and beloved disciples, and through them on their descendants, He, through that visit, had bequeathed a priceless heritage – a heritage which carried with it the sacred and primary obligation to arise and carry on in that fertile field the work He had so gloriously initiated.[3]

> During these sombre days . . . 'Abdu'l-Bahá . . . was moved to confer once again, and for the last time in His life, on the community of His American followers a signal mark of His special favor by investing them, on the eve of the termination of His earthly ministry, through the revelation of the Tablets of the Divine Plan, with a world mission, whose full implications even now . . . still remain undisclosed, and whose unfoldment thus far, though as yet in its initial stages, has so greatly enriched the spiritual as well as the administrative annals of the first Baha'i century.[4]

The Tablets were extraordinary in their scope, though the first Tablets published in 1916 gave only a mild hint of what was to come. Of those first published Tablets, four were addressed to distinct areas of the United States and one was addressed to Canada and Greenland. In them, 'Abdu'l-Bahá encouraged the Bahá'ís to travel-teach to areas where there were few or no Bahá'ís. The Tablet to Canada and Greenland also emphasized the importance of teaching the Inuit peoples.

It wasn't until after the war that the rest of the Tablets reached their destinations and their full impact was felt. The remaining Tablets were – to put it simply – a plan for the spiritual conquest of the entire planet, and they were addressed solely to the Bahá'ís of North America, except for one short passage that said the German Bahá'ís should send travel teachers to America, Africa, Japan and China. These Tablets were to reshape the Bahá'í world under the guidance of Shoghi Effendi and would, during the Ten Year Crusade, involve all the Bahá'í communities of the world, not just those of North America.

The Tablets of the Divine Plan originated in the calls sent by both the Báb and Bahá'u'lláh to the Americas. The Báb had written:

> Issue forth from your cities, O peoples of the West and aid God ere the Day when the Lord of mercy shall come down unto you in the shadow of the clouds with the angels circling around Him, exalting His praise and seeking forgiveness for such as have truly believed in Our signs. Verily His decree hath been issued, and the command of God, as given in the Mother Book, hath indeed been revealed . . .[5]

Bahá'u'lláh's call was more specific:

> Hearken ye, O Rulers of America and the Presidents of the Republics therein, unto that which the Dove is warbling on the Branch of Eternity . . . Bind ye the broken with the hands of justice, and crush the oppressor who flourisheth with the rod of the commandments of your Lord, the Ordainer, the All-Wise.[6]

To Shoghi Effendi, Bahá'u'lláh's Tablet of Carmel, the Will and Testament of 'Abdu'l-Bahá, and the Tablets of the Divine Plan formed the three Charters that 'set in motion three distinct processes, the first operating in the Holy Land for the development of the institutions of the

Faith at its World Centre and the other two, throughout the rest of the Bahá'í world, for its propagation and the establishment of its Administrative Order . . .'[7] The Tablet of Carmel was Bahá'u'lláh's design for the Bahá'í World Centre while the Will and Testament contained the elements of the Bahá'í Administrative Order. The Tablets of the Divine Plan were for the diffusion of the Faith over the whole globe.

The United States and Canada, as the recipients of the Tablets of the Divine Plan, were therefore given the responsibility to carry out their instructions. Shoghi Effendi made it clear why these communities were chosen:

> Little wonder that a community belonging to a nation so abundantly blessed, a nation occupying so eminent a position in a continent so richly endowed, should have been able to add, during the fifty years of its existence, many a page rich with victories to the annals of the Faith of Bahá'u'lláh. This is the community, it should be remembered, which, ever since it was called into being through the creative energies released by the proclamation of the Covenant of Bahá'u'lláh, was nursed in the lap of 'Abdu'l-Bahá's unfailing solicitude, and was trained by Him to discharge its unique mission through the revelation of innumerable Tablets, through the instructions issued to returning pilgrims, through the despatch of special messengers, through His own travels at a later date, across the North American continent, through the emphasis laid by Him on the institution of the Covenant in the course of those travels, and finally through His mandate embodied in the Tablets of the Divine Plan.[8]

Though 'Abdu'l-Bahá had issued the marching orders, it wasn't until the time of Shoghi Effendi that implementation truly began. After the First World War, a few souls arose in response to the Master's call. Martha Root began her world-encircling journeys, Hyde and Clara Dunn left America and opened the Australian continent, and Emogene Hoagg and Orcella Rexford travelled to Alaska, but few others arose to answer their specific call. No one other than the Master appreciated the power and scope of the Tablets of the Divine Plan during His lifetime.

The process of implementation began in 1922 with a 'period of incubation' during which Shoghi Effendi introduced principles of

Bahá'í administration and established an initial contingent of local and national spiritual assemblies. Travel teachers and pioneers began to fill the internal national goals of the first five Tablets. Full implementation of the Plan didn't begin until 1937 when Shoghi Effendi gave the North American Bahá'í community the mission of the First Seven Year Plan: to open every country and island group in both American continents to the Faith. The succeeding teaching plans and the Ten Year Crusade were all part of the Guardian's efforts to implement the grand scheme of taking the Faith to every corner of the world. But even the Ten Year Crusade was just the beginning. Shoghi Effendi wrote that the Tablets would lead to the 'penetration' of the light of Bahá'u'lláh,

> in the course of numerous crusades and of successive epochs of both the Formative and Golden Ages of the Faith, into all the remaining territories of the globe through the erection of the entire machinery of Baha'u'llah's Administrative Order in all territories, both East and West, the stage at which the light of God's triumphant Faith shining in all its power and glory will have suffused and enveloped the entire planet.[9]

The liberation of Haifa and Wellesley Tudor Pole's role

Ahmad Sohrab described the privations they had been through during those war years:

> For years we had not seen an Englishman and we were forbidden to speak the language even in our own homes. We had almost forgotten that there were countries like England, France and America, as no news reaches us from those regions. Daily we were fed on so many falsehoods and lies that we could digest it no longer. When there was a glut in the market, the Agence Nationale had to mix its dishes of lies with some condiments of Mohammedan rising in India, Irish Rebellion, Afghan ranging herself against England and famine in London – thus these new spices might please the already satiated tastes of the worn and long-suffering public . . .[10]

In early 1917, rumours began to reach London that 'Abdu'l-Bahá was in great danger, but since there had been no communication with

Palestine for a long while, no one was sure what was actually happening there. At one point, 'Abdu'l-Bahá wrote a Tablet and needed to send it to Tehran so that it could be copied and distributed to the Bahá'í world. Getting a messenger from Haifa to Tehran was exceedingly difficult, but a volunteer stepped forth. Ḥájí Ramadán was 75 years old, partially blind, and had no family. 'Abdu'l-Bahá accepted his offer and Ḥájí Ramadán walked to Tehran, arriving safely after 45 days. His return to Haifa was even more difficult because on that trip, he was carrying gold in the bottom of his bag and letters sewn in the lining of his *'abá*. Arriving back in Haifa, 'Abdu'l-Bahá embraced him saying, 'Behold by what poor and humble children of God are great events served.' Resting for a short while, Ḥájí Ramadán set out on another mission, but never reached his destination.[11]

By late 1917, the war in Palestine was going on against the Turks. On 24 December, Wellesley Tudor Pole, who had met 'Abdu'l-Bahá in Alexandria in 1910 and with whom 'Abdu'l-Bahá had stayed in Bristol on His English visits, was then a captain working for Military Intelligence in Egypt. He wrote to Sir Mark Sykes, a Member of Parliament, about the danger to 'Abdu'l-Bahá's life. The letter, however, did not reach its intended recipient until 6 February 1918.[12] Lady Blomfield received a phone call about this same time and the caller said, "Abdu'l-Bahá in serious danger. Take immediate action.'[13] She quickly went to Lord Lamington, 'a frequent speaker at the House of Lords on questions affecting the East', who immediately wrote to the Secretary of State for Foreign Affairs, Arthur Balfour. On 24 January 1918, Balfour wrote, 'I have been asked to intervene in the interest of Abdul Behar . . . I enclose a Memo about him and I should be grateful could the action be taken.'[14] The Memo stated:

> Abdul Behar sometimes known as Abbas Effendi, leader of the Bahai movement, having for its object the true peace of the world is believed to be at his home in Haifa, or else on M. Carmel. In the past he has undergone much persecution at the hands of fanatics and anxiety is felt by his many friends in Gt. Britain and America lest he, his wife and family should not receive adequate protection during the British advance owing to his identity not being known to our authorities. His friends therefore would be grateful if instructions would be cabled to secure on his behalf the good offices of those in command.[15]

On the same day this letter arrived, another arrived at the Department of Foreign Affairs from Frederick Whyte, a member of Parliament and son of Jane Whyte, a Bahá'í in Edinburgh, saying,

> I have just received a letter from my Mother saying that she understands that Abdul Baha is living in some risk of his life at Haifa. My Mother's correspondent, as you will see from the enclosed letter, seems to think that we could do something to save him. I presume I need not waste your time in giving an account of Abdul Baha himself, whose personality and work must be well known to you . . . I know that at one time Lord Curzon was very deeply impressed with the Bahai Movement in Persia itself and he may be willing to interest himself in the matter now.[16]

In a note appended to Whyte's letter, R. Graham wrote: 'The Bahais are splendid people, but I do not see how we can help Abdul Baha unless and until we get to Haifa . . .' All of this led to a telegram being sent to Sir Reginald Wingate for the British High Commissioner in Egypt on 30 January which said: 'My attention has been called to the presence at Haifa of Abdul Baha, head of the Bahais. Please warn the General Office Commanding that he and his family should be treated with special consideration in the event of our occupying Haifa . . .'[17]

In late September 1918, General Sir Edmund Allenby began an offensive directed at liberating Haifa and ʻAkká. The speed of the British attack up through Palestine caught the Turkish forces unprepared – Allenby's forces covered 50 miles in three days.[18] As the sound of artillery fire and fighting reached Haifa, the small Bahá'í community was terrified that Jamál Pá<u>sh</u>á's death threat against ʻAbdu'l-Bahá might be carried out. ʻAbdu'l-Bahá calmed them and called them to pray. He told His followers that no British shells would cause death in Haifa, and that turned out to be the case.[19]

On 23 September, both Haifa and ʻAkká were captured. ʻAbdu'l-Bahá had predicted that Haifa would be taken with little loss of life and that ʻAkká would surrender without a fight. Both of these happened as He predicted. The capture of ʻAkká was surprising because the British expected to find a fortress full of Turkish soldiers. Unknown to them, however, the Turks secretly evacuated during the night, leaving the ancient city empty of troops. The next morning, two lost British soldiers arrived in front of 'Akká, mistakenly thinking that the town was already in British hands. 'Akká's mayor, seeing the British soldiers, immediately rushed out and presented the startled men with the keys of the town and welcomed them.[20]

After the capture of the two towns, 'Abdu'l-Bahá and His family were found to be safe and on that same day word was quickly sent to London saying, 'I have now received a telegram from the Chief Political Officer in Palestine, reporting that on the occupation of Haifa, Abdul Behar was found to be still in the town in good health, and that he is being well cared for.'[21]

Ahmad Sohrab joyously sent a letter to Joseph Hannen on 26 September that told the news of the Master's safety:

> The victorious British army came down from Nazareth like unto a mighty irresistible whirlwind on September 23, and at 3 p.m. took possession of our town, after a battle of twenty-four hours, the picture of which shall never be effaced from the page of my memory. The army that captured Haifa were all English and Indian cavalrymen, and they showed courage, invincibility and heroism in the very jaws of death . . .
>
> As soon as I heard this morning that our new postal authorities would receive letters for the outside world, I was beside myself with joy and hastened to write you this note, so that you and the friends may know that we are all well, awaiting anxiously to receive your news of how things are going with you and the friends.[22]

In another letter to Pauline Hannen, he told how 'Abdu'l-Bahá was found to be safe:

> When on September 23rd, the conquering General and his English and Indian Cavalry entered Haifa, one of the first questions that he asked of the President of the Municipality was about the health of 'His Excellency' Abdul-Baha, the head of the Bahai Movement and whether the Turks in any way had in the past few years molested his tranquillity and quiet life. Being assured that God has protected him and his followers, the General was satisfied and later in the afternoon of the same day, he sent his aid-de-camps [sic] to Abdul-Baha's home to meet him and make personal inquiries about his

health. Next morning he called himself and had a pleasant interview. Three days later, Col. Stores [Storrs], the Military Governor of Jerusalem, who was acquainted with Abdul-Baha when in Egypt, came to Haifa in his own automobile to meet him and after his warm reception informed the Cairo believers by cable that Abdul-Baha was enjoying good health.[23]

Colonel Sir Ronald Storrs wrote of his second meeting with 'Abdu'l-Bahá (he had previously spent an hour with the 'patient but unsubdued prisoner and exile' in 1909):

> I called upon 'Abbás Effendi on the day I arrived and was delighted to find him quite unchanged . . . His conversation was indeed a remarkable planning, like that of an ancient prophet, far above the perplexities and pettiness of Palestine politics, and elevating all problems into first principles.
>
> He was kind enough to give me one or two beautiful specimens of his own handwriting together with that of Mishkin Kalam . . .[24]

'Abdu'l-Bahá was in Haifa during the British invasion, but as soon as it was safe, He went immediately to the Shrine of Bahá'u'lláh and then stayed in 'Akká.[25]

On 25 September, Tudor Pole sent £200 of food supplies to 'Abdu'l-Bahá, requesting at the same time that the Master come to Egypt where He could be cared for more easily. Colonel Storrs replied on 29 September that 'Abdu'l-Bahá and His family had plenty of food. 'Abdu'l-Bahá said He didn't need the money for Himself so he asked that it be given to the poor.[26]

In another letter dated 8 October, Sohrab wrote to Georgie Ralston:

> This letter was written to you nearly two years ago, but returned to me from Constantinople because war was declared between the United States and Germany. Because it contains the words of Abdul-Baha as well as the translation of his Tablet to you, I only change the envelope, add these few words of greeting and mail it again, hoping that this time it may reach you safely. During this long period of silence we have been waiting for this day, so that we might correspond with each other with the utmost freedom.[27]

The conquering British were mesmerized by 'Abdu'l-Bahá and many went to see Him:

> Abdul-Baha, after four years of silence and isolation, was again pleased to meet and speak with men who understand his ideas and respect his conviction. English officers of all ranks, Major General, Brigadier General, Colonels, Majors, Lieutenants, Captains and non-commissioned men and privates have called on him and drank tea with him and listened reverently to his words of wisdom. The military Governors of Acca and Haifa have often met him; the former being his guest at dinner. Once about eight members of the Australian Flying Corps, who have their aerodrome at the foot of Mount Carmel, were his guests all day in Bahje, near Acca. They visited the tomb of Bahá'u'lláh, listened to the lecture of Abdul-Baha on the history of this Cause and its principles, and left in the evening in their large auto with glad hearts and beaming faces. Never were they so royally received in Palestine! They were overwhelmed with the extreme kindness and attention of the Master. Surely they will never forget what they heard and saw . . .[28]

The British army had advanced so quickly to Haifa, however, that it had outrun its supply train, so there was a huge problem with food supplies.[29] Because of this problem, a British officer went to consult with 'Abdu'l-Bahá. The Master said, 'I have corn.' In surprise, the officer asked, 'But for the army?' to which 'Abdu'l-Bahá replied, 'I have corn for the British army.' 'Abdu'l-Bahá had taught the Bahá'í farmers how to grow corn, which resulted in abundant harvests. The extra corn was stored in covered pits, some of which the Romans had originally dug. So, when the British needed food, 'Abdu'l-Bahá had corn.[30]

Wellesley Tudor Pole arrived to see the Master on 21 November:

> The Master was standing at the top waiting to greet me with that sweet smile and cheery welcome for which he is famous. For seventy-four long years Abdul-Baha has lived in the midst of tragedy and hardship, yet nothing has robbed or can rob him of his cheery optimism, spiritual insight and keen sense of humour.
>
> He was looking little older than when I saw him seven years ago, and certainly more vigorous than when in England after the

> exhausting American trip. His voice is as strong as ever, his step virile, his hair and beard are (if possible) more silver-white than before.[31]

After lunch, 'Abdu'l-Bahá and Tudor Pole drove to the Shrine of Bahá'u'lláh. 'Abdu'l-Bahá

> approached the Tomb in complete silence, praying with bent head – a wonderfully venerable figure in his white turban and flowing grey robe.
>
> On reaching the portal to the Tomb itself, the Master prostrated himself at length, and kissed the steps leading to the inner chamber. There was a majestic humility about the action that baffles description . . .[32]

When they returned to 'Akká, they found about three dozen people had gathered. The Master served them tea, then told them about His visit to Tudor Pole's hotel in Clifton, Bristol. Later, Tudor Pole went to meet the Military Governor and see what he thought about 'the greatest religious personage in Asia today'. He arrived to find the Governor deep into the arrangements of the next day's World Peace celebration. He had found a band that would accompany many notables of 'Akká in a parade through the town. The Governor himself would give a speech from the balcony of the Town Hall. The one thing the Governor had not done, however, was to invite 'Abdu'l-Bahá. When Tudor Pole asked about the omission of inviting the one person Who had dedicated His whole life to peace, the Governor said that, well, his name hadn't appeared on the list of important people in 'Akká that he had been given. The omission was quickly rectified.[33]

The next day, Tudor Pole gave the Master a pile of letters from all over the world that he had brought, to which 'Abdu'l-Bahá dictated replies for Tudor Pole to take with him. Tudor Pole also gave 'Abdu'l-Bahá a Persian camel-hair cloak, which 'greatly pleased him, for the winter is here, and he had given away the only cloak he possessed. I made him promise to keep this one through the winter, and I trust he does.'[34] At lunch that day, 'Abdu'l-Bahá and Tudor Pole talked on a variety of subjects. After a while, another English-speaking person joined them and Tudor Pole suddenly realized that, although he neither understood nor spoke Persian, 'Abdu'l-Bahá had been speaking in Persian during the whole of their conversation and that he had understood every word.[35]

Shoghi Effendi wrote to Lotfu'lláh Hakím on 19 November about Tudor Pole's visit. He wrote that 'Abdu'l-Bahá

> was so glad to look at his radiant face and feel, from shaking his hands, the fresh fragrances of the ablazed Bahais of England . . . The Beloved has been sojourning for a month and a half at Acca, visiting almost daily the Tomb of his father and offering his thanksgivings for the bounty, care and protection of the Blessed Perfection . . .
>
> The past four years have been of untold calamity, of unprecedented oppression, of indescribable misery, of severe famine and distress, of unparalleled bloodshed and strife, but now that the dove of peace has returned to its nest and abode a golden opportunity has arisen for the promulgation of the Word of God. This will now be promoted and the Message delivered in this liberated region without the least amount of restriction. This is indeed the Era of Service.[36]

Ahmad Sohrab had called on the Persian Consul General on 28 December in order to get a new passport. The Consul General had met the Master before the war and was strongly attracted to Him. Sohrab noted:

> He is an enthusiastic lover of Persia, and free from the narrow prejudices of many bigoted Persians. He praised the Bahais very fervently, especially Agha Mohamad Taki. 'Although he is a Bahai,' he said, 'yet I believe as truth all that he tells me, because I know that he is essentially a good and righteous man; but there are many important Persians in this city who are Moslems, still I cannot trust them because their lives are not straight and their aims are selfish.' He desired the Bahais to render a most concrete and practical service to Persia.[37]

At the end of 1917, 'Abdu'l-Bahá sent a Tablet to Mason Remey about the war, America and the great receptivity of people everywhere to the message of the Faith due to the ravages of the war:

> Praise be unto God, that throughout this violent storm the Ark of the Covenant hath attained unto the shore of Salvation. The danger

was imminent and the occasion for fear and apprehension prepared. The friends in all the regions remained safe and preserved under the shade of divine protection, particularly in the Holy Land where the danger and calamities were infinite and limitless. Every day brought a new trial and every hour carried with it a special difficulty. In brief, had not divine protection been extended, existence for a single day would have been absolutely impossible. This, verily, is one of the miracles of God that I and the friends in the Holy Land should remain safe and protected while being held in the strong grip of a group of sanguinary persons.

Prior to the war, numerous letters were dispatched to America wherein it was manifestly recorded that a severe commotion was ahead and a great agitation lay in the near future; that the people of the world would be involved in crucial danger and affliction, and trying tests would come to pass; that the pillars of comfort would quake from the intensity of commotion and that blessed souls would shine resplendently like unto the stars of the Supreme Horizon.

Praise be to God, the showers of the blessing of the Blessed Beauty (Baha'o'llah) are abundantly pouring and the grace and bounty of the loving Lord are complete. At present these gloomy clouds are in the process of dissipation from the horizon of the world. The friends of God must, in accordance with the prescribed directions which have formerly been sent, forget everything, hasten to different lands and regions and promulgate the divine teachings. For this blood-thirsty war has made the world of mankind tired of life, all ears eager to hearken to the call of universal peace, to the declaration of the oneness of the world of humanity, to full understanding, to the annihilation of estrangement and the hoisting of the standard of affection. The majority of the people are ready to listen to the divine teachings. Opportunity must not be let slip away for at another occasion such a capacity will not be found and endeavor and effort shall be in vain. Today is the day of teaching, for all men are athirst and divine teachings are as the refreshing water. Later on, the thirst shall not remain so severe. Hence one should seize the opportunity so that possibly all races and creeds shall unite and this enmity and rancor may vanish from among men.[38]

Shoghi Effendi

In the summer of 1918, Shoghi Effendi returned to Haifa from the Syrian Protestant College, where he had spent most of the previous five years studying English and other subjects. He had earned his Bachelor of Arts degree in June 1917, then spent an additional year doing graduate studies. With the end of the war, letters and pilgrims began to flow into Haifa and Shoghi Effendi quickly found his English skills to be a great help to 'Abdu'l-Bahá; for the next two years he acted as one of the Master's translators. The young man soon found himself translating letters to Bahá'ís in Japan, and to such well-known Bahá'ís as Marion Jack, Agnes Alexander, George Latimer and Jessie Revell.[39] Shoghi Effendi described the excitement of his new work:

> Every day carries with it fresh tidings and happy news. From the Far-Eastern land, the centre of news has shifted today to Persia, in the Middle East, and thence to the extreme West in the U.S. of America. Many telegrams have arrived, and each contributed its share of consolation and solace . . .
>
> Early this morning I was ushered to His Holy presence, and there facing the Beloved on the sofa, enwrapped in His mantle with masses of supplications scattered around Him, I sat, the pen in my hand, putting down the words that flowed from His lips.[40]

1919: JANUARY–NOVEMBER

In 1919, a stream of Tablets flowed from 'Abdu'l-Bahá's pen to the world as a flood of pilgrims poured in. Shoghi Effendi wrote on 29 January that the Master had written almost a hundred Tablets to the friends in America alone.[1]

Because of the lack of food and other problems throughout the general population, the Haifa Relief Fund was established, 'composed of the heads of the different religious denominations and acting under the surveillance of the British authorities'. On 10 February, Ahmad Sohrab wrote that at the first meeting, all the religious leaders gathered, 'from the bishop to the Jewish rabbi'. 'Abdu'l-Bahá donated £50. He later sent Shoghi Effendi with an additional contribution.[2]

Tudor Pole wrote that 'Abdu'l-Bahá had driven with General and Lady Allenby, General Bols and Colonel Stanton to 'Akká and that they had taken tea at Bahjí. Tudor Pole said that Allenby 'was deeply impressed, and asked for literature on the Bahai Movement'. By this time 'Abdu'l-Bahá had been visited by every important military commander in Palestine including the Commander-in-Chief, General Sir Arthur Money, and General Ronald Storrs.[3]

Shoghi Effendi's diary letters

Early in 1919, Shoghi Effendi began writing diary letters which he typed himself (using the 2-finger method[4]) on a manual typewriter. Using carbon paper, he made multiple copies of these letters and began sharing them with Bahá'ís around the world.[5] On 8 February, Shoghi Effendi wrote that Captain Agal Khan, from Lahore, Punjab, came to see 'Abdu'l-Bahá carrying a newspaper article on the Bahá'í Faith and Bahá'u'lláh, published by 'Abbás 'Alí of Rangoon and reprinted in a Punjab paper. 'Abdu'l-Bahá spoke with him for over an hour about how 'under chains and fetters Bahá'u'lláh propagated his teachings, the mutual arrangements of the rulers of Turkey and of Persia to quench his light and the utter failure of their plans'. The captain was amazed to learn that the remains of the Báb had been interred in the Tomb on the hill above and he said that his next goal was to visit that holy site. He left promising to return with some of his friends.[6]

The next day, Shoghi Effendi wrote:

> This afternoon being bright and warm, Abdul-Baha ascended the mountain and visited the Tomb of the Bab where the friends had assembled for their weekly Sunday gatherings, where he inquired regarding the spiritual activities of the S. P. C. students [Syrian Protestant College in Beirut] to which one of its members, Mr. Bahader [Bahádur], who is still here for a short visit to Abdul-Baha, replied that their weekly Sunday gatherings are uninterruptedly held within the college grounds. This leading to a certain statement made by the president of the college with respect to his Sunday morning Bible classes, Abdul-Baha referred to the relative standing of the Holy Books and their adaptation to their respective environment. The Old Testament, he said, is largely historical and partly states various commands and regulations. The Gospel, on the other hand, in addition to these two subjects, reveals a whole set of admonition and exhortation, of counsels and of advice. The Koran embodies all three of these and in addition reveals abstruse, scientific and mathematical problems. He then spoke in detail of the variety of the branches in mathematics and astronomy as expounded by the Egyptian, Babylonian, Greek, Roman and Persian leaders and scientists. He then referred to the rise of Ptolemy, his compilation of the different theories of past mathematicians, his school in Alexandria, his book being the essence and gist of previous laws and theories and his founding the well-known Ptolemaic system. He told us how all astronomers and philosophers believed in his system and although Pythagoras and Plato revealed contradictory facts, that the Ptolemaic system was considered the immutable and correct law. Then arose that illiterate, young, inexperienced Arab leader in the Arabian peninsula, who revealed his Koran wherein the following words are incorporated: 'The sun moves in a fixed place and each star moves in its own heaven.' These bodily challenged the whole Ptolemaic system and shook it down to its very foundation. However, it was not until the 15th century, when the famous Copernicus discarded the baseless interpretation of the ulemas in their explanation of the

> two above-mentioned verses, overthrew the Ptolemaic system and asserted the truth of the statement of the illiterate Arab youth, who declared the movement of the earth and the immobility of the sun. The whole scientific world arose to the consciousness of this truth. What clearer and stronger proof may be stated for the establishment of the truth of the Mohammedan Revelation?[7]

Ḥájí Muḥammad Yazdí arrived a few days later from Damascus, and Shoghi Effendi wrote that he had

> brought with him many a good news. When the permission to visit the holy sites was granted to our eager visitor . . . the means of facility were miraculously provided. Within an exceptionally short period of time he secured his pass, was assigned a comfortable and uncrowded compartment in the train, enjoyed splendid weather and sunshine all throughout his travel, the latter lasting only ten hours – an exceptionally swift and comfortable journey.
>
> This morning he was ushered into Abdul-Baha's presence and the first thing he did was to offer a supplication from an erudite Arab, a native of Medina, an influential and responsible personage in Damascus, an authority in the Moslem creed, who had been attracted and moved to write to Abdul-Baha as result of the interview and discussions with Sheikh Aliasqae, that seemingly cold, indifferent and powerless soul . . .
>
> In short, the news of our dear visitor, Agha Haji Mohammed Yazdi, was refreshing, numerous and significant. With a smile and a nod of appreciation Abdul-Baha greeted every bit of news and was glad to know that a reaction from the passiveness and inactivity of the past had set in. ‘Deliver the divine message with prudence and wisdom’, was his recommendation to the teachers who are serving in these regions. Having said this he arose, again welcomed our guest and regained his room to correct the Tablets that had been revealed, leaving us with our friend whose source of news and glad tidings seemed inexhaustible,
>
> Abdul-Baha remained in doors until 3 P. M., when Major Nott came and motored him to the house of the Commander-in-chief, Sir Edmund Allenby. This was the second time Abdul-Baha had called on the General and this time the conversation centered around the

> Cause and its progress. Interest seems to have been stimulated and eagerness to learn more of the Truth intensified. This time, as well as last, was particularly noted for the warmth, the reserve and the respect which characterized the conversation of General Allenby with the Master. He is a very gentle, modest and striking figure, warm in affection, yet imposing in his manners.[8]

Major Wellesley Tudor Pole had written an introductory article about the Bahá'í Faith which was printed in the *Palestine News* early in the year. On 14 February, Shoghi Effendi wrote that because of the article, 'inquirers and seekers multiply with astonishing rapidity, a keen interest is aroused and a wide demand is being pressed more and more.' The addresses of Elinor Hiscox in Cairo and Ethel Rosenberg in London had been included and they found themselves in correspondence with many people, mostly in, or formerly in, the military.[9]

After 'Abdu'l-Bahá had spent that morning correcting and signing 60 Tablets, there was a knock at the door. When it was opened, there stood Private Sinclair, bearing a copy of Tudor Pole's article, which included an invitation 'to quaff from the fountain-head'. The young man worked at the Red Cross Egyptian hospital in Haifa and had found some Bahá'í literature in Cairo, after which he had read Tudor Pole's article. From these, Private Sinclair's interest had been raised 'to its highest pitch and henceforth he became an ardent inquirer'. 'Abdu'l-Bahá's first words to Sinclair were, 'I am glad to meet thee for thy face is illumined, thy brow is pure, thy heart is clear and thy purpose is right.' Shoghi Effendi wrote:

> A search so sincere, an interest so lively, an earnestness of tone so genuine has hardly been remarked in any of the previous callers and inquirers. In view of his earnest inquiry and his lack of any preconception, the Master spoke in detail of the main purpose of the Bahai teachings, the idea of peace and reconciliation, the most immediate need of mankind. He told him the futility of men's effort to establish a lasting peace, resting on secure foundations, through material means. Whenever such efforts have been exerted they were doomed to failure. History affords a striking illustration. 'From what I can gather from the events during my life', said Abdul-Baha, 'history clearly shows the wars that have been waged, the peace measures that were subsequently adopted, have proved inevitable failures . . .'

> Our attentive visitor listened and was absorbed. He was glad to listen to this remarkable talk and was furthermore grateful to receive a copy of Mr. Remey's *Some Vital Bahai Principles* which Abdul-Baha put in his hands. When he retired, he was inwardly moved and outwardly satisfied and assured.[10]

The next day, Shoghi Effendi wrote that 'No less than a score of callers from prince and pasha to a simple private soldier have sought interview with Abdul-Baha.' Private Sinclair, whose 'eyes sparkled as he shook hands with the Beloved', had read Remey's pamphlet and was back for more. 'He seemed,' wrote Shoghi Effendi, 'full of the spirit of Baha'o'llah, absorbed in meditation, and ablaze with His love.' As he left, 'Abdu'l-Bahá embraced him saying, 'Thou art my son, my dear son, I love thee, and I pray for thee.'[11]

'Abdu'l-Bahá was at Bahjí on 18 February and Shoghi Effendi wrote that

> The Beloved has again decided to tarry for a time at the vicinity of the tomb of his father. Here he is, in the adjoining room, sitting by the candle light, viewing from his window the solitude from afar, the silent surroundings, which nothing breaks save the distant roar of the waves which die away in the immensity of space. He is engaged in his meditations, absorbed in his prayers, thinking of his friends across the seas, remembering their prayers and their supplications and communing with his heavenly Father on behalf of such souls. What a vivid contrast does this vicinity of the Holy Tomb represent with the increasing activity of the life in Haifa. The air over there was filled with gases and vapors which steam and motor engines continuously discharge, while the atmosphere here is as pure, as clear and as fragrant as it can be. The traffic accompanied with its deafening noise and bustle, gives way here to a stillness, a calmness and a quietude which nothing interrupts but the stillness of nature. The dazzling lights of the city are gone and nothing but a flickering taper's light cheers this cold and starless night. The constant movement and circulation witnessed in the Beloved's house has stopped, and tonight everything is at a stand still, everything quiet and at rest. The morning hour of prayer is maintained and even lengthened for twice a day, the Beloved visits the holy shrine, kneels in reverence

and devotion, orders communes to be chanted and often spends an hour or more in silent prayer. His attendants, friends and relatives are absent and no one save Kosro, Esfandiar and myself, the two vigilant guardians of the Tomb, and Ali Eff, a friend who will leave tomorrow for Beirut, form his small retinue.

Everything, the environment, the atmosphere, the view, the stillness, all are uplifting, elevating and inspiring. One feels to have forgotten his cares and his concerns, his mind is refreshed and his burden alleviated. No matter how long the Master will tarry in this sanctified place, no feeling of monotony, and ennui overcomes the soul. It is the Spot which so many souls crave to attain and long to visit. Particularly is it magnificent at such a time when nature is smiling, the sky above is no more gloomy and threatening with clouds but serene and blue, the plains and meadows as if covered with a multicolored carpet, the shrubs sparkling with roses, jasmins, lilies, narcissus embalming the pure and refreshing air; the grass growing luxuriantly everywhere and the breeze wafting in every direction. Often is the Beloved seen in the open air, majestically walking to and fro upon the verdant plains and amid the wild flowers that abound in this gifted region. He treads the same ground that the blessed feet of his heavenly Father have trodden, circumambulates the shrine where for many years He has lived, waters the flowers and plants, many of which have been blessed by His hands and lives and moves and has his being in an atmosphere which fully reminds him of His manners and His conduct. What a dear and blessed spot to be privileged to live in![12]

Military visits and pilgrims

Wellesley Tudor Pole was in Haifa and 'Akká from 25 to 27 February and was met by Mírzá Aḥmad Yazdí, who was then the Persian Consul in Port Said and had recently married 'Abdu'l-Bahá's daughter, Munavvar Kh̲ánum. Tudor Pole wrote that 'Abdu'l-Bahá's 'influence is doing much to lessen the friction between various important religious communities in Palestine and elsewhere'. When Tudor Pole left Haifa, he carried a hundred Tablets from 'Abdu'l-Baḥá to be mailed all over the world.[13]

Though communication with the rest of the world had improved dramatically, it was still curtailed by the residue of the war. In spite of that, wrote Shoghi Effendi,

> Supplications from every corner of the globe, of different length and character, written in different languages, enclosing clippings of papers, pamphlets, typewritten reports, petitions, etc., are ceaselessly pouring in and the time for their perusal is sufficient to exhaust all the time that one might possibly have at his disposal. Although the ways have not yet fully opened and communication with all parts has not yet been restored, one is baffled at the amount of letters, books and magazines that the post office daily delivers.[14]

And beyond correspondence, pilgrims were arriving again. By April, Hippolyte and Laura Dreyfus-Barney had come from France; Muḥammad-Taqí Iṣfáhání and others arrived from Cairo; and Husayn Ikbal, Zia Bagdadi's brother from Adana, Turkey, came with his family.[15]

'Abdu'l-Bahá had no sooner returned from his journey to Europe and America than He began receiving supplications that He visit one place or another. The believers in India had long been begging for the Master to visit and 'Abdu'l-Bahá began suggesting that He desired such a visit. According to Shoghi Effendi, He had declared that He was planning a journey to India, Indo-China, Japan and Hawaii before crossing the American continent for a second time and proceeding to Europe.[16]

Two 'enlightened' British officers, Colonel Cash and Major Fitzgerald, called on 'Abdu'l-Bahá on 5 June. They were hurrying to Egypt, but thought it important enough to spend two hours with the Master before they left. Their main question was, 'Is it at all possible for those who have sacrificed their lives so freely on the battle field to communicate with their relatives and kindred from the world beyond?' 'Abdu'l-Bahá replied:

> This spiritual communication and mutual exchange of thoughts is conditioned upon certain facts that prepare the person in this world to communicate with the spirit of his departed ones. A clear mind, a pure heart and a concentrated attention are the requisites for that spiritual inter-communication. Like unto a mirror, man's heart and mind must be purified, clarified and polished. Any dust or rust that may be on it such as attachment to this nether world, the turning of man's face away from God, sin or lust, animosity and rancour – all these must be removed that the rays of the Sun of Truth may shine upon it in full splendor and may be reflected therefrom with full effulgence. If such state or condition is attained, communication

> with the world above will be made possible. Purity of purpose and concentration with prayer are the essential requisites.[17]

In November, Mrs Jean Stannard asked a similar question 'concerning the state of all those young men souls who have fallen so suddenly and tragically during or world war. Could they affect our present living conditions in any way?' 'Abdu'l-Bahá explained:

> God treats these people with His mercy, not with his justice, since God is against war. But as many did not will the war, but were obliged to go to the battle field by force of circumstances, therefore God has mercy for they suffered much and they lost their lives. These deserve the forgiveness of God. As they suffered in the world and were afflicted by great calamities and their blood was shed and in reality they were treated unjustly and thus died unwillingly, therefore God will have mercy and forgive their shortcomings and will reward them. He will compensate them for loss. Is it just to be so afflicted and killed and suffer and have no reward? This is contrary to the Kingdom of God. We supplicate God that these murdered ones will become and stay alive in His Kingdom and be submerged in the sea of His mercy.[18]

On 19 June, Colonel Criton, Colonel Bentwitch and Major Kerr, three British officials associated with the administration of Palestine, came to meet 'Abdu'l-Bahá. Each came with a specific question regarding legal principles of the courts and international law and each received a convincing answer. Colonel Criton had been commissioned to go to 'Akká and inspect the portion of the prison where Bahá'u'lláh had been incarcerated and to ensure that no damage was done to it during the conversion of the buildings into a prison. He said that Britain felt that it had the duty to preserve that portion of the prison as a memorial for future generations. 'Abdu'l-Bahá then gave a short talk on Bahá'u'lláh's exile from Persia to 'Akká which his visitor found very touching.[19]

A journalist, Marion Weinstein, visited 'Abdu'l-Bahá in June or July. She wrote of her visit in the *Globe and Commercial Advertiser* of 17 July:

> While the league of nations is hailed or attacked here as a Wilsonian project, out in Palestine is a religious leader who claims it first saw

the light in the writings of his father fifty years ago. He is Abdul-Baha, the son and successor of Baha'o'llah, founder of the modern cult, Bahaism.

Abdul-Baha, or Abbas Effendi, as he is widely known in the Near East, counts hundreds of followers in America. He made a tour here in 1912, preaching his doctrine of universal love in churches and halls from coast to coast . . .

I met Abdul-Baha lately in his home in Haifa. He has many friends among the British, including General Ronald Storrs, military governor of Jerusalem, and it was a British officer who took me to him. His influence is considerable in the Holy Land, but it is almost impossible to reduce it to actual numbers. I went to him curious as to his views of the future of Palestine, but he seemed more eager to talk of a matter of world importance – the league of nations.

He spoke in Persian, a well trained secretary interpreting his low, soft words in good English. Through the open windows of the large sunny salon of his modern house came the trill of songbirds in the Effendi's lovely garden. In white galabieh and turban, he fitted into the summery scene, his voice falling on the silence like a woodland echo. An ancient, venerable patriarch he seemed, with his snowy beard, a kindly patriarch, but with little of the Biblical fire.

'Fifty years ago,' he began, 'BAHA'O'LLAH wrote that there must be a league of nations to establish universal peace. He worked his idea out on practical lines, too. He said every nation must choose representatives, approved by the senate, the cabinet and the ruler of the country. They were to meet to found a universal peace congress to be forever a world court of arbitration.

'BAHA'O'LLAH saw even then, half a century ago, that unless universal peace is established, the world of humanity will continue in a state of barbarism. For it is a world of struggle for existence, of sensualism, a world of nature. Only when universal peace comes to stay will it become a world of spirit . . .'

For Palestine Abdul-Baha has the brightest hopes. 'It will develop day by day now,' he declared, 'in industry, in commerce, in agriculture, under an enlightened government. Up to the present the people of this country were like lost sheep. Now they have found their shepherd.

> 'If the Zionists will mingle with the other races and live in unity with them, they will succeed. If not, they will meet certain resistance . . .
>
> 'The Zionists should make it clear that their principle is to elevate all the people here and to develop the country for all its inhabitants. This land must be developed, according to the promises of the prophets Isaiah, Jeremiah and Zachariah. If they come in such a spirit they will not fail.
>
> 'They must not work to separate the Jews from the other Palestinians. Schools should be open to all nationalities here, business companies, etc. . . .
>
> 'This is the path to universal peace here as elsewhere – unity. We must prevent strife by all means. For 6,000 years man has been at war. It is time to try peace a little while. If it fails, we can always go back to war.'[20]

The number of pilgrims increased as the year went on. In the autumn. a group came from Persia who had travelled for about five months to reach 'Abdu'l-Bahá. They had met and overcome many dangers, delays and exorbitant charges for accommodation, spending 20 days on a ship in the monsoon season, during four of which they had no food. Finally, when they approached the port at Haifa and their spirits soared at the thought of reaching their cherished goal, the ship did not stop but sailed right past and on to Beirut. They could see the Shrine of Bahá'u'lláh, but they were forced to watch it pass astern. Just the sight of the Shrine was enough to give them the strength to wait out a quarantine stay in Beirut. When they were 'finally ushered into the presence of Abdul-Baha, scenes of inexpressible joy were witnessed at the meeting, some of the younger members gazing on his face for the first time in their lives.'[21]

More of Shoghi Effendi's diary letters

Shoghi Effendi continued sending his diary letters through the summer of 1919. Much of his time was now spent translating Tablets for 'Abdu'l-Bahá. His increased workload forced him to condense his diary letters into a single weekly one instead of his previous daily reports. On 3 August, Shoghi Effendi wrote that

This day was eventful. The Master made several significant statements. He revealed a Tablet for the ex-governor of New York City in which He presented the basic teachings of the Faith and praised the humanitarian actions of the government officials.

Consul Abella who had been in charge of British interests in Haifa, came to visit the Master. The Master spoke to this visitor about the oppression and misery in the region during the war.

Before noon more visitors, the deputy governor of 'Akká and his wife, came to see 'Abdu'l-Bahá. The conversation centred on topics that interested the deputy governor including social reconstruction, the industrial crisis, the spread of Bolshevism and so on. The deputy governor and his wife had lunch with the Master during which 'Abdu'l-Bahá spoke of the sacredness of Mount Carmel and the unique position of the Shrine of the Báb. At two o'clock the deputy governor and the Master were driven to the Shrine of the Báb. There, near the middle gate facing 'Akká, they sat and discussed the spiritual significance of Carmel.

In the afternoon . . . Mrs Stannard, the friends and pilgrims arrived. They sat in the presence of the Master and listened to His important discourse. Mrs Stannard said to the Master that she was happy to see Him so comfortable. In response, the Master said: 'I have always felt at rest. Hast thou ever seen me uncomfortable? It does not make any difference to me. Do you want me to tell you the truth? At a time when I was confined, I felt much more comfortable and was much happier . . .'[22]

On 9 August, Shoghi Effendi reported that Major Moore, a correspondent for the *Times of Teheran,* and a supporter of the League of Nations, came to see the Master. He talked about the failure of war to create peace. The next day, the Major returned with a question about whether prayer and concentration could have an effect on another person. Shoghi Effendi wrote that 'Abdu'l-Bahá answered the question by saying that

man cannot stimulate and awaken others if he is speechless and inactive. His prayer can only bring a change through divine power. However, as soon as the person puts his thoughts into actions his hearers can be inspired.

Regarding the condition of prayer, the Master said that the best time for prayer is at dawn and dusk. The power of will draws one to the condition of prayer. When one is not in a receptive mood and is rather immersed in one's worldly affairs, he can pull himself into the condition of prayer by an act of will: 'By a force of will and an effort of mind, man turns his attention to God, to His knowledge, His wonderful creation, His wisdom and His Omnipotence, and then by thinking frequently and deeply of Him, attains the state of Love, of desire for prayer, of supreme ecstasy. But sometimes one finds that Divine power and not human effort transports man into that condition.'[23]

On 1 October, 'Abdu'l-Bahá celebrated the twin birthdays of Bahá'u'lláh and the Báb according to the lunar calendar. Shoghi Effendi described the event:

> . . . the large number of pilgrims, including men, women and children, representatives of Persia, India, England and Egypt, that had flocked during past months to Haifa, were all summoned by their Master to come and celebrate this anniversary day in the vicinity of the Sacred Shrine. A concourse of sixty to seventy souls, pilgrims as well as residents of Haifa filled almost all the compartments of the morning train that left on that day for Acca. When they reached their destination the friends of Acca, likewise men and women, who had gathered in that same Spot in anticipation of their arrival, raised the number of the participators in the great jubilee to well nigh a hundred. Although the night before they had hardly slept a wink, so eager and impatient were they to catch the early morning train, yet when at last they found themselves on their way to the Sacred Spot, they manifested by their songs, exclamations, clamour and movements, a joy that amazed everyone even the conductor of the train. Not a minute did elapse in quiet and calmness from the time the train pulled away from the station of Haifa to the time it stopped at Acca. Amid the uproar and the jubilant songs that rent the air, the chief of the train was seen as if carried by an irresistible torrent, clapping, applauding and cheering. All the day was spent in the demonstration of such fervid and unbounded emotions, displaying thereby a scene that exerted its clear effect upon

a group of British officers, who in that hour of stir and animation, had motored from Haifa to meet specially the Master of whom they had heard so much. It was indeed a picturesque as well as imposing and significant scene, to witness again after these dreadful and perilous years of war, in the close vicinity of the Tomb of Bahaullah, the Beloved sitting with majesty and confidence with British officers in His presence and His far-away devoted friends sitting side by side on the ground or crowding the adjoining hall and corridors – all beaming with thanksgiving and joy at this happy and sudden turn of events. When twilight had set in and all outsiders had gone and nature seemed to present the opportune moment for prayer, the Beloved dressed in white, came out and proceeded with reverence and majesty toward the Sacred Shrine, followed by a long retinue of friends, marching all with a look on their faces and an expression in their countenance, that are exclusively attributed to the ablazed and steadfast believers of Persia. In the interior of the Sacred enclosure, all fell prostrate on the ground and then with their supplicant and tearful eyes directed toward the interior of the Tomb, plunged all into a moment of silent prayer.

This fervent meditation was broken by a most excellent and thrilling melody, sung by the well-known poet Kabil, a believer of Abadeh, who was bidden by the Beloved to address the opening prayer at the Sacred Threshold. This was followed by the chanting of the prayer of visitation, after which all retired to receive from the hands of the Beloved the various sweetmeats and fruits that were prepared for this remarkable occasion.

After that with hearts refreshed, with souls inspired and with mouths sweetened, they sat in the open air and gave vent as never before to their intense feeling of joy and of gratitude. Their leader who at every turn stirred and animated them had composed a poem in honour and memory of these two consecutive feasts, with a most charming chorus and a lovely tune and in the chanting of which all participators, young and old, heartily joined and swelled the chorus with the clapping of their hands and the tramping of their feet.

Joy was indeed unconfined . . . At dawn they awoke and in a mood of prayer hastened to the garden encircling the Tomb, plucked its flowers, circumambulated the shrine and visited again its interior.

Having partaken of the morning tea in the presence of the

> Beloved, and having received His blessings and favours they returned to their pilgrim-house on Mount Carmel . . .[24]

Three days later, the British battleship *S.S. Marlborough* was anchored off Haifa and the commander requested 'Abdu'l-Bahá to 'give him the honour of visiting the battleship in person'. The Master accepted and was greeted upon boarding by a group of naval officers, the Bishop of Haifa and the Mufti of 'Akká. Ship's officers gave Him a tour of the ship, including the turret, the interior and the 13.5-inch guns, after which He joined the Commander and the military governors of Haifa and 'Akká for tea. After joking about the comparative weathers of London and Haifa, 'Abdu'l-Bahá told those gathered:

> It is the first time that I have come on board of a man-of-war. I hope and trust that all these implements and means of warfare will be turned into factors that shall promote peace and industrial prosperity, that these men-of-war will be turned one day into merchant ships, stimulating thereby trade and industry. This is my hope.[25]

The following day, a pair of Italian liners arrived in port. One brought Mírzá Maḥmúd-i-Zarqání, one of the Master's secretaries in America and Europe, and Indian pilgrims Set Yousef and his daughter Ashraf. The other ship carried seven pilgrims, including Hand of the Cause Ibn-i-Aṣdaq and Fáḍil-i-Mázindarání. This second group had had a difficult passage, but 'Abdu'l-Bahá told them that whatever hardships they suffered in the path of God should be welcomed and accepted. He continued, saying:

> Difficulty under such circumstances was turned into happiness and ease and alarm converted into tranquility and contentment. Viewed from the standpoint of consequences, both are the same and if the object is attained without experiencing any hardship, it is undoubtedly preferable. This world is likened to a general market, 'bazar', in which one man is seen tranquil and restful while another is restless and active. Towards the end of the day the former as a result of his inactivity and rest is deprived of any gain and is thus gloomy and disheartened, whilst the latter in view of his toil and labor has gained and is as a result hopeful and glad.[26]

Later in the month, two soldiers of the 20th Deccan Horse Calvary came to see 'Abdu'l-Bahá. They had read about Him in their native town of Hyderabad. The Master warmly welcomed them and took them to the Shrine of the Báb, where they met several Bahá'ís and pilgrims. One of the soldiers returned the next day and spent more time with the Bahá'ís. The soldiers were followed by an Indian captain and a lieutenant. 'Abdu'l-Bahá told them:

> Although this war was terrible and fearful yet it led to our interview and made possible this meeting. I hope that ye will return in safety to India and there having laid down your arms ye will engage in another warfare – a war that ye will wage against self and passion. Waging war against human beings is an easy matter, what is difficult is resistance and a successful war against the evil passions of the heart. He who gains victory over his self and over Satan is the real conqueror, has proved his power and will become the recipient of God's blessing.[27]

Shoghi Effendi completely threw himself into his work for the Faith in a manner foreshadowing his work as Guardian. He worked whatever hours were required to do whatever the Master needed done and, as it did later, this affected his health. Shoghi Effendi suffered from repeated attacks of malaria throughout 1919. When he left to study at Oxford in April 1920, 'Abdu'l-Bahá sent Dr Lotfu'lláh Hakím with him and they spent the first three months at a sanatorium in Neuilly, France, before Shoghi Effendi was ready to continue to England.[28]

Dr John Esslemont, and Corinne and Edna True

In November, there was an influx of Western pilgrims. The first were Corinne and Edna True and Dr John Esslemont. They were followed by George Latimer, Harry and Ruth Randall with their 12-year-old daughter, Bahiyyih (Margaret), Arthur Hathaway, Albert Vail and Sachiro Fujita, along with a Colonel Allison and his wife, who had become intrigued about 'Abdu'l-Bahá after learning of Him on the ship with the Randalls. In addition to the Americans and British, there was a group of Eastern pilgrims that included Dr Sulláyman Rif'at Bey from Constantinople (Istanbul), Mírzá Feizullah Subhi and Ibn-i-Aṣdaq from

Tehran, Mírzá Muḥammad Sahib from Qazvin as well as 'Azízu'lláh Khán Varqá and Mírzá Asadu'lláh Faḍl from Mazandaran.[29]

Corinne had joined her daughter, Edna, in Paris, where Edna was serving after the war. There they met Ali-Kuli Khan and, on the day they were leaving Paris, also met the five members of the Randall group and had just enough time for dinner together.[30] Arriving in Naples, Corinne looked up Sachiro Fujita. Fujita, who had lived with the Trues for seven years, had received an instruction from 'Abdu'l-Bahá to 'come to [the] Holy Land in way of [the] Atlantic'. He had travelled with the Master in America in 1912. But now Fujita was waiting for a visa to enter Palestine and the Trues were forced to leave him and continue alone.[31]

In order to get to Egypt, the Trues first had to travel to Brindisi, on the boot heel of Italy. Eating breakfast in that city, Corinne noticed a 'distinguished-looking man' at a nearby table. Turning to Edna, she said:

> 'I think I know who that man is.'
>
> 'Who do you think he is?' Edna asked.
>
> 'I believe it is Dr Esslemont.'
>
> 'The Scot who is writing a book about the Faith?'
>
> 'Yes.'
>
> The stranger glanced their way, as if he sensed he knew them. But there was no communication between them in the dining room. Soon after returning to their room there was a knock on the door. It was the same man.
>
> 'Could you by chance be Mrs True?' he asked.
>
> 'Could you possibly be Dr Esslemont?' Corinne responded.[32]

The three Bahá'ís spent the next two days together. Edna especially enjoyed walking with Dr Esslemont on the Appian Way because he was an expert on Roman history. On 23 October, the Trues and Dr Esslemont both sailed for Haifa, but on different ships at different times.[33]

Corinne was still a poor traveller, but Edna, who loved to travel, helped her along. One trauma she did not have to undergo this time was the trip from ship to shore in a rowing boat that she had suffered in 1907 on her first pilgrimage. This time there was a train, but to ride it meant getting a permit from military headquarters in Cairo. Corinne suffered the delay, but Edna took complete advantage to explore around Cairo.

Finally, at 6:15 p.m. on 2 November they boarded the train and set out for the overnight trip to Haifa. It was not the pleasantest of journeys for Corinne since there were 'no comforts whatever on the train, only a bunk to wrap oneself in a steamer rug and stretch out for the night'.[34] The two women were befriended by a group of soldiers who reassuringly took the compartment next to theirs. The train had a notorious reputation – thieves targeted people, especially women and the elderly.[35]

Corinne and Edna arrived in Haifa at 11 the next morning and stayed in the pilgrim house across the road from the Master's home. Corinne noted that the Master's house even had a garage to house the Cunningham automobile sent to Him by Helen Goodall of California. Unfortunately, the car was quite big compared to Haifa's narrow streets and was confined to one-way roads. It was also too large to drive through 'Akká's city gate.[36] When the car arrived in cargo, the Master had put Shoghi Effendi in charge of clearing it through customs. The vehicle arrived at the beginning of the weekend and none of the officials were working, but Shoghi Effendi took the paperwork to the home of each one, getting signatures and the order for the car's release. 'Abdu'l-Bahá was quite surprised when Shoghi Effendi told Him that the car was outside and ready for Him before the weekend was over.[37]

Corinne and Edna learned with delight that Shoghi Effendi would be their guide to the Holy Places the next day. They were very taken with the 22-year-old young man they knew from 1907, when he was but ten, but now was on the verge of going to Oxford University. Rúḥíyyih Khánum later said that even as a youth, Shoghi Effendi showed the qualities he would later need to be the Guardian:

> Once the Master came into a room and found the Guardian alone memorizing tablets. The Master asked him what he was doing. The rest of the family was downstairs drinking coffee or tea and talking. 'Abdu'l-Bahá looked out of the window at them and said to Shoghi Effendi, 'I don't want you to be like them'.
>
> Shoghi Effendi asked 'Abdu'l-Bahá if he might go and study in England. He had been serving the Master as interpreter and sometimes as Secretary. When he went to England with the Master's permission he never dreamed it would be the last time he would see his beloved Grandfather. The object of his going was to perfect his English so he could translate the Writings of Bahá'u'lláh.[38]

Most mornings began with the pilgrims and others gathered in the Master's living room at 6:30 a.m. when there was the chanting of prayers followed by 'those far-famed cups of tea, which seemed like veritable draughts of life'. On some days, the pilgrims asked questions while on others He talked to them with that 'marvelous flow of divine knowledge and wisdom'. After the talk and a visit with the Greatest Holy Leaf or the Holy Mother, the pilgrims usually went back to the pilgrim house. Commonly, after they had returned to the pilgrim house and been served a European breakfast, the pilgrims would go out on the front balcony. The Eastern pilgrims would then join them and share stories of the early history of the Faith. At 4 p.m. the pilgrims returned to the Master's house for tea. At 6:30 the American women were permitted to meet with the men who gathered each evening to meet with 'Abdu'l-Bahá for an hour. Then came dinner, with Edna seated on the Master's left and Corinne on His right, together with a dozen of the Eastern pilgrims.[39]

'Abdu'l-Bahá talked with Corinne about the American House of Worship, of which she was the driving force. Corinne worried about the slow pace of the project. In 1919, the American community was still trying to raise sufficient money to start construction and was still a few months from choosing a design.[40] 'Abdu'l-Bahá, however, seemed unconcerned and assured her that the Ma<u>sh</u>riqu'l-A<u>dh</u>kár would become a great teacher of the Faith. The Master praised her for the development of the Bahá'í Temple Unity administrative body.[41]

Hand of the Cause Ibn-i-Aṣdaq one day spoke to Corinne about contributions for construction of the House of Worship. Describing the sacrifices of poverty-stricken Bahá'ís in villages across Persia, he said that

> in the furthest corners of Persia, in the outlying province of Khorassan, there is a village consisting of some 30 families who have all converted to the Cause and who are wonderfully enkindled. They live in extreme poverty to such an extent that a single rug is owned by a group of families and whenever a guest that is a travelling Bahai teacher arrives this rug is passed around that it may be used by that teacher and secure for him a partial comfort . . . Notwithstanding this misery and need and although their bread is made out of barley and their food is hardly sufficient, yet they manage to gather a cent

> or half cent every day and send their humble contribution every now and then for the Mashrekul Azkar in America.[42]

On this pilgrimage, Corinne had the bounty of spending a lot of time with the ladies of the Holy Household.

> We were permitted more intimate association with the Greatest Holy Leaf and the Holy Mother, Munírih Khánum. Almost daily we were received by them in the Master's garden where questions were asked and instructions given to us, clearing up many things that had puzzled the American friends. Here we saw this beloved wife of 'Abdu'l-Bahá as a most wonderful teacher, and through her we grew in the knowledge of the Cause. In the early days one of the greatest privileges of the visiting women pilgrims was this intimate association with these two divine maid-servants of Bahá'u'lláh, Bahíyyih Khánum, the Greatest Holy Leaf, and Munírih Khánum, the Holy Mother. We seldom saw one without the other.
>
> These holy women had sacrificed everything to be the companions of Bahá'u'lláh and 'Abdu'l-Bahá in Their imprisonment. Could we have found in all the world a greater privilege than this: to sit at the feet of these holy women; to hear from them, first hand, the thrilling recital of their prison lives, of how God had sustained them when deprived of the very necessities of life; and to learn that they regarded this prison life with the Blessed Perfection and 'Abdu'l-Bahá as infinitely more valuable to them than all the comforts and luxuries of life! These women are God's great heroines and we were indeed conscious of the great privileges that were granted us in their presence. The seeds of conviction that were born in our souls by this association planted roots of faith that assisted everyone to return to the outside world and lift the Banner of the Greatest Name before the eyes of all.
>
> On our second visit we saw Munírih Khánum not only as a Universal Mother loving every child of God, but as a great teacher and expounder of the principles of Bahá'u'lláh. She was a teacher who lived these principles before our eyes. Religious history had never known greater examples than these of devotion and sacrifice to God's Holy Messengers! Should we praise God throughout the coming centuries, we could not render praise sufficient for the

priceless spiritual heritage bequeathed to us by these holy women. They are the archetypes for the Bahá'í womanhood of the world.[43]

Dr John Esslemont arrived in Haifa on 5 November, but didn't see 'Abdu'l-Bahá until the next day. Dr Esslemont had started a book about the Faith, which came to be known as *Bahá'u'lláh and the New Era*, in about 1916 and by the time he reached Haifa, it was nearly half finished.[44] Dr Esslemont had a difficult pilgrimage from a health point of view. He was forced to stay in bed on 17 and 18 November and then again from 20 to 23 November with dysentery. On the 23rd, he finally asked 'Abdu'l-Bahá to help him. The Master replied: 'I will pray for you. I will pray for your spiritual health – that is the essential thing. I suffered much when I came here (in the prison at Acca, where he had dysentery very badly) and you must have a portion. You must suffer a little too.' When Dr Esslemont replied that he would be content with whatever was the will of God, 'Abdu'l-Bahá said, 'You are confirmed' then gave directions about what he should eat. He also sent over a rug from his own bed.[45]

But his illness didn't limit his time with 'Abdu'l-Bahá because the Master went to the Pilgrim House almost every day for lunch. He mixed humour with wise counsel. One day he told about a lady who was a very good Bahá'í, but overly reserved and lacking in enthusiasm. The Master said, 'In Persia we take sour milk, add a little water, shake it well and then we get very good butter from it. Mme ___ wants a good shaking up and then will yield very good butter.'[46]

After eleven days with 'Abdu'l-Bahá, the time of leaving arrived for the Trues. Corinne was already in the carriage when Shoghi Effendi hurried up and said the Master wished to see Edna. 'Abdu'l-Bahá had Edna sit in a chair next to His and then He looked into her eyes. Very quickly, she began to sob uncontrollably. 'Abdu'l-Bahá lovingly told her that she was His own daughter. When Edna returned to the carriage, Corinne knew what had taken place, because the same thing had happened to her in 1907.[47]

A future president visits

Sometime in about 1919, a poor young Israeli couple walked to Bahjí. They had been recently married and were walking the length and breadth of the country. As they passed the Shrine of Bahá'u'lláh they met 'Abdu'l-Bahá, who was very warm and courteous, taking them into Bahá'u'lláh's Shrine and serving them tea. The young couple were very impressed with 'Abdu'l-Bahá and 34 years later recounted the story to Leroy Ioas. The Israeli man was Itzhak Ben Zvi, who in 1952 was elected President of Israel and would make the 'first official visit paid by the Head of a sovereign independent State to the Sepulchres of the Martyr-Prophet of the Faith and the Centre of Bahá'u'lláh's Covenant' in 1954.[48]

1919: NOVEMBER–DECEMBER

The Randall family, George Latimer, Arthur Hathaway, Albert Vail and Fujita

As the Trues left, George Latimer, the Randalls, Arthur Hathaway, Albert Vail and Sachiro Fujita arrived with Colonel Allison and his wife.[1] Though the Randalls, George, Arthur, Albert and Fujita all ended up coming together, their journeys were different. George had been serving in the military in France when his invitation reached him. The Randalls and Albert Vail were told: 'In case travel to the Holy Land may be accomplished in the utmost comfort and happiness, your visit will be the cause of the rejoicing of hearts.'[2] Fujita left well in advance of the others but was delayed in Naples by his visa troubles.

The Randalls and Albert Vail left New York in October and, when they arrived in Naples, found Arthur Hathaway and Fujita already there. Fujita was still stranded in Naples trying to get his visa, but had run out of money. Fujita had written to 'Abdu'l-Bahá that he was returning to America. 'Abdu'l-Bahá immediately contacted General Allenby who wired the consulate in Rome to issue the passport and visa.[3] With that problem solved, Fujita and Arthur Hathaway found that it was very difficult to get a ship to take them to Haifa.

While in Rome, the Randall family was invited to meet Pope Benedict XV. Fujita was with the family when they met the Pope and he had felt forced to kiss the Pope's ring. When 'Abdu'l-Bahá heard about this, He is reported by George Latimer to have said, in substance: 'The Pope's Palace is worth 60,000,000 while His Holiness Christ was living with all his clothes in rags. He was in the wilderness . . .' He then talked about a Cardinal in America who had come to see Him and wanted Him to speak at a meeting, though behind His back he was publishing things against the Faith. The Master paid him no mind. When 'Abdu'l-Bahá was in Washington, the Cardinal was distributing leaflets against the Cause, but they seemed just to make more people want to hear Him and the Master continued to ignore him. Finally, when the Master was in Denver, where the Cardinal openly declared that 'Abdu'l-Bahá was the enemy of Christ, He decided it was time to respond. George Latimer recorded:

> There was a large demonstration for the dedication of a new chapel. This cardinal had arrived three days before to assist at the services. Now was the time to strike so the Master went to a very large crowd and said he had been made very grateful because of this large demonstration. His Highness the Cardinal had opened the church and he was exceeding grateful because this religious demonstration is exactly like the one 1900 years ago in Jerusalem. Exactly like it. But consider the matter carefully and one can find there is a little difference.
>
> That gathering was in the utmost humility while this one is in the utmost pomp and ceremony. On that occasion, the people were all blaspheming while at this one they were all glorifying. At that one a wreath of thorns was laid on the head of Christ, while at this one a jewelled crown was placed on the head of the Cardinal. The leader of that gathering was in rags while this one wore glittering robes, with a sceptre . . . In Jerusalem it was held in the utmost lowliness while here in the utmost pride. That one was held on the top of the Cross, this one on a stage in the Temple. That one there were the blasphemers, here 15,000 souls knelt down. What is the connection between the two? What similarity? That was the real one while this one was worldly.
>
> After this the Cardinal became silent.[4]

The Randalls brought Fujita into their party and sailed for Alexandria. Arthur was going to look for a later boat. The Randall’s ship, the *Karlsbad*, was a dirty vessel that had transported troops during the war. ‘When Margaret entered her stateroom, she thought the pattern on the wallpaper was quite strange. And then the pattern began to move, and she realized that the room was alive with insects. When she lay down, bugs crawled all over her – it was too much!’ She promptly put on all her clothes, and with socks over her hands announced she was sleeping on deck. The next day, the captain told them that the secret for getting rid of cockroaches was to put a piece of raw meat just outside the door. They tried that and it worked.[5]

When the group arrived in Cairo, Mírzá Muḥammad-Taqí came

to meet them and invited them to come to his home that evening for a meeting. During the day they also met Elinor Hiscox, Jean Stannard, and Corinne and Edna True, who had just left the presence of the Master. That evening, 'a large number of friends had gathered awaiting our coming', wrote George Latimer; 'words were scarcely needed for the spirit of love and understanding, the real language of the heart, was so strong between us'.[6]

They spent several days in Cairo where they all went to see the Pyramids. Their guide, who had been called 'Good for Nothing' by some sailors, was short on camel transport, having just four, so Bahíyyih had to ride a donkey. The donkey suddenly bolted with Bahíyyih clinging desperately to its back. The guide was frantic, but only because the donkey was very valuable. The next day, they took a tour of the bazaars. Suddenly a 'shouting crowd of men' surged around the corner and surrounded the party's carriages. The situation looked desperate until one man in the crowd saw an American flag pin on George's coat. Someone asked if they were American and, after an affirmative answer, the crowd cheered and let them proceed.[7]

Later in Alexandria, they met Muhammad Said Adham, 'an enkindled Egyptian believer. There were a number of Egyptian Bahais, quite new in the Cause and wonderfully full of fire and enthusiasm.' Proceeding to Port Said, they were greeted by Aḥmad Yazdí. The group were only a few hours there, but they suddenly encountered Arthur Hathaway, who was trying to find a ship to Haifa. He succeeded in joining the Randall party on the old *Karlsbad*.[8]

After 40 days of travel, the Randall group finally arrived at their destination at 6:30 a.m. on 16 November. Unlike the Trues, who had taken the train, arriving by ship meant taking a rowboat to shore. Bahíyyih remembered the 'thin-looking' rope ladder they had to climb down to get to the boats and said that it was scary and that her mother almost fell.[9]

The pilgrims were welcomed by Lotfu'lláh Hakím, who took them to the pilgrim house. When Bahíyyih stepped out of the carriage,

> it was as if a magnet drew my head to the left and I looked into 'Abdu'l-Bahá's eyes. He was in the little turret house built on the wall opposite our gate . . . He looked at us, and yet beyond us, as if He were looking out at the whole world. There was compassion and love and with it wisdom. I was momentarily lost in such an

> experience, which was beyond description, because it was like facing infinity.[10]

The group was taken into the pilgrim house where they met Dr Esslemont. Soon 'Abdu'l-Bahá swept up the stairs 'majestically and greeted us with the utmost love'. He spoke with them for half an hour, then said He had to leave as he had an appointment with a fanatical priest. When He left, He took Fujita with Him.[11]

Fujita remembered that there were many Persian believers present when they reached the Master's house. 'Abdu'l-Bahá called to him:

> 'Come on, I will introduce you to My family.' Then I went in Greatest Holy Leaf's room and met all the ladies of the Household . . . Although I haven't served very much, you see I stayed with 'Abdu'l-Bahá . . . two years. I used to go around everywhere. Always He ask me to go with Him. Even on the Christmas Day, we have a little church here, behind the Master's house, we call on them. Have taken a picture too, with Master and . . . minister and myself.[12]

In the afternoon, the pilgrims were joined by Colonel Allison, his wife and Mr Denham, all passengers on the ship who had become interested in the Faith and wished to meet 'Abdu'l-Bahá. At 3 o'clock, Shoghi Effendi called them to the presence of the Master. George Latimer wrote about the conversation:

> Across the street we hurried in joyous expectation. We entered a garden, approached a large stone house, entered a hall, severely simple, and a salon, large, bright, carpeted with a beautiful Persian rug of rich crimson pattern. On the chairs were plain linen covers and a small table stood in the centre of the room which was beautiful, yet simple, without other ornamentation. As we took our seats a wondrous peace and content descended upon us. We were at home in the home of the Master.
>
> Soon the Beloved entered the door. He had just been lunching with the Bishop of Haifa and apologized for delaying us. We could have waited forever in his home for He seems to fill the whole house with the light of His Presence. He centered all his love, his kingly courtesy that afternoon upon Mr. Denham, his English visitor. He

was so gracious, so brilliant, his smile so loving that Mr Denham's face simply shone in response.

'Abdu'l-Bahá: 'Here is the Holy Land. It is a very good place. From all parts of the world people desire to come here. This Mount Carmel has a very good climate. It is picturesque and has an ideal setting. Here at Haifa they need a good number of physicians. Its well-known physician is a Jew. There is no popular physician here.'

Mr Denham asked: 'Should the fundamental truths of this Cause be taught to children in the schools?'

'Abdu'l-Bahá: 'In childhood it is easy. Whatever a child learns during childhood, it will not forget. There is a proverb in Arabic that says: 'Teaching a child is like carving upon stone. It can never be erased.' A child is like a fresh branch. It is tender. In whatever way you wish you can train it. If you want to keep it straight it can be done. But when it grows up, if you want to straighten it, it cannot be done except through fire.'. . .

'Although the Christians say that all the world is for the Christians, yet this is the Bounty of God for all the people. Enough of these superstitions! People are so antagonistic to one another and wish to defeat each other. Praise be to God the Century of Light has come! It became evident that these ignorant superstitions are the causes of destruction. Why should not the children attend schools other than their own, so long as He has created all as human beings? All are the sheep of God and He is the kind shepherd. This is the Divine Policy. He would not leave any sheep unattended and is kind to all. The Divine Policy must be followed and therefore universality should be the rule.'

Mr Denham: 'Should truth be spread verbally or by writing?'

'Abdu'l-Bahá: 'Both. Real teaching is by action. Action has effect. One act is better than a thousand words. Jesus Christ says "by their fruits" (actions) and not by their words. What is the effect of words alone? The real thing is action . . . Action has made man eloquent. There is no eloquent language better than action. As long as the sun is bright, is it necessary that it should say "I am bright?" There is no need for that' . . .

Colonel Allison asked if the war would have any spiritual reaction in the United States and in the world.

'Abdu'l-Bahá: 'Yes. In the first place, people were very negligent.

Especially in Paris no one would mention the name of God. I used to speak about God to many people and they would ask me to take another topic. It had reached to such a state, but now they realize and are better than before. The hearts have become a little more tender.’

Colonel Allison: ‘Since the cessation of war the spiritual impulse seems to have abated.’

‘Abdu’l-Bahá: ‘Those whose sons have been killed, naturally, their hearts are affected. They would like someone to talk to them about God and the spirit. For instance, a father and mother having had a son who might have been killed, they would like to know whether the soul of their son is immortal. As soon as they hear that his soul is immortal, their hearts are consoled. There were Germans here, some of whom had lost their sons, and they would come to me and ask me to talk to them about spiritual things. “Give us proofs of the immortality of the soul.” I would ask them: “What for?” They would say: “If the spirit is immortal, then our hearts are really consoled.”

‘This war has been instrumental in partly awakening mankind and it has exposed the virtues of Universal Peace. All people are desirous of having Universal Peace because they have suffered from this universal war. They do not want another war like it. Gradually racial prejudice will be dispelled. There will come a day when the German will say to the Frenchman: “I am a Frenchman.” And the Frenchman will say: “I am a German.” If the Government should like to wage war the people would not agree to it. They would say: “If ye leaders have any war go and fight it out. We will not go. Why should we go? What is the use? If there is any use, it is for you; but there is no result for poor people like us. Our sons and property are taken while ye are in palaces and pavilions, enjoying delicious food and drinking wine. If war is good, go yourselves and fight. Ye simply eat and enjoy yourselves.”

‘Ultimately all men will say we have no quarrel. This war has brought about these sentiments; such as sentiments of Universal Peace; also the abolition of religious superstitions, patriotic superstitions and all these which have gradually gathered together – and caused the war. It will reach such a state that if anyone is in any place, he will say this is my home, and you (Col. Allison) will say Syria is my home.

'All have understood that war is the destruction of the foundation of humanity. It has no benefit save loss.'

Mr. Randall: 'This war has made all the nations poor.'

'Abdu'l-Bahá: 'The loss in this war will be felt in the future. All these strikes in Europe and America are the results of the war. Had there been no war, there would have been no such strikes. In Egypt the strikes caused an increase of thirty per cent in wages.

'His Holiness Bahá'u'lláh fifty years ago mentioned the evils of this war and said these things would happen, and that the cure is Universal Peace and the establishment of Universal Arbitration and that all nations should be included to solve these disputes. If the letters which His Holiness Bahá'u'lláh sent to the rulers of the world had been put into action, this war would not have occurred. What is the result? France needs fifty years to recover and become as before, likewise Belgium, Roumania, Bulgaria, Montenegro, Servia and Turkey, even Persia. Although Persia did not fight, yet her loss was great.'

In the midst of this wonderful interview, the whistle of Mr. Denham's boat blew to call the passengers aboard. 'Abdu'l-Bahá urged Mr. Denham to stay two or three days. When he replied that he must go, 'Abdu'l-Bahá said 'perhaps' he would come back to Haifa on his return from Damascus. He went away with the words: 'The Master has the most magnetic personality I have ever known in the world.'[13]

The pilgrims joined 'Abdu'l-Bahá at the Shrine of the Báb in the afternoon. At the door, everyone took off their shoes and Bahíyyih wondered if any were ever stolen or if anyone ever took the wrong shoes. She stood by 'Abdu'l-Bahá's side as the pilgrims entered the Shrine and watched as He put rose water on the hands of each. She was impressed: 'He had a very small bottle, and I watched. There was always enough, even for me at the end. How could it be? Maybe it was a miracle.'[14] 'Abdu'l-Bahá had given Bahíyyih her name, which was the same as that of the Greatest Holy Leaf and meant 'full of light'. He told her parents that their 'daughter has a sincere heart, very sincere and pure. She should have a Bahá'í education so as to develop a heavenly character and become a proficient teacher. She will become eloquent and speak in large gatherings and I will supplicate the Blessed Beauty that He may confirm her so that she will attract many souls.'[15]

At the evening meal were the Randalls, George Latimer, Arthur Hathaway, Fujita, Dr Esslemont, Ibn-i-Aṣdaq, Sulâyman Rif'at Bey, 'Azízu'lláh Khán Varqá, Mírzá Muḥsin, a son-in-law of the Master, Maḥmúd-i-Zarqání, Mírzá Asadu'lláh Fáḍl from Persia, and Shaykh Faraju'lláh 'the fiery but peace-loving Kurd', Dr Lotfu'lláh Hakím and Shoghi Effendi. 'Here we were', wrote George Latimer, 'Persian, Arab, Kurd, Turk, English, American, Hindoo, Japanese, Mohammedan, Christian, Jew and Buddhist, gathered at one heavenly table by the power of the Covenant of Bahá'u'lláh.'[16]

After the evening meal, 'Abdu'l-Bahá returned to the topic of the recently terminated war saying, 'There is no doubt that Germany will fight again. Whenever she gets a chance she will go to war.'[17] George asked the Master about Mason Remey: 'What did you do with Mr Remey? He was teaching in the New England states. Altho' he longs to be here yet he is happy in teaching there.' 'Abdu'l-Bahá replied that

> Mr Remey is very good. He works very hard. He is very restless. He is continually travelling from city to city. He has not left a place unvisited. He has gone everywhere, even to India. I am going to send him to Persia so that he may be one day in the East and one in the West. His father and his mother rebuked him very much, but he did not cease working. He respects them and obeys them. But when they would say 'Why are you a Baha'i,' he would not listen to them. In everything he would obey them, except in this. Notwithstanding that his father and mother are rich and would not deny him of anything, yet he lives in the utmost economy. He never asks them for anything.[18]

During the time of 'Abdu'l-Bahá, Mason Remey was a tireless teacher of the Faith. He had gone on pilgrimages in 1901, 1907, 1908 and 1914. He had been a travel teacher in Europe in 1907, had gone to England, Germany, Iran and Turkestan, including making the first visit by a Westerner to the House of Worship there, in 1908. The next year he and Howard Struven spent seven months travel-teaching in Hawaii, Japan, China, Burma and India. During the years 1906 to 1911, he crisscrossed the United States visiting everywhere he could teach the Faith. In 1914, he and George Latimer were sent to Europe to counter the efforts of Dr Fareed who had become a Covenant-breaker. Interestingly, in view of his end, in 1918, Mason was appointed to a Committee of Investigation in Chicago to look into Covenant-breaking. In 1951, Mason was appointed to the International Bahá'í Council by Shoghi Effendi and also named a Hand of the Cause of God the same year. But after Shoghi Effendi's passing, Mason began to insist that the Hands of the Cause appoint another Guardian, even though it was not possible according to the provisions of the Will and Testament of 'Abdu'l Bahá. When they did not, he, in 1960, appointed himself the next Guardian and was consequently expelled as a Covenant-breaker.[19]

Bahíyyih learned many new things in Haifa. At dinner, she sat on 'Abdu'l-Bahá's left across from the Shaykh. Bahíyyih said she 'was fascinated because I had read about such men. I wondered if he had tents filled with silk pillows and women lying on them.'[20]

At the end of their first day in Haifa, Ruth Randall showed Bahíyyih a few things. The first was the toilet. It was, she wrote, 'a small building the size of a clothes closet. Inside, it had a wooden shelf with a hole in the middle. That is where we sat, over the hole. I was afraid that something underneath would bite me.' Ruth showed Bahíyyih her room's light: 'There was a drinking glass that was two-thirds full of water. On top of that was a thin layer of oil, and on top of that was a little round piece of stiff, pink paper. Later, after dinner, it would light my room enough so I could see to get ready for bed. I was told it would burn a long time. It was a gallant little wick!'[21]

'Abdu'l-Bahá jokes with Bahíyyih and Fujita

'Abdu'l-Bahá loved to joke with Bahíyyih and Fujita. Fujita had moved from Japan to San Francisco in 1903 when he was 17 years old. He learned about the Faith from Kathryn Frankland.[22] After accepting the Faith, he received a Tablet from 'Abdu'l-Bahá praising him for becoming a Bahá'í and thought it had been sent to him by mistake. After receiving a third Tablet, Fujita realized that the Tablets really were intended for him, so he wrote and asked what he could do to serve the Faith. The Master told him to continue his education. Fujita met 'Abdu'l-Bahá in Chicago in 1912, then travelled with Him to California and back. Afterwards, the young Japanese lived with Corinne True for seven years during which he completed his studies in engineering. Now, in 1919, the Master had called Fujita to Haifa where he became His servant. After a time, not using his education in Haifa began to bother Fujita and he decided to return to America in order to work in his field. While he was packing, 'Abdu'l-Bahá called for him and asked what was troubling him. Fujita replied that he wasn't using the learning that the Master had told him to get. 'Abdu'l-Bahá responded with, 'Fujita, if I wanted a mechanic or engineer I could have gotten one easily. The work you are doing for me is what 'Abdu'l-Bahá wishes you to do.'[23] Fujita joyfully served both 'Abdu'l-Bahá and Shoghi Effendi for many years.

One day, the Master took Fujita up Mount Carmel. Fujita remembered that

> Once we . . . drive up to the college, up to top of mountain. There used to be a German hospice and . . . we had a key and looking over, I says, "Abdu'l-Bahá, this is a wonderful place, and, I like have such a place like this.' 'What?' he said, 'You small man, you want a big house like this? Little chicken coop is good enough for you!' He laughed, and then He said 'Never mind, in the future you will have the best place in the world.'[24]

With Bahíyyih, 'Abdu'l-Bahá always spoke in English. Bahíyyih loved eggs, so one day He asked if He should order some ostrich eggs for her. Then He said that

> if she liked to eat camel's meat he would send out and have one killed for her. He then wanted to know which she preferred (after her bright answer that she would rather have the camel alive so that it might be of service to someone), to ride on an ass or a camel.
>
> Then He turned to Fujita with a beaming smile and asked how he got on a camel when he was so small. Fujita replied, 'I jumped on it.' Then the Master said he would send him to Japan on a camel. Later he said it would be better to send him on an elephant to Japan, a large one that would eclipse him . . . He said to Fujita he should grow a beard, a long one (pointing to his own stomach) which would counteract the shortness of his stature.[25]

When Fujita finally grew the beard, 'it was at best a thin collection of long hairs . . . The Master enjoyed stroking Fujita's wispy beard, usually making Him laugh.' Fujita and the Master had a special relationship and usually ate their breakfasts together alone, usually to gales of laughter.[26]

'Abdu'l-Bahá tried to get Fujita to teach Him how to eat with chopsticks, with the result that, according to Bahíyyih, 'we all laughed, even the Master'.[27]

The pilgrimage continues

On 17 November, Bahíyyih was awakened by bagpipes. Apparently, the British army in Haifa had replaced bugles with bagpipes. At 7:30, a maid brought Harry Randall a large cup of black coffee, leaving him amazed and wondering how they could know his morning routine.[28]

Alma Knobloch was mentioned at 'Abdu'l-Bahá's table that day. He quickly responded: 'Consider the power of God. Such a small woman! She is confirmed in service. She is greatly assisted. When a person compares her success with her physical body, a hundred people will not be so assisted as she. This woman is so short. That is why confirmations of God are necessary . . . There is a large man, Mr Herrigel, very large. She converted him.' Later He said that 'little Miss Knobloch. She is the sister of Fujita in size.'[29]

Each of the Randalls had a private interview with 'Abdu'l-Bahá on 18 November. The elder Randalls wanted to know if they could pay for a 20-room Western Pilgrim House. The Master agreed and told them to talk with 'Abbás-Qulí, the custodian of the Shrine. 'Abbás-Qulí was excited about it and soon thereafter, the Master asked Mason Remey to draw up a design for the building.[30] Before long, construction began, but because of financial difficulties, work had to be suspended. In 1923, Amelia Collins offered the funds to finish the building. In 1951, the building became the home of the International Bahá'í Council and in 1963 the seat of the Universal House of Justice. When the House of Justice moved into its permanent Seat in 1983, the building was occupied by the International Teaching Centre. Today, the building contains offices.[31]

When Bahíyyih's turn came for her final meeting with 'Abdu'l-Bahá, she surprised herself by asking, 'What can I do to serve the Faith?' 'Abdu'l-Bahá was silent for a while and then said, 'study, study, STUDY'. She remarked that when He wanted to emphasize something, the Master would repeat it three times, with His voice getting louder each time.[32]

On 19 November, Bahíyyih decided to go visit the neighbours, but before she got out of the door, a message came from 'Abdu'l-Bahá saying she should not visit them because they were His enemies. 'I was grateful He had stopped me,' she thought, 'but how had He known? I had not told anyone. Living there under the protection of the loving Master was a gift never, never to forget.'[33] At lunch Ruth noted that the Master was very tired, apologizing that He could 'not be fresher'. She wondered what tired meant to Him.[34]

The next day, Bahíyyih helped the ladies of the household to clean wheat. The work consisted of pulling wheat out of large bags and removing the little stones. When finished, Bahíyyih passed the partially open door to the Greatest Holy Leaf's room. She tried to go by quietly, but Bahíyyih Khánum heard her and invited her in. Though she spoke little English, 'her eyes talked. Her face looked dreadfully tired, but her eyes were like the Master's, so alive and expressive. She was not like the other ladies.' Before she left, the elder Bahíyyih gave the younger Bahíyyih a decorated Persian pen box.[35]

The Randalls had brought a trunk full of gifts, but when they opened it, they found that a bag of yellow bug powder had broken open and everything was coated with yellow dust. The gifts included a typewriter for Shoghi Effendi, a pocket watch for 'Abdu'l-Bahá, and three lengths of soft wool for the Greatest Holy Leaf to make into coats for the Master. When a coat was made, 'Abdu'l-Bahá modelled it for them, but the next day, the very same coat was seen on a poor man walking down the street.[36]

On 22 November, the pilgrims went to 'Akká, the Garden of Riḍván and Bahjí. At 7:30 in the morning, the Randalls, Dr Suláyman Rif'at Bey, Arthur Hathaway and Lotfu'lláh Hakím climbed into the Master's carriage while Albert Vail, Fujita, Shoghi Effendi and George Latimer followed in a second. When they arrived at the Barracks in 'Akká, a special guide was called to give them their tour. He was Áqá Ḥusayn Ashchí, the only surviving member of the party who had arrived with Bahá'u'lláh in 1868, other than 'Abdu'l-Bahá and the Greatest Holy Leaf. Áqá Ḥusayn had been a cook for Bahá'u'lláh and 'Abdu'l-Bahá for 66 years and was now 77 years old.[37] George Latimer described their visit when they entered the Barracks:

> Immediately to the right of the entrance was the room where Bahá'u'lláh stayed the first night . . . At the opposite end of the

> courtyard were two long narrow rooms where the 70 odd followers were kept. It was here that they were so sick . . . Then we . . . mounted up some steps with vaulted roof to the room where Bahá'u'lláh's secretaries lived and copied Tablets. We passed on thru a small courtyard to the room where Bahá'u'lláh passed two years . . . We then mounted to the terrace on the roof where He also walked and where Abdu'l-Bahá's brother, the Purest Branch [Mírzá Mihdí] in failing to keep count of his steps one night, fell thru the skylight and was mortally hurt.
>
> When we left the Barracks we went to the Tomb of the Purest Branch, near the Barracks . . . and we mounted into the carriages for the drive to the Rizwan Garden. Here we had a delightful lunch . . . of delicious pilau, dates, and Turkish sweet-meats with various fruits from the garden. In this sacred and most beautiful spot, Bahá'u'lláh revealed many Tablets. We visited His simple room and walked thru the Garden which are really on an island divided by the two branches of a small stream. Words cannot express the beauty of this spot after one had driven thru the barren plains . . . Oranges, lemons, grape-fruits, tangerines, dates, pomegranates are all growing in great abundance. The fountain was playing and the air wafting the song of birds. The branches of the two mulberry trees covered the area where Bahá'u'lláh revealed His Tablets.[38]

When they first arrived at the Garden of Riḍván, the fountain was not functioning. Bahíyyih asked about it and the gardener took her to one corner and showed her a donkey and a small, circular track around a block structure. He harnessed up the donkey and blindfolded it (the donkey wouldn't walk unless it was blindfolded) then started it walking around the track. With the donkey walking, 'the fountain came alive, making a soft sound'.[39]

They left the Gardens at about 1:30 p.m. and made the short drive to the Pilgrim House near Bahjí. The caretaker met them and 'with a shining and happy face prepared Persian tea . . .'[40] At the Shrine of Bahá'u'lláh, Albert Vail was one of the few people who was able to put his feelings down in words:

> As we took off our shoes and approached the holy Threshold I was like one whose breath was caught away. The room was gloriously

lighted, brilliant with sunlight, full of flowers, still as the silent hush of eternity. But the wonder was the living presence in the air. The atmosphere was alive with a Divine Presence. It filled the place. A marvellous vibration trembled in the sunbright room, so tremendous my every limb shook, every atom was athrob with this spiritual electricity, the power that held me in its grip and almost crushed me with its majesty, its omnipotent touch. To bow flat on the floor was a relief before the glory. I poured out my heart's longing in prayer . . . Then dear Shoghi motioned us to draw near the inner room. I walked as one who could scarce move for the wonder, the descending currents of omnipotence, the heavenly majesty. I was not on earth but in heaven. At the threshold, the holy, the precious, the shining – this little child cowed and kissed the wondrous Threshold and prayed for annihilation, to die in Him that He might live in me. Oh, what ecstasy to prostrate oneself at the divine Threshold! Oh, what joy to be nothing at His feet, to die for Him! Then with an effort – I could have lain at that Threshold in joyous wonder for ages, I arose and silently as if in a divine dream moved backward . . . every prayer seemed alive, ablaze with penetrative light, as though each one were in the living Presence of the Most High. Never had prayer been so sublimely real, so immediate the response. It was in the living ear of God.

Then Shoghi chanted with heavenly sweetness the Visiting Tablet. All the flowers, the supernal sunlight sang in rhythm, it seemed their praises to the Glory of God, the Ancient of Days, the Blessed Beauty. Shoghi silently motioned us to approach the inner room. In unbelievable wonder, now rising through the crystal tears that dropped down our cheeks into waves of joy, with awe, and the desire to walk so slowly, that the divine ecstasy might last a long, long time, we one by one approached again the shining Threshold, bowed in joy, kissed its holy whiteness, and then entered the most holy Place.

This servant God blessed, for as I looked at the pale green velvet cover of the tomb, there among the vases, there shone forth a living presence of colossal size in outlines of light, trembling with power . . . I dropped on my face almost bowed down by the glory, kissed the hem of the velvet cover, touched my brow to its wondrous softness . . . Oh, how I would have loved to have bowed there with my face to the Holy Floor forever! . . .

> Then with aching longing to remain there forever we withdrew with faces turned to the Holy of Holies, the glorious resting place. We put our shoes on in a sort of sublime dream, withdrew through the garden in awe-subdued wonder.[41]

That evening, dinner was delayed until, unexpectedly, Colonel and Mrs Allison arrived from Damascus. Their arrival didn't seem to surprise 'Abdu'l-Bahá and He welcomed them as though they had been expected. The discussion quickly turned to Damascus where there had recently been a 'disturbance'. When Colonel Allison mentioned this, 'Abdu'l-Bahá said, 'This is childish play. They did these things so that the English would not evacuate.' He told the Colonel all about the situation in Damascus and its meaning. 'Abdu'l-Bahá's knowledge baffled the Colonel and he asked Harry, 'By what power does He know all these things?'[42]

On the afternoon of 23 November, the pilgrims went to the Shrine of the Báb. Bahíyyih wasn't impressed with the 'awful rocky road' they used to get there. When they arrived, 'Abdu'l-Bahá, looking over the panoramic view, said that

> someday the drive to 'Akká and the Shrine of Bahá'u'lláh would be beautiful with orange groves. A great breakwater would be built to form a harbour, and ships from all over the world would come. The Shrine of the Báb would be lighted and would be a landmark for ships and airplanes.[43]

Part of this vision, a 1.2-mile breakwater, had been constructed by 1933.[44]

As the pilgrims entered the Shrine of the Báb, 'Abdu'l-Bahá gave everyone a little rose water. Again, Bahíyyih was baffled by how the bottle never seemed to empty. George described the visit:

> He ['Abdu'l-Bahá] drove up early with Mr. Randall . . . Others of us followed later on foot. Soon we overtook Mírzá Noureddin, the gifted scribe who engraved so beautifully the Great Teaching Tablets. 'Tis hard,' he said, 'to climb the Mountain of God but very easy to come down.' It did seem hard, the rocks rose so abruptly one above the other. But when we thought of our Beloved just above us on the mountain, wings rose beneath our feet.

A fathomless stillness surrounds the Tomb of His Highness, the Supreme Báb, the 'Gate' to the City of God, the New Jerusalem of Light. One would like to rest there forever on the terrace in front of the Tomb overlooking the sea, breathing deep the silence of the Kingdom. The view from that Holy Mountain, that 'Vineyard of God' is ravishingly beautiful. The city of Haifa lies below, white stone houses with red-tiled roofs, planted amid walled gardens; the great bay swings in a perfect semi-circle around to the north. 'Akká, white, dazzlingly bright in the resplendent sunlight of that holy land, lies like a jewel on the blue sea. But the atmosphere, silent, luminous, like a living spirit, is the true garment of wonder. It is as though Elijah, Isaiah, the Christ, Muhammad, the Blessed Beauty – 'the Feet of Him around Whom all names revolve' – had all left their foot-prints not only on the mountain soil of that 'Garden of God', but in the shining air and had diffused the fragrance of their holy garments over all its flowers and grass, and made even the dust reflective of a hidden and heart-subduing beauty.

As we turned and entered the great central room of the Tomb we saw engraved on the doorway the symbol of the Cause of God, two stars standing at each side of the Tree of Life. The Báb was the morning star of the Day of God on earth.

In one corner, sitting on the beautiful Persian rug that covers the floor and part of the wall, was the blessed Haydar-'Alí. How we had longed to meet him! With what wonder had we read of his years of service, his twelve years imprisonment in a dark, solitary cell, at Khartoum, his being carried in a bag head downward over the desert and singing for joy as they beat him. Now he was here before us! He embraced us with heavenly love and said. 'How wonderful to be living in the day prayed for by all the prophets of God. They all wrote and dreamed of this day.'. . .

When the Master entered the room, now filled with friends, Persians, Arabs, Egyptians, Americans, joy swept our hearts. Haydar-'Alí, like an eager child in the presence of the Master, tried to rise but 'Abdu'l-Bahá prevented him. The Master in his humility does not allow anyone to bow before Him or show Him special deference. Soon after, Haydar-'Alí was ill and had to leave the room. As the friends lovingly helped him out, 'Abdu'l-Bahá said: 'He is a blessed soul. From his youth he has had no thought but the service of the Kingdom.'

Presently we all rose and followed the silent steps of the Master out and around the terrace to the holy room where the body of the Blessed Báb lies in its age-long rest. The Master stood at the door and anointed our hands with rose-water as we entered, a symbol of the new reality, brought into the world by the Holy Spirit of the Báb. We lifted the rose water to our foreheads and then bowed with our Persian brothers just inside the Threshold. The atmosphere of that holy place was marvellous. The air was vibrant with a living presence. It pressed upon us, overwhelmed us with the Power of that Light which shone through the Báb as through a gate. At the same time a peace that passeth understanding broke over us.

One by one, silently, the Persians, those pure, wonderful servants of the God who is Most Glorious, approached the inner room and dropped their heads on the shining Threshold, while Shoghi chanted impressively the Tablet of Visitation. Our hearts were aglow with the thought of the bounty of God. The very heavens seemed to open; and when 'Abdu'l-Bahá – that star that never sets, the Star of the Covenant – with sublime tenderness helped Haydar-'Alí down the centre of that room, supporting and leading him, and then with kingly majesty walked back again – the effect was indescribable.

After we left the Tomb we watched the majestic figure of the Master, with black flowing abá, shining white turban and silver hair, finding his way down the winding stony path. The friends followed in silent love and wonder.[45]

When they descended, Harry Randall wrote:

And now the Master leads the way, walking down the mountain. The friends all following, conspicuous in His white turban and 'abá – just ahead – one can only think, this is Galilee of 2,000 years ago as Christ, followed by His Disciples, walked down to the sea, and yet the Centre of the Covenant is the Manifestation of the Beauty of Bahá'u'lláh . . .[46]

On 26 November, the Greatest Holy Leaf sent Shoghi Effendi with a small gift for each pilgrim. The gift was just a small envelope, but when Shoghi Effendi asked what we thought it might be, no one had any idea. He then informed them that the envelopes contained a tiny dried drop of Bahá'u'lláh's blood. The pilgrims were thunderstruck. Bahíyyih wrote that 'I felt sort of numb. I could not grasp having such a thing. We were all silent. It was the most precious gift in the world. How do you say thank you for such a thing?' The Greatest Holy Leaf later told them that it had been considered healthy to draw out a little blood each spring. When Bahá'u'lláh's blood was drawn, it had been stored in a vase where it dried.[47]

Later, the pilgrims went to the room of the Greatest Holy Leaf to see the photograph of Bahá'u'lláh. Harry, as other pilgrims had, noted that 'the Master grows more to look like Bahá'u'lláh. To me His tender face is like the love in the face of Bahá'u'lláh.'[48]

The Carmelite Monastery

The subject of the Carmelite Monastery came up on several occasions. 'Abdu'l-Bahá related that much of the land around the Monastery had been public and used by the poor to graze their flocks and cattle in the meadows and from which they collected firewood until the monks prevented them from doing so. When the people complained to the Governor of 'Akká, he went to the Master and asked Him to accompany him to speak with the monks. When they demanded to see the lease, they discovered that the Monastery had leased only a small portion of what they were claiming. George Latimer wrote, 'The leaders apportioned vast property around [the Monastery] for their own use. They used coercion to get it.'[49]

At first, the monks tried to bribe the Governor, but he was not moved. The monks then invited him to a 'sumptuous' banquet with his family. Again the Governor begged 'Abdu'l-Bahá to go with him. The Master agreed, but since He had not been officially invited, He sat in a corner and watched. The Monastery was 'decorated most lavishly, the lights were burning most brilliantly and the banquet hall was embellished with the most delicate Oriental arts and drapery. The table groaned under the load of steaming dishes, delicious viands and most palatable and savoury food. There were all kinds of fruits and candies . . .'[50]

> They all sat around the table and the Master sat in one corner. On one side sat the governor and his officials, on the other the monks

> and priests, while facing them were the notables of Haifa. One of these notables addressed the governor saying that these monks were the people of God . . . The monks were always kind and they clothed the naked . . . The Governor said 'yes' to all of this, and asked 'Have you finished? To whom are these monks related?' He answered, 'To Christ.' Then the Governor replied, 'Christ was in the wilderness without a home. He had no lamp save the stars, no bed save the ground, no food save the herbs, while with these monks it is exactly the opposite. Their food is sumptuous, their residence palatial, the view so splendid! They are in the utmost comfort and their wealth is immense. Consider how they have used force to accomplish this. What connection does this have with Christ?' They all remained silent at this. Afterwards the monks said Abbas Effendi had told the governor what to answer.[51]

'Abdu'l-Bahá had indeed suggested the initial line of reasoning, but then concluded the argument Himself by stating three times that 'the standard is deeds'.

On a later occasion, in January 1920, 'Abdu'l-Bahá described the luxury enjoyed in the Monastery to Mrs Parsons and Dr Esslemont:

> When the Turks came and attacked the place they brought out wines of all descriptions, a great number of barrels of wine, wines of twenty years old. The Turks sated themselves with drink and wine and said, 'No matter how much we drink the store is not exhausted.' They brought out boxes of tinned beef, salmon, etc, so it became evident that the monks used meat. Sweets and chocolates also they found. The Col. declared, 'In all my life I have never tasted such wine.'[52]

Departures and arrivals

Harry Randall had not seen the Greatest Holy Leaf at any time during the pilgrimage; unfortunately, the social protocol of the day kept them apart. But Harry greatly desired to see her. At about 4 o'clock one afternoon, 'Abdu'l-Bahá called for Harry. When Harry opened the front door of the Master's house, there across the room standing in a doorway, was the Greatest Holy Leaf. She smiled and, for a few seconds,

Harry was given his heart's desire. That night, 'Abdu'l-Bahá informed the pilgrims that it was time to leave, so at 3 p.m. on 27 November, the Randalls, George Latimer, Albert Vail and Arthur Hathaway departed from Haifa.[53]

When the pilgrims arrived in Alexandria on 3 December, they unexpectedly encountered Dr Zia Bagdadi and his wife Zeenat, who were on their way to Haifa, and Dr Basheer, who had studied medicine in Chicago and was now working in Port Said. The Bahá'ís of Alexandria quickly gathered and all of the friends had 'a splendid and memorable meeting'. The Egyptian friends were wonderfully amazed at the 'spirit with which they were returning from Haifa. We noticed that they had become new creatures, full of spirit, life and love, charming and attractive, affecting, with their burning soul, every one who came into contact with them.' According to Muhammad Said Adham,

> Each one of the friends gave us a short talk of what they saw and heard in Haifa, which was translated immediately. A new Egyptian beginner in the Cause was amazed at seeing the American friends associating with us with love and harmony, as if we were intimate friends who had known each other and met often before. After the chanting of the Tablets in Arabic and Persian by Zeenat Khanum as well as the readings of a supplication in English by Mrs. Randall, supper was served.
>
> The next day I went to the boat to bid them farewell. I saw two young Egyptian students who were on their way to Germany to study medicine and introduced them to our American friends who received them with Bahai cordiality. The students, seeing my friendliness with the Americans, expressed their wonder to me in Arabic saying, 'How did you come to know such sincere Occidentals?'[54]

John Esslemont and the Bagdadis

Dr Esslemont oscillated between being healthy and being ill. When he was ill, he was unable to attend 'Abdu'l-Bahá's talks, but Lotfu'lláh Hakím would come over and share them with him. After all of the American pilgrims left, Esslemont wrote in his diary:

> I am glad that for a time I am left alone with the Eastern Bahá'ís, so

I shall have a better opportunity of studying them and getting an insight into the differences between their mode of life and religious customs and our Western ways.

Last night the difference caused by the departure of the Americans was at once obvious. When they were here there was always bustle. At meal times there were always many questions put to the Master. Generally two or three were taking notes. Afterwards they were very busy transcribing and completing their notes and discussing what the Master said or meant about this or that.

At the meeting last night the initiative was left entirely to the Master. If a silence occurred, as at a Quaker meeting, no one seemed to feel the slightest awkwardness. The Persian believers seem to be quite happy to be in the Presence of their Lord even when nothing is being said. The Master talked more, however, than I have ever heard him do before at a meeting. I could understand only a word here and there, but the whole atmosphere of the whole meeting was so restful and spiritual that I was very happy just listening to the tones of the Master's voice, watching his eloquent gestures, seeing the rapt expression on the faces and realizing, although very dimly and feebly, the presence of Bahá'u'lláh and the Supreme Concourse . . .

At supper the difference was also obvious. The supper was much simpler. The company numbered only 12 instead of the usual 17 or 19. Evidently the somewhat elaborate suppers we had been having were out of compliment to our American visitors, and we had now reverted to the simple meals of the household.[55]

On 5 December, Esslemont went for a two-hour drive with 'Abdu'l-Bahá in the rain. During the drive, the Master taught him a few words in Persian and Esslemont taught 'Abdu'l-Bahá a few words of Esperanto. Three days later, Shoghi Effendi, Lotfu'lláh Hakím and Esslemont went with 'Abdu'l-Bahá's servant, Isfandíyár, to 'Akká, the Garden of Riḍván and the Shrine of Bahá'u'lláh. When they returned to Haifa, they found that an American lady, Dr Couch, had arrived; she remained in Haifa for the rest of Esslemont's two-and-a-half month stay. Throughout Esslemont's time in Haifa, he and 'Abdu'l-Bahá talked about his book and the Master gave the author many suggestions.[56]

On 9 December, Zia and Zeenat Bagdadi arrived in Haifa, 12 years after Zia's last pilgrimage. Zia wrote:

> Oh! what a difference between now and twelve years ago. At present the light of justice is shining, in the past there was only injustice. Now, for the first time in the history of the Holy Land, religious freedom is given; people's lives, property and chastity are safeguarded.
>
> The face of the Master is radiant as the sun, and the multitudes around him are as butterflies, and he is the luminous lamp. He says the people of the world will enjoy the blessings of the Most Great Peace only when they accept the Bahai Message.[57]

In addition to the Western pilgrims, there were many Eastern pilgrims at the end of the year – so many, in fact, that when 18-year-old Hassan Safa Bagdadi, Zia's nephew, arrived on 27 December, there appeared to be no place for him to stay. There were about a hundred Eastern pilgrims, so the Eastern pilgrim house was full of the men, while all the women were accommodated in the Master's house. Safa was very surprised to find himself, along with Fáḍil-i-Mázindarání, given the front room in the Shrine of the Báb (which is today the Shrine of ‘Abdu'l-Bahá) for his 19-day stay. Safa remembered that one of the pilgrims asked ‘Abdu'l-Bahá whether the Treaty of Versailles, which had ended the first World War, would end war forever as the newspapers were claiming. The Master said no, the treaty ‘contained the germs of the next war, and that war would be so terrible that the 1914/18 war would seem like child's play in comparison’.

The young pilgrim learned many things from the Master, how he had a joyous sense of humour, but that he could also be very serious. One day, an English official came to see Him. ‘Abdu'l-Bahá introduced him to the gathered friends by saying, ‘You see, I'm gathering all the friends here, with me, to protect them, and save them from spending all their evenings in the casinos.’ On another occasion, ‘Abdu'l-Bahá was asked about comments made by some pilgrims from America that there would be another war which would destroy half of humanity. The Master replied, ‘Yes.’ Zia Bagdadi wrote, ‘I was so terrified by the Master's reply who, seeing the anguish of the friends present, changed the subject and turned to amusing stories.’ On another occasion ‘Abdu'l-Bahá, when asked about the possibility of a religious war, replied that there would be an economic war but no religious war.[58]

Mírzá 'Isá Khán Iṣfáhání

A Persian pilgrim named Mírzá 'Isá Khán Iṣfáhání was in Haifa from about 14 December 1919 until 11 January 1920. His pilgrim notes consist mostly of recorded comments by 'Abdu'l-Bahá and the Master's answers to his questions. John Esslemont, who was writing *Bahá'u'lláh and the New Era* at that time, was there at the same time and is mentioned several times in these memoirs. At one point, 'Abdu'l-Bahá asked Zia Bagdadi to read a part of his translation of Esslemont's book. The Master corrected some of the sentences, then said, 'There is so much work and so little time. However, this book must be translated as I do not wish this person [Dr Esslemont] to leave this place unhappy.'[59] One day, Mírzá Haydar-'Alí was with Dr Esslemont and asked him why he had flattened the back of his shoes. He replied, 'After my arrival in Haifa, it so happened that at the time I attained an audience [with 'Abdu'l-Bahá], as I was removing my shoes, other companions would go inside and I would remain by myself and would be sad. Therefore, I prepared this means so that at the time of attaining His presence, I would not fall behind.' He had turned his regular shoes into slip-ons.[60]

'Abdu'l-Bahá made the Western pilgrims think. One night at dinner, bread, butter and honey were served, but there were no knives or forks, so the Western pilgrims ate with much difficulty. The Master commented:

> How wonderful it would be if a person were not seized by habits. When I was in the blessed presence [of Bahá'u'lláh] going from Baghdad to Istanbul, preparation of all provisions for the companions was in My charge. After conclusion of all the work, I would be very tired. Sometimes, I was so fatigued that I would put a rock under My head and fall sleep on the ground. Since I was under the shadow of His blessed bounties, when I woke, the fatigue had disappeared and a special delight had overcome Me.[61]

'Abdu'l-Bahá also spoke about Haifa and 'Akká and their future. On 21 December, He gave the pilgrims a short history lesson about 'Akká. When Mírzá 'Alí Khán Fírúz asked the question, 'When Prophet Joshua states that the valley of Achor is the door of hope, is that about 'Akká?' 'Abdu'l-Bahá responded:

> Yes, Achor is this same 'Akká. The Westerners refer to 'Akká as Achor. Over the course of history, it has acquired many names. At first it was 'Aúk, then became 'ákúr [Achor] and afterwards 'Akká. The Phoenicians raised this city and their custom was that when they built a town, whatever geometric figure it resembled, they would call it by that name. Since this city was triangular with curved sides, then they called it 'Aúk, which had this meaning. Moreover, Haifa was known as Hayfú, meaning 'a town on the skirt of a mountain'. And Lebanon in the Phoenician language means 'white mountain' since it is covered under the snow. The city of 'Akká was build fifteen hundred years before Christ.[62]

Describing the arrival of Bahá'u'lláh and His followers in 'Akká, The Master stated that when they arrived at the military barracks,

> one day the governor sent word that someone on behalf of Bahá'u'lláh should come to hear the Sultan's decree. The Blessed Beauty sent me as His deputy to the government house. They placed Me where the criminals would stand. The announcer went behind the table and read the decree of the Sultan, which was in Turkish. The essence of that order was that the family of Bahá'u'lláh would be imprisoned until the end of eternity in the city of 'Akká and were not permitted to leave the city.
>
> After hearing this command, I laughed. Those present were most astonished and asked, 'Why do you laugh?' I said, 'Because the statement about us not leaving the city is meaningless, since we will not be alive till the end of time.'[63]

On 4 January, 'Abdu'l-Bahá described Mount Carmel being 'entirely covered in light'. Haifa and 'Akká would be connected by roads and on each side trees would be planted. It would become the most important port in the world. Then Agnes Parsons asked, 'Where will the Mashriqu'l-Adhkar be built?' 'Abdu'l-Bahá replied: 'Near the Shrine of the Exalted One. On one side, the largest and most important scientific school will be raised. On the other side, there will be an asylum for invalids and on the opposite side an orphanage.'[64]

Ḥájí Mírzá Haydar-'Alí was very old and weak at this time and one night, 'Abdu'l-Bahá spoke to John Esslemont, Agnes Parsons,

Mrs Dodge, the Eastern pilgrims and the resident believers about this amazing man who was known as the Angel of Carmel. With Shoghi Effendi translating for the Westerners, He pointed to Haydar-'Alí and said:

> You see this old man; he has devoted his entire life in service to the Cause of God. He has dedicated all his energies and thought to the exaltation of the Word of God. Never has he considered his own comfort. In Iran, the friends have passed the tests very well: They have offered their heads, their lives, and their families. The Mir-Ghazab [executioner] would say, 'Curse [the Faith] or I will separate your head from your body;' but they would respond, 'We will not curse; do what you please.' In America, such tests have not occurred yet. If tests occur and the believers remain constant, then that means something.[65]

On Christmas Eve, 'Abdu'l-Bahá told about visiting some Christian friends. He said:

> Today was the birth of the Christ. I went to visit some of the Christian friends. In accordance with Bahá'u'lláh's utterance, I associate with all people in the spirit of friendliness and fellowship. In Divine Verses it is revealed, 'Consort with the followers of all religions in a spirit of friendliness and fellowship'; moreover, elsewhere, He [Bahá'u'lláh] states, 'Beware, beware, not to associate with the rebellious.' If someone wants to instill doubt in hearts or invite them for carnal pleasure and debauchery, then of a certainty one must avoid such a person and avoid association with him.
>
> One of the Christians said to Us, 'You claim divinity!' I replied, 'If I succeed in servitude to the Sacred Threshold, then I have attained unto a mighty station. It is your priests who advance claim of divinity. He asked, 'How so?' I said, 'They take a piece of bread, recite something and blow on the bread, and then say, "This bread has become the blood and the flesh of Jesus." Therefore, these individuals are even mightier than God, as they are able to blow on bread and turn it into the flesh and blood of Jesus.'
>
> He also stated: In 'Akká we had a neighbor who one day said, 'Tomorrow I want to baptize my daughter.' He also invited Me.

> Therefore, I went. I saw that a bowl was filled with water and placed before the priest, who recited something. He read so much that it tired everyone. Then he said, 'This water is made holy.' He took the hapless little girl, and holding her mouth, immersed her twice in water. The third time he submerged her, she polluted the water. Even funnier and more ridiculous was that the priest said, 'Do not pour this holy water somewhere unsanitary; pour it in the sea!'[66]

Since the Great War had only recently ended, many pilgrims asked about the possibility that there would be another war. 'Abdu'l-Bahá said:

> Yes, since they have disobeyed the blessed instructions [of Bahá'u'lláh]. Only a few countries have representatives in the League of Nations, whereas the representatives must be appointed and ratified by the nation, the government, the monarch and the Senate. They do not even consult. On the other hand, some governments are deprived of membership, and this has precipitated their fury and prompted their feeling of revenge. Governments have secret alliances with each other of which no one is aware, but these schemes will reach nowhere.[67]

On 1 January 1920, an Egyptian crashed his car into the wall. The driver was very embarrassed and 'Abdu'l-Bahá had to call him into His presence. When the driver arrived, the Master, instead of chastising him, said, 'Where were you? Did you want to deprive us today of your company? Do not be saddened at all. If one person's heart is happy, it is worth more than any automobile. A vehicle is for the comfort of the friends. I will not barter the delight of one of the friends for the entire world.'[68]

On another day, a man from Shiraz arrived and introduced himself as a Bahá'í. 'Abdu'l-Bahá immediately responded:

> I said to him, 'Since you are not a Bahá'í, tell the truth: What is your purpose [in introducing yourself as a Bahá'í]?' He . . . told the truth, saying, 'There are Bahá'ís everywhere. I identify myself as such, so I could benefit from their humanity and kindness.' I was most pleased with his truthfulness in this regard. The point is that, praised be God, the friends are vigilant in every locality and prepare the means of comfort for new arrivals.[69]

1920

Many pilgrims and others came to Haifa during 1920, including King Feisal of Iraq. It was also a year when the British government recognized the efforts of ‘Abdu'l-Bahá by giving Him a knighthood.

Agnes Parsons and John Esslemont

On Christmas Day of 1919, a group of pilgrims arrived in Haifa including Agnes Parsons and her son Jeffrey, of Washington, D.C., Leone Barnitz and Frank Chant. They stayed for several weeks. ‘Abdu'l-Bahá had the new car sent Him by Helen Goodall, and Frank Chant became His daily chauffeur. Frank also taught Fujita how to drive the car. One day, Frank drove the Master and Mírzá Haydar-‘Alí up to the Shrine of the Báb. Mírzá Haydar ‘Alí was quite old and Frank had to keep his arm around him to support him.[1]

Mírzá Maḥmúd-i-Zarqání, one of ‘Abdu'l-Bahá's secretaries on His Western journey, was married on 1 January 1920 and that led to a discussion among the pilgrims of the differences between marriages in the East and in the West. The wedding followed Eastern traditions where deputies stood in for the bride. ‘Abdu'l-Bahá noted that in the East, the bride had no say in the marriage; everything was arranged by her father without her knowledge or consent. This easily led to disharmony. In Western marriages, He said, the bride and groom made the decisions together, but sometimes without the consent of the parents. This also led to disunity. ‘Abdu'l-Bahá stressed that the couple should choose each other, but that the parents had to approve. That formed the basis of unity.[2]

While Agnes Parsons was there, a Mr Shirazi acted as a tutor for Jeffrey, doing so without payment, something that bothered Agnes. One day, she brought this up with ‘Abdu'l-Bahá, asking Him to request that Mr Shirazi accept payment for his efforts since he had already spent three weeks tutoring Jeffrey. The Master responded saying that it would be better not to since it would be like ‘asking a person who wishes to be straightforward, to tell a lie . . . Now this matter is for you to decide, whichever way you wish can be carried out. The present arrangement is the cause of his progress. He becomes more self-sacrificing daily. If I tell him (to accept payment) this will prevent his progress.'[3]

Agnes and Leone Barnitz asked many questions about the organization of the Bahá'í Faith because of the upcoming Mas͟hriqu'l-Ad͟hkár Convention and Bahá'í Congress in Chicago. A small teaching booklet on the Faith by Roy Wilhelm, entitled *Big Ben*, contained the passage, 'The Bahai Revelation is not an organization. The Bahai Cause can never be organized.' This was causing confusion among the Bahá'ís and within a few years would cause another crisis within the American Bahá'í community when some, particularly Ruth White, rejected the efforts of Shoghi Effendi to build the Bahá'í Administrative Order. 'Abdu'l-Bahá responded, 'How is it possible that there should be no organization? Even in a household if there is not organization there will be hopeless confusion.' He then proceeded to describe the Universal House of Justice and local spiritual assemblies.[4]

On 16 January, Dr Esslemont had his final interview with 'Abdu'l-Bahá. One of the questions he asked was which of the caves of Elijah the Master had lived in after the passing of Bahá'u'lláh. 'Abdu'l-Bahá replied that He had stayed for three weeks in the lower cave, the same one Elijah had used. He noted that the cave had been enlarged since the days of Elijah.[5]

Most of Dr Esslemont's time with the Master had been spent discussing his book. At the end of his stay, 'Abdu'l-Bahá told him, 'London is lighted but it is quiet. I want you to go and make it aflame.' With his marching orders, Esslemont departed Haifa on 23 January.[6] During his almost three months in Haifa, Esslemont had developed a close friendship with Shoghi Effendi. Esslemont's *Bahá'u'lláh and the New Era* was finally published in September 1923. When his health deteriorated the next year, Shoghi Effendi invited him back to Haifa. He arrived in 1924 and assisted Shoghi Effendi in the translation of a number of publications, including the Tablet of Aḥmad and the Hidden Words. He passed away in Haifa in November 1925. After his passing, Shoghi Effendi named him a Hand of the Cause of God.[7]

The discussion at supper on 17 January centred on the relations between black and white people. 'Abdu'l-Bahá reminded Agnes Parsons that when He had asked her in Washington why she did not have meetings with both black and white, she had replied, 'If the colored people come here, the white ones will not come. We had appointed a special place for the colored people, but they do not go there.' 'Abdu'l-Bahá said that the black people had felt slighted by this and He spoke about how the blacks and whites had helped each other even when they didn't realize it.[8] 'Abdu'l-Bahá then told Agnes to organize a Racial Amity campaign for the Bahá'í community to overcome the problems of racial inequality, saying, 'I want you to arrange a Convention for unity of the colored and white races.' Agnes always tried to obey the Master and consequently she threw herself into the task, working with Louis Gregory, who later, after his passing, was named a Hand of the Cause.[9] The Parsons party returned to America in mid-February.

Sir Herbert Samuel

Sir Herbert Samuel was appointed the British High Commissioner for Palestine in 1920. Soon after taking up the position, he visited 'Abdu'l-Bahá for two reasons, one personal and one official: he had long been interested in the Bahá'í movement and had previously met the Master and wanted to meet Him again; and he wanted to show the British commitment to tolerance and respect for all religions. He wrote:

> I was impressed, as was every visitor, by 'Abdu'l-Bahá's dignity, grace and charm. Of moderate stature, his strong features and lofty expression lent to his personality an appearance of majesty. In our conversation he readily explained and discussed the principal tenets of Bahá'ísm, answered my inquiries and listened to my comments. I remember vividly that friendly interview of sixteen years ago [actually 1909], in the simple room of the villa, surrounded by gardens, on the sunny hillside of Mount Carmel.[10]

C. R. Ashbee

In March, C. R. Ashbee, who was a Civic Adviser to the City of Jerusalem, visited Haifa with his wife, Janet. In his book, *A Palestine Notebook*, he wrote about meeting 'Abdu'l-Bahá:

> On the ramparts, among the old masonry to a background of crumbling golden stone there was an impressive little figure, white

bearded, with waving hair. He wore a white *‘emma* and an *‘abaya* of tender brown over his gray *galabia*. It was Abbas the Bahai. Later on, thanks to the courtesy of one of our Syrian schoolmasters, we were invited into the house. Word came that he would be very glad to see Mr and Mrs Ashbee, and we spent a wonderful hour with him. He was quite willing to talk and our interpreter was clear and true in his English. Old Abbas curled himself up in the corner of his divan, looked at us with his wonderful illuminating eyes that radiate love, and set forth the cardinal point of Bahaism.

I have rarely come across a man who so completely sums up the saint, or let us say saint and philosopher combined, for the presence and image of the man are of the Middle Ages, their spirit of personal holiness, while what he says has the lucidity of the Greek, is disruptive of all religions and mediaeval systems, is philosophic, modern and synthetic.

‘First,’ said he, ‘we must get rid of all the glosses, Talmuds, codes of divinity, and clerical law. Get back to the revealed word of God where we can. Christ had the revealed word, so had Muhammad, so had others before them, but – and here’s the point – those revelations were for their own day and environment. You cannot always take the literal interpretation of first-century Syria or eighth-century Arabia and say that in its application it is true now.’

He gave the impression of being very modest about his own teaching, adding that the East was in a bad way, needed light, and had to be told these things. That was the reason for Bahaullah and the Bab.

‘Then,’ said he, ‘all the nations must come together, there must be a league of nations for the government of the world.’

He sketched out a sort of council appointed by the presidents, the kings, and the democracies.

‘And the existing League?’ we asked.

He smiled and shook his head. ‘That is only the merest beginning. It is not representative of all. It palliates the disease, the disease of discord. It is no remedy.’

But Bahaism went much further, and here it cuts itself free from the orientalism of Pauline Christianity and from Mohammad. There must be equality of the sexes. ‘Humanity,’ said old Abbas as he took a pinch of snuff from a little enamelled box, ‘is as a creature with two wings – man and woman – you must not cripple either, or you impede flight. Humanity needs both for progress.'

'And the common tongue that is to make it possible for man to speak with man?'

'It will come,' he said.

Janet suggested that the tongue might be English. He accepted the suggestion with a look of warm-hearted love that seemed to imply: 'We all of us would like to have our own, but God has found a tongue before.'

Who knows but it may be English yet? Still the last language in which God revealed himself was not Aramaic, nor Greek, nor Hebrew, nor Egyptian, but Arabic. And don't you make any mistake about it! But the languages of God are many.

He tells somewhere in his teaching: Release comes by making the will a door through which the confirmations of the spirit move.

And those confirmations of the spirit? They are the powers and gifts with which some are born, and which men sometimes call genius, but for which others have to strive with infinite pains. They come to that man or woman who accepts his or her life with 'radiant acquiescence.'

A good phrase, 'radiant acquiescence.' Let's remember it!

As we motored back across the sands, we saw Lord Milner's destroyer lying outside the harbour. 'War,' old Abbas had said, 'is not of God because it does not unify.'

. . . When they offered Abbas his title, with whatever bit of ribbon or strip of paper it was accompanied, he said:

'As it comes from the British Government I accept it, as a teacher of God's word it will make no difference to me.'

It is pleasant to think that English administrators go to this wise old man for help and counsel. We dined in the evening with Colonel Stanton, the Military Governor of Haifa, Lord Milner, and Herbert Samuel. The two last were rather envious of our afternoon with Abbas, and Colonel Stanton told us how he often went to get his advice. 'Of course,' he added in the characteristic manner of the British Administrator, 'I have to listen for half an hour or so first to the beauty of the flowers and the wings of the mind; after that we get to business.'

I thought of the destroyer lying outside Akka, and waiting to take Lord Milner back to England. Somehow I rather wished he could have put his journey off another day and come with us if we went again to Akka. He was a little melancholy and pessimistic, but he always takes a big sweep . . .

Yes, say his friends, but Lord Milner is getting old, Abbas is older, and his sweep is bigger; for his is – shall we say? – a less bounded, because more oriental, faith in the goodness of God and the destiny of man.

But it is noteworthy, is it not, that while the political vision is from the Englishman, the spiritual vision is not from the Christian, nor from the Jew, but from the Moslem.

'You must learn,' says old Abbas, 'to distinguish the sun of truth from whichever point of the horizon it is shining! People think religion is confined in an edifice, to be worshipped at an altar. In reality, it is an attitude.[11]

Later in his book, Ashbee writes, 'I'll even take you to old Abbas, the Bahai, at Akka, one of the wisest men, I should say, that ever lived. . .'[12]

'Abdu'l-Bahá visits 'Adasíyyih

'Abdu'l-Bahá visited 'Adasíyyih in 1920. Up to that time, because of the war and the lack of food in Haifa and 'Akká, the Bahá'í farmers there had been sending Him one-third of their harvest as rent for the land. On this visit, with the war now over, He reduced their harvest rent to one-fifth of the harvest, but noted that a portion of each harvest should be shared with their workers 'or one day these day workers and farm labourers would come and take their share of the income'. 'Abdu'l-Bahá only stayed for a day and a night, but He emphasized the importance of holding nightly prayer meetings and consulting on local problems to resolve them. This allowed them to elect their first Local Spiritual Assembly four years later.[13]

Inez Cook

About 21 April, Inez Cook (later Greeven) and her sister, India, arrived for their pilgrimage from America. Inez had recently divorced and one day the Master asked her, 'Where is your husband?'

This was the one question she did not want Him to ask. She replied,

> 'Well, he's not here, 'Abdu'l-Baha.' 'Yes, I can see that he is not here. Where is your husband?' She replied that her husband had left her for another woman. 'Yes, I know,' the Master said. 'And because you have forgiven him, God has forgiven him.'[14]

'Abdu'l-Bahá told her that she was not to feel like a guest in His house, but as His own daughter and that He loved her very much. He promised that He would pray for her.[15]

> One night, she was asleep in the same bed with her dear sister India, in the pilgrim house . . . In the middle of the night she awoke, and something was different. She couldn't put her finger on it. Then as she awoke more fully, she could see that she was floating several feet above the bed. She was startled, and got down, and began to walk around the room. She bumped into things and the noise awoke her sister. 'What's wrong?' her dear sister asked. 'I was floating in the air!' she said. 'And I don't understand why . . .' and as she reflected on it, she knew for a certainty that at that very moment, 'Abdu'l-Bahá was praying for her in the Shrines. Later that day she was walking in the streets of Haifa, and she saw the Master. He saw her, and walked over to her, smiled and asked, 'Did you know I was praying for you?' She said yes, she did.[16]

Though saddened by her life's difficulties, 'Abdu'l-Bahá told her that she had

> great capacity and he prayed for great results from me in the future – that I should be as a flame when I left here & so intense that He could feel the heat in Haifa. I should be as a flaming candle – no, as a star, as the moon and light the night. The people in America must say that I had changed completely from this visit.[17]

One day at breakfast, 'Abdu'l-Bahá saw Inez with a cup of coffee and said, 'You, drinking coffee? Drink tea, good, very good. Coffee has the particles pulverized in the liquid and is disintegrating, while tea is clear, aids digestion and stimulates the spiritual qualities.' He then said that in the future, all countries would become tea drinkers.[18]

One day when Inez and the other pilgrims sat down for lunch,

'Abdu'l-Bahá had already eaten so He personally served them. Then He began to speak and

> what He said was so profound and so lofty, that it filled her soul. She said it reached the point that her heart was so filled with spirit that she could not bear to hear another word. And at that moment, He stopped, and moved His head-gear back on His head, and then He began to tell funny stories. She said, 'He was the funniest man I ever met.' She said that He was so funny, that everyone was practically falling off of their chairs. She said, 'Our sides hurt from laughing, we couldn't bear to laugh any more.' Then, she said that Abdu'l-Baha moved His cap forward, and again began walking around the table, and speaking on lofty matters.[19]

When Inez returned to America, she was eager to share her experiences with two friends of hers who were not Bahá'ís. She was so eager that she arranged for her friends to go to the Holy Land and meet 'Abdu'l-Bahá. As Brent Poirier has recounted following an interview with Inez, when they returned she could hardly wait to hear what they thought of the Master:

> One of her friends said, 'Oh, our trip was wonderful!'
>
> 'Well, tell me all about it!' Inez said.
>
> 'Well, first of all we visited the pyramids in Egypt.'
>
> 'Yes, yes, go on,' Inez said somewhat impatiently.
>
> 'And then we went to the Holy Land.'
>
> 'Yes, yes!'
>
> 'And we went to Jerusalem and visited all the holy places.'
>
> 'Yes, yes!'
>
> 'And then we went to Mount Carmel, and we met your Master.'
>
> 'YES!'
>
> 'And he invited us into his home, and we had meals with him and his family. Why, they were the *nicest* people! And he told us funny stories. And they took us to beautiful gardens and shrines. It was wonderful.'
>
> Inez paused. 'Is that all?'
>
> 'Is that all? What do you mean!? We had a wonderful time! Thank you for arranging it!'

So neither of her friends had become Bahá'ís, and she did not understand this . . . The following year, in 1921, Inez returned to the Holy Land for a second Pilgrimage . . . During this second visit, she decided to ask him why her friends had not become Bahá'ís . . . 'My friends came here, and they met you, and they visited the Holy Places, but they were unaffected. When I came here I was completely intoxicated with the greatness of the Cause. Why didn't they become Baha'is?'

'Abdu'l-Bahá's answer was,

'At the gate of the garden, some stand and look within, but do not care to enter. Others step inside, behold its beauty, but do not penetrate far. Still others encircle this garden, inhaling the fragrance of the flowers; and having enjoyed its full beauty, pass out again by the same gate. But there are always some who enter, and becoming intoxicated with the splendor of what they behold, remain for life to tend the garden.'

The translator wrote this down for Inez . . . after her return to New York, she met with her friends, and told them exactly what had happened. She then gave both of them a copy of 'Abdu'l-Bahá's beautiful statement about the gate of the garden . . . One of these two women was attracted to the Cause, and became a Bahá'í. Her name was Frances Esty. She became a lifelong devoted Bahá'í. She compiled a lovely book of the Writings of 'Abdu'l-Bahá which she titled *The Garden of the Heart*. In the front of this book, which is extremely rare, she quotes this pilgrim's note, and thanks Inez Cook for it. It is often wondered where in the Writings this beautiful passage came from, and to whom it was revealed. It is not from the Master's Writings, it is a pilgrim's note from Him to Inez Greeven [Cook].[20]

'Abdu'l-Bahá's knighthood

'Abdu'l-Bahá was awarded a knighthood of the British Empire on 27 April in recognition of His humanitarian work during the war. When General Sir Arthur Money first brought up the idea of decorating 'Abdu'l-Bahá, Badi Bushrui, the General's private secretary and a Bahá'í, told him: "Abdu'l-Bahá does not receive decorations from Kings, he decorates Kings. However, inasmuch as he has accepted the persecution by the Turkish Government for 40 years, he will no doubt accept the honor you wish to bestow upon him.'[21] Actually, 'Abdu'l Bahá at first refused, but finally accepted because it was the wish of the British government.[22]

On 18 July 1919, General Money sent an official recommendation to General Allenby that 'Abdu'l-Bahá be given the Order of the British Empire with the grade of Knight Commander. The reason for the award was that 'Abdu'l-Bahá:

> Has given consistently loyal service to the British cause since the occupation. His advice has been most valuable to the Military Governor and officers of the Administration in Haifa, where all his influence has been for good.
>
> He was for many years placed in captivity by the Turks in the Citadel at Acre.[23]

When the recommendation was received at the British Foreign Office, E.W. Light wrote that

> Perhaps this paper might now be sent on to Sir Frederick [Ponsonby] with a view to obtaining H.M. sanction for the award of a K.B.E. to the Head of the Bahai religion – Abdul Baha . . . I suppose we may take it that Sir A. Money in recommending Abdul Baha for the K.B.E., does not think that any injury will be done to that gentleman's religious susceptibilities by giving him a cruciform decoration, but perhaps the War Dept. w[oul]d. advise on this point, which seems one of some special importance in this particular case.[24]

G.P. Churchill, a senior official at the Foreign Office and the one who signed the knighthood document, was more worried about political ramifications and suggested that the British Ambassador in Tehran and the Persian Minister for Foreign Affairs be consulted. Neither had any objection. The knighthood was approved by the King on 7 November 1919.[25]

Shortly before the presentation on 27 April 1920, the British sent a large automobile to collect 'Abdu'l-Bahá. The Master, however, was nowhere to be found. While everyone searched for 'Abdu'l-Bahá,

Isfandíyár, who had driven His carriage for many years, lamented his apparent uselessness; 'No longer am I needed.' But when 'Abdu'l-Bahá appeared, He signalled to Isfandíyár to ready the carriage. It was the motorcar that was not needed.[26]

The ceremony was held in the beautiful garden of the house of the British Governor, Colonel Stanton. Other officials, Muslim, Christian and Jewish leaders were present as well as other notables and local officials. English troops stood on the borders of the garden and a military band played music. 'Everyone was waiting for 'Abdu'l-Bahá to drive up in great pomp and ceremony. The walk to the Governor's house was lined with soldiers ready to make the guard of honor. To everyone's surprise, 'Abdu'l-Baha quietly came in at the back and took the seat allotted for him.'[27]

The surprised General Allenby quickly recovered. Standing behind 'Abdu'l-Bahá, he gave a short speech, after which the Master said a few words and offered a prayer for the British government.[28] When the ceremony was over, 'Abdu'l Bahá left the same way He had entered and General Allenby realized that it was his government which had been honoured by 'Abdu'l-Bahá, and not the other way around.[29]

King Feisal

At some point during 1920, King Feisal of Syria visited 'Abdu'l-Bahá. When interviewed by Martha Root in 1930, the King remembered 'Abdu'l-Bahá, saying, "Abbás Effendi, for that was the name I always used in speaking with 'Abdu'l Bahá, impressed me as a very great, intelligent, wise man. I had great respect for him because he was working for the welfare of humanity.'[30] Feisal had been declared King of Syria in March 1920, but was expelled after a defeat by the French in July. The next year, the British, whom he had fought for during the world war, made Feisal the King of Iraq.[31]

Though King Feisal thought highly of 'Abdu'l-Bahá, he proved to be incapable of controlling the Shí'ih Muslims when they moved to appropriate the House of Bahá'u'lláh in Baghdad during the 1920s. Despite promises to ensure that ownership remained with the Bahá'ís, the King did not fulfil his pledge.[32]

More pilgrims

Sir Patrick Geddes had first met 'Abdu'l-Bahá when he gave Him a tour of his Outlook Tower in Edinburgh, Scotland, in 1913. During 1919 and 1920, Sir Patrick was involved in town planning in both Jerusalem and Haifa and had proposed, along with the Haifa City Engineer, Dr Ciffrin, a town scheme that included the Bahá'í ground on Mount Carmel. The scheme called for two roads to cross the Bahá'í property. 'Abdu'l-Bahá not only approved the roads, He refused compensation and even presented them with a 4,000 square-metre piece of ground for a school. Dr Ciffrin also submitted a plan to the Master for a 'monumental stairway and cypress avenue leading uphill from the Templar Boulevard upon the level plain, to the central meeting place of the Bahá'í community', the Tomb of the Báb. 'Abdu'l-Bahá gladly accepted this plan. Sometime in late 1920 or early 1921, the Society of Citizens, a group formed to unite all religions 'in the work of social service and of civic and regional improvements', asked 'Abdu'l-Bahá to be its President, a post He gladly accepted.[33]

A young Bahá'í from India, Kaushal Bhargava, passed through Haifa on his way to England to study soaps and oils on a government scholarship. Like all other pilgrims, Kaushal was greatly taken by 'Abdu'l-Bahá. One day, the Master told him that he should study sugar instead of soaps and oils. Kaushal cried, 'Beloved Master, this is not possible. It is the decision of the government . . .' 'Abdu'l-Bahá simply said, 'It will be so.' The Master then sent a telegram to Lady Blomfield to get the subject changed. Before Kaushal even left Haifa, he received word that his field of study had been changed to sugar.[34]

Kaushal's wife, Shyamdulari, was a Hindu from a Brahmin family and not happy with his becoming a Bahá'í. By 1929, things reached a crisis and Shyamdulari said that if Bahá'u'lláh came to her in a dream, she would become a Bahá'í. Otherwise, Kaushal would have to convert back to being a Hindu. After three days of fasting and praying with an open heart, Bahá'u'lláh came to her in a dream, put His hand over her head and said that what Kaushal believed was true. She woke up a Bahá'í.[35]

Many people served 'Abdu'l-Bahá in Haifa. In 1920, Zia Bagdadi was there and he noted that his time was divided into three parts: learning from the Master, medical service to the community and meditation and prayer.[36] He later reported that there were usually about 50 guests in Haifa in addition to approximately 100 members of His family and those who lived with them. He said that mail came in 'boxes and baskets' and even with four secretaries it was impossible to read everything. One of the secretary's main tasks was to select which letters to pass to 'Abdu'l-Bahá.[37] Zia left in September after spending a year in service to the Master in Haifa.

Emogene Hoagg

Emogene Hoagg arrived in Haifa on 7 June and stayed until the end of October. 'Abdu'l-Bahá's first question was whether she was tired after her long journey. When Emogene said no, He said that it was because her aim was good and not material. Had she made the journey for material reasons, she would have been very tired.[38]

One day, 'Abdu'l-Bahá called Emogene into His presence and asked her about the Faith in America. She described the disunity affecting the Bahá'í community. 'Abdu'l-Bahá 'laid His hand on a book beside Him', and said:

> In this book is a story of a man who went to a doctor for treatment. He told the doctor his symptoms. First, he told him of the pains in his head, and of his not being able to sleep. To which the doctor replied,
>
> 'That is due to old age.'
>
> Then, the man told him that he had a great deal of pain in his stomach, and couldn't digest his food. The doctor replied,
>
> 'This is also due to old age.'
>
> 'Oh, but my arms and legs and back pain me constantly,' said the man testily. And the doctor said,
>
> 'This, too, is old age.'
>
> Then the man grew very angry, and asked how it was possible that a doctor, who had studied for years to learn how to cure people of their ills, had nothing more to say to a patient than that his illness is due to old age.
>
> And the doctor replied, 'Your anger, too, is due to old age.'
>
> "Abdu'l-Bahá, rising, replied to Emogene's question as to the cause of the lack of unity in America, "The condition in America

> is due to lack of steadfastness." And He strode out of the room. When relating this story, Emogene added, 'Steadfastness means faith, knowledge, obedience.'"[39]

What they needed most, He said, was firmness in the Faith, adding that all of the trouble in America was because they were not firm in their Faith. 'Abdu'l-Bahá assured her that the Bahá'ís there would become united. When she asked if that unity would come soon, He said no and she must pray for them.[40]

On 29 June, 'Abdu'l-Bahá called in Emogene and Mrs Culver. He told them that though they hadn't spent much time together, they had a spiritual connection. Then He talked about the problems created when people asked Him questions:

> Often when questions are asked I must reply – such as: An American woman came here [and] she does not like another woman and asks 'Is it well to sleep too much?' I say 'no' – Then she returns to them and says to someone who sleeps much, A. B. has said that one is not good who sleeps too much and thus much trouble is made.
>
> The talks I give without questions are the important ones, for then the person receives what he needs. Each bird has a special melody, and does not sing the melody of another kind of bird.[41]

A month and a half later, 'Abdu'l-Bahá told Emogene:

> I am growing to love you very much – more and more each day so that it will be hard for me to have you leave – Your heart is pure, your thoughts only of Bahá – you are sincere. Nothing! Nothing, but the Cause is in your heart. You are very dear to me – you are like one of my family. If you would remain always it would make me happy, but you have work to do.[42]

'Abdu'l-Bahá then told Emogene to tell Anne Apperson, one of the first Western pilgrims in 1899, that she should always remember their meeting in 'Akká and the advice He'd given her (Anne had married a non-Bahá'í and, though remaining a Bahá'í in her heart, had become inactive in the Faith because of her husband). 'Abdu'l-Bahá added that Anne should remember that

> Mrs Hearst while a very rich woman, had many difficulties and sorrows; she did much work in the world, – but nothing in her life was as important as her visit to Acca – in the K[ingdom] of G[od] this visit is remembered. Tell her to be very kind to the third grand child of Mrs Hearst – this boy Mrs Hearst bro't to me and I have prayed for him . . .[43]

'Abdu'l-Bahá sent Emogene to Naples, but Rúhá Khánum protested that she knew no one there. He replied, 'God will be with her.' Initially, Emogene was lonely, but then came an unexpected letter from the Borghese family in Rome inviting her to come and give a talk about the Faith. Signora Borghese arranged for an evening in her home with twenty guests. One of the guests, a Count, was impressed and invited her to speak at his mother's home. When she arrived, she found a roomful of men, but no women. That talk led to an invitation by General Piola Caselli to talk to a group of about thirty in his sister's home in Naples. From this came a call to address students at the University in Naples which resulted in a study group being formed. Then she was invited to Milan and Turin.[44] 'Abdu'l-Bahá had been right.

Mabel and Sylvia Paine, Cora Gray and Genevieve Coy

On 1 September, four American women arrived for pilgrimage: Mabel Paine, her 11-year-old daughter, Sylvia, Cora Gray and Genevieve Coy. The group arrived from Cairo by train, making a customs stop at Kantara, the entry point for Palestine from Egypt. Mabel wrote that 'we had to get porters to carry our many pieces of baggage to the customs officer . . . After a rather exciting melee of porters, officers, crowds, all enveloped in well nigh Egyptian darkness, we stumbled into a sleeping car, and, after some English soldiers had been evicted from our berth, settled down for the night.'[45]

Cora had heard that the best way to offload baggage when they reached Haifa was to pass it out through the train window. Just as she was about to engage a porter to do this, she heard a voice calling, 'Are there any American Bahá'ís here? Miss Gray?' When she turned, she found a 'fine looking man in a fez'. Rúḥí Effendi, the Master's grandson, 'Azízu'lláh Khán, Lotfu'lláh Hakím and Fujita were there to collect them and take them to their accommodation. Fujita climbed in through the window and passed their bags out, then 'staggered out the door with a huge basket of fruit sent by some friends in Cairo and my suit case, stoutly denying that either was in the least heavy.'[46]

When they reached the Pilgrim House, they were met by Emogene Hoagg and Malcolm McGillavrey. Malcolm had arrived a week before. Emogene acted as the hostess and Fujita did everything else: he brought breakfast in the morning, served the lunch, waited on the table for dinner, washed the dishes, cleaned and filled the lamps.[47] Mabel described the Pilgrim House and their room:

> The large central room, which one enters first, is used as a dining room. It contains an oval extension table, bent wood chairs and a sideboard. Out of the dining room open three sleeping rooms and a passageway. Out of the passageway open another sleeping room and the kitchen. We occupied the bedroom opposite the entrance. It contained two iron beds with mosquito nettings, two rugs, a medium-sized table, with looking-glass over it, and an iron washstand. There were four windows, two opposite the door, looking up Mt. Carmel, and one on each of the other two sides of the room. There were outside blinds and dotted Swiss curtains. The windows had iron gratings on the outside and against one of these was a clay water bottle.[48]

At 7:30 in the evening, Emogene escorted them to the house of the Master where they met the ladies of the household: the Greatest Holy Leaf, Munírih Khánum, Túbá Khánum and Rúhá Khánum, and a few little girls. Cora noted, 'I remember almost nothing of what they said, but one does not soon forget the love, the kindness they shower upon the visitor, nor the sweet beauty of their faces.'[49]

At four the next afternoon, the four ladies climbed aboard a carriage for the ride to meet 'Abdu'l-Bahá at the Shrine of the Báb. Genevieve was worried about meeting the Master. Before leaving New York, she had talked with Juliet Thompson who

> had said with deep earnestness, 'When you are in the Master's presence do not be self-conscious, if you can help it. Do not be afraid. There is nothing to fear. He is all love and kindness. Pray, pray, all the way on your journey, that your hearts may be freed from all self-consciousness. Go to him freely, gladly!'

> I had tried to remember that, I had prayed for purity of heart that I might learn the lessons the Master will teach those who are ready to learn. And yet as we rode up the steep road toward the Tomb, there was a strange mixture of love and dread and longing in my heart. The way seemed very long![50]

Arriving at the Shrine, Emogene led them around to the front of the Tomb where they found about 30 men. One was a tall, majestic Bahá'í teacher from Ashgabat who had 'the most beautiful laughter-wrinkles around the eyes . . . for he smiled almost all the time'. Five chairs awaited the four pilgrims and Emogene. Suddenly, everyone stood and turned toward the east. The Master had arrived.[51]

Cora's first thought was how tired and frail He looked.[52] Genevieve thought the same and was surprised when one of His secretaries said that He looked better than He had a few days before. Genevieve said, 'it hurt poignantly that any face of such beauty should be so weary.'[53]

Sylvia remembered that 'Abdu'l-Bahá 'walked with a great deal of energy and he was radiant and loving and smiling. As He talked, He looked out across the bay of Haifa – you could see 'Akká in the distance – and His eyes just seemed to penetrate into that distance. His eyes were very expressive . . .'.[54] She was 'a shy and self-conscious child' and remembered that

> I felt very much on my best behaviour because here I was having gone months to get there . . . We left Illinois in July and it took us until the first of September . . . it took us two months to get there. So, here we were with all of these delays and difficulties in travel having gone all this way and I knew that it was something very important and that I was to be very much impressed, but I wasn't quite sure how and what. But I was self-conscious and afraid that I would do the wrong thing at the wrong time as a child is likely to feel in such circumstances. My memory is that there was an instant in which, when the Master greeted me, for just an instant that all that feeling of self-conscious left me. I felt, I can't say a force of power, but it was as though these artificial things which come from a child's insecurity were gone. Just for that moment. Because I was not a person who rushed up and hugged people. I was brought up to be very reserved, we were in our family, but I would never rush

> up and hug anybody that I didn't know. But with Him I did and I didn't know why. For just an instant, it took that self-consciousness away from me. I don't know if I was completely accepted, but I was rid for the moment of my childish anxieties and self-consciousness and insecurities. For just that moment. I can't say that it lasted long, but that was my memory. I have a very strong memory of that.[55]

Sylvia also wrote: 'I was excited, in awe of Him, but longing to be with Him. I remember the moment when He spoke to me, holding out His arms, and I spontaneously rushed into them. For a moment I felt truly selfless – forgetting my customary reserve and fear of demonstrating emotions.'[56]

After about half an hour, 'Abdu'l-Bahá left to see some English visitors and Emogene took the ladies into the Shrine. Genevieve wrote:

> We removed our shoes, and then the caretaker poured rose-water on our hands, from a little glass cruet. We followed Mrs. Hoagg into the first room. It was perhaps fifteen feet square, and the floor was covered with a beautiful dark Persian carpet. There was no furniture of any kind. Directly in line with the outer door was a second door that led into an inner room. That was also covered with beautiful rugs. Standing on the floor were exquisite glass vases with candles burning in them. They were in groups, perhaps of three, and they gave the impression of flowers of living flame. I think there must have been other objects, a few, in the room. But the whole impression was one of exquisite beauty, simplicity, and peace. The inner room was raised several inches above the outer, and the raised threshold was covered with an embroidered cloth.
>
> Mrs. Hoagg walked slowly up to the threshold, knelt there a moment in prayer and then came back to a corner of the room. Cora followed her, and then came my turn. I had heard of the custom of prostrating oneself at the threshold of the Tomb, and I had wondered whether it would not seem stilted and formal. But it did not in the least! Perhaps it was the dignity and majesty of the Tomb, perhaps it was because we had been with the Master so recently. I was filled with a feeling of humility, with a longing to be 'evanescent at His threshold,' and the kneeling in prayer seemed the most natural thing in the world! After that moment at the threshold, I

> walked to the back of the room while Sylvia and Mabel in turn went forward. We knelt in prayer a long time. I cannot guess what was in the hearts of the others, but my own was filled with a great longing to lose my old selfish self, and to acquire the unselfishness of service. It was a wonderful time. I thought of that 'radiant youth called the Bab,' who had given everything, friends, family, life itself, to prepare the way of the Lord. I thought of the Master and the years of imprisonment and hardship that he had spent in the service of the Blessed Beauty. For the first time, since coming to Haifa, I was almost ready to weep, not from sorrow, but from the sense of the greatness of the power of God.[57]

No sooner had the pilgrims walked out of the Shrine then 'Abdu'l-Bahá suddenly appeared from around the corner followed by a group of men. He picked up the rose-water cruet and held it out to the ladies and they realized He wished them to go back inside. The Master Himself anointed each person's hands as they entered. Inside, Rúḥí Effendi chanted the Prayer of Visitation. The Americans were the last to leave and 'Abdu'l-Bahá was waiting to say goodbye, greeting them individually.[58]

On 3 September, the American pilgrims visited the ladies of the household, but did not see the Master. That night, they had watermelon for dessert. Genevieve wrote:

> When the Master is not there to give the signal for leaving the table, it is the custom for all to watch until everyone has finished eating; then all rise at once. But that evening, Malcolm and Mirza Lotfullah lingered over their watermelon longer than the others! I *think* Mrs. Hoagg and Mirza Badi were responsible for flashing a signal down the table, that we should rise and leave them there! So some twenty-three people rose and looked on while Malcolm and Mirza Lotfullah finished their watermelon, while everyone laughed at them! We were all like the simplest children who had played a prank on two playmates![59]

Cora and Genevieve rose at 4:30 a.m. on 4 September in order to visit the Shrine of the Báb before the heat. The caretaker, 'Abbás-Qulí, let them into the Shrine. After an hour, they went out and wandered in the gardens where they met Rúḥí Effendi and Lotfu'lláh Hakím. They had told Rúḥí Effendi they were coming up early, but he was still surprised to see them there: 'You *really* came! I didn't think you would! Americans never get up early.' Lotfu'lláh then took them to the circle of cypress trees where Bahá'u'lláh used to sit. They had only been there a few minutes when Rúḥí Effendi rushed up saying 'Abdu'l-Bahá wished to see them. When they arrived at 'Abbás-Qulí's house, they found the Master sitting on a divan. Cora stopped in the doorway, unsure of what to do so 'Abdu'l-Bahá stood and indicated a chair in which she could sit. Cora asked if He was feeling more rested. He said He was not, but that 'physical weariness was a matter of small concern'. After tea, figs, olives, honey and bread, 'Abdu'l-Bahá rose to leave. Cora and Genevieve went to see Him leave in His carriage and were greatly surprised when He motioned them to join Him.[60]

The next day at dinner, Cora found that her napkin had been placed in the seat of honour beside 'Abdu'l-Bahá. Thinking that a mistake had been made, she quietly moved her napkin to the side, but 'Abdu'l-Bahá, seeing her do so, quickly put it back.[61]

The 6th of September was their day to go to 'Akká and the Shrine of Bahá'u'lláh with Ḍíyá Khánum as their guide. Sylvia described the journey to the ancient city:

> And we went right along on the beach. Haifa was really just a small Arab village and instead of going on a road, we went right along on the edge of the water, all the way around the bay with the horses hooves in the water much of the time. We came to a place where a river emptied into the sea, so to escape the strength of the current, we went out with the horses in about up to their knees, right out into the sea and then back on the beach. It was right around that way on the beach the whole way to 'Akká, which was really a wonderful way to go. It was really very beautiful and very thrilling.
>
> And we came to the gate and one of the horses had something wrong with its shoe. There was someone there near the gate outside 'Akká and the shoe was repaired. I remember particularly a train of camels . . . and I think some donkeys, too, who had arrived in 'Akká from someplace and they were waiting to have work done on the camels' feet by a blacksmith. . . . I, as a child, was very impressed to see a train of camels waiting to get into the gate in 'Akká. We went in to this rather narrow gate and in the streets. 'Akká seemed

> thousands of years older than Haifa, although Haifa just seemed like an old Arab town, but 'Akká had far more antiquity – the cobblestoned streets, rough and everything very dirty.[62]

When they arrived at the Barracks in 'Akká, a soldier met them and insisted on showing them the whole fortress before finally taking them to the only part they were interested in. Sylvia, again, described their visit:

> We went first to the Barracks where the Friends were first imprisoned . . . We went into a long room . . . with open arches which led out on this court. The Barracks were built around the court . . . in which was a pool of rather stagnant water . . . I was very impressed . . . that seventy people or so all crowded into this room. We had been told by members of the family and by the Greatest Holy Leaf what it was like . . .
>
> What made an impression on me was this great, long Barracks room . . . it was just a great, long, dark place . . . and I thought how in the world did these people ever manage with just that dirty water out there. They told us about how terrible the water was and it was all they had to drink. The Greatest Holy Leaf . . . said she used her handkerchief to strain the water before she drank. It was August and they were so thirsty and hot and they weren't given any food at all. Then the next day they were given some dirty bread.[63]

Afterwards, they visited the House of 'Abbúd. Sylvia remembered eating melons on Bahá'u'lláh's porch and that there were families living in the house at that time. From there, the group went to the Riḍván Garden:

> We drove around the streets of 'Akká . . . then we went with the carriage out to the Riḍván Garden which was very, very beautiful. That made an impression on me because of the running water and the little fountain and a blind mule which went around and around pulling this rope which made the fountain run. And the mulberry trees and the benches. We sat on the benches and had a picnic lunch and took little naps under the mulberry trees . . .[64]

From the Garden, the pilgrims went to the Shrine of Bahá'u'lláh. Sylvia said, 'We never entered Bahjí because it was not in the hands of the

Bahá'ís, but they never told us this. They just said that is where He lived. They never emphasized these negative things at all.'[65]

When they entered the Shrine of Bahá'u'lláh, the door to the inner Shrine was closed. They all wished the door to be opened, but accepted its closure and said their prayers. Each seemed to feel that they were unworthy of entering that inner room. Then, as they began to leave, Ḍíyá Khánum returned and opened the door. Genevieve wrote, 'I do not know how long we knelt there. Time's passing ceased for us. My very breathing was a dedication of myself to our glorious leader, Bahá'u'lláh.'[66] Sylvia remembered:

> We went into the Shrine of Bahá'u'lláh and that made a tremendous impression on me because I realised that this was probably the most Holy place I would ever be in and here was an opportunity to get closer to Bahá'u'lláh and to get more understanding of God and whatever part I might have to play in this Faith. It was about 4 o'clock and we went in . . . The remarkable thing to me was that we were there all by ourselves. We knelt at the Threshold. Then they opened the door and we all went in, clear in to the very place. We were all allowed . . . We stayed as long as we wished and it seemed like a long time to me. I think there was chanting, probably some of the daughters of the Master chanted. I just remember praying and thinking that, in my rather childish way, that whatever we prayed for in all sincerity at that spot would be granted. As a child we think of these things. As a child my vision was very, very limited. That made a very great impression.[67]

They returned to Haifa and arrived in time for dinner with 'Abdu'l-Bahá. After eating, 'Abdu'l-Bahá got up and went to a basin and pitcher at the side of the room and washed His hands and face, after which He was given a towel. Then He said to the pilgrims, 'Go and rest' and then He left.[68]

Two days later, Genevieve went early to the Shrine of the Báb. As she was leaving, she met Lotfu'lláh Hakím and the two collected jasmine blossoms for the Pilgrim House. As they walked down the mountain, he told her that 'Abdu'l-Bahá 'works all day long, interviewing callers, etc. He goes to bed possibly by 9:00 or 9:30, but often he is up again at midnight, chanting and praying. Then he may correct Tablets for a while, and then sleep two or three hours more. And at 6:00 a.m. he rises for the day's work'.[69]

Later in the day, 'Abdu'l-Bahá called for Sylvia and gave her a Bahá'í name, Badia, meaning something new and wonderful. When they met the Master for the last time that night, He was radiant and laughing and said, 'Silvia! – Badia Khanum! – *Miss* Badia!' So came the end of their pilgrimage, and they left the next morning on the train.[70]

After the pilgrimage, Mabel reflected on her experience and what she had learned:

> The experience of being in Haifa and meeting Abdul-Baha is so great that it cannot be contained in the narrow bounds of the few days spent there. After the pilgrimage is over new beauties are revealed, new strength is derived. Every scene, event, and circumstance partakes of the eternal world and so continues to grow and develop in our hearts. The sojourn there is like being on a spiritual mountain top where broader, more spiritual views are spread before us. Or better, it is like having the water of life flow with its penetrating, life-giving, cleansing power into every last part of one's heart and life . . .
>
> Abdul-Baha himself is the Living Word, the very embodiment of the spiritual life. His whole bearing, his every attitude of body and expression of face mirror forth spiritual truth. How precious are the mental pictures of Abdul-Baha which remain with the returned pilgrim! I see him standing a little apart from the rest and in his bearing is absolute independence and majesty. It is evident that he can stand alone against the whole world. It comes to me that this great power and independence of aught save God is with him because he is so entirely selfless. It is a part of his station, the wonderful station of servitude.
>
> Again I see him . . . He is walking. The head is a little bent. The eyes are full of that wonderful compassion which all spiritual artists have tried to portray in paintings of great spiritual beings. There is a great freshness of early dawn, the purity of the child, a look of wonder as of one sojourning in a strange and foreign world. Such a look may have been in Christ's eyes when he said to his disciples, 'How is it that you have so little faith?' But a look too of great compassion, such compassion as must have existed from the beginning which hath no beginning and which will endure to the end which

hath no end. Then what compelling, active power in those eyes when sometimes they flash a summons from this world to the other!

What a blessing comes to the pilgrim to Haifa from being able to watch the daily life which is the active counterpart of these heavenly pictures! The following incident related by M. Azizul-lah Khan Bahadur [ʻAzízu'lláh Bahádur] illustrates the unfailing kindness which Abdul-Baha showers so freely on everyone with whom he comes into contact. M. Azizul'lah spoke in some such way as this:

'One morning I was in Haifa with the Master. We entered a store. Here we found a group of people and among them a German missionary, a resident of Haifa. At first this man was talking in such a way as to display his knowledge of classical Arabic literature. Then the subject of his conversation changed. He spoke of his personal affairs. He was no longer receiving remittances from the missionary board in Germany. This was during the war. He was in need of money. When the Master heard the man speak of his need, he promptly gave him a generous sum of money.'

Mirza Azizullah continued: 'All the time I was feeling critical of the Master and at the same time blaming myself for feeling critical. This missionary I knew had no love for the Master. He had opposed the Master and would oppose him again. 'Still,' I said to myself, 'if that is not the Master, I don't know who is.'

How often while in Haifa were we sharply confronted with this contrast between the human and divine way of thinking! 'My thoughts are not your thoughts, neither are your ways my ways, saith the Lord. For as the heavens are higher than the earth, so are my ways higher than your ways and my thoughts than your thoughts.' One morning some pilgrims were sitting in a small room on the ground floor of the Master's house. One of the pilgrims, a Mohammedan, was pouring over the pages of the Bible. He had recently become a Bahai and since that time could not read the Bible enough. Soon Dr. Lotfullah Hakim entered. He brought a message from the Master to the Mohammedan pilgrim. It directed him to go to the hospital. He had not been well for several days and the Master, like a kind father, was watching over him and advising him for his best welfare. But the pilgrim answered that he had not seen the Master for three days and that he would not go to the hospital until he had again seen the Master. In the mind of one of the

> pilgrims who was watching this little scene, sprang up a feeling a little critical and consequently a little hostile to this Oriental brother (Why was he not obeying Abdul-Baha?) But we were soon to see the Divine way of regarding the man. Dr. Lotfullah carried the man's message to the Master and returned immediately with directions to the man to step outside. He did so, the rest of us following. We went by the gravel path around to the front of the house. Soon Abdul-Baha appeared on the porch just above us. He looked down on the sick man with laughing kindly eyes and his beautiful musical voice fairly rippled with laughter as he again advised him to go to the hospital. The man's face beamed with pleasure and he went off to the hospital satisfied.[71]

Mabel, Sylvia and Genevieve left Haifa soaring in spiritual clouds, but Cora was later to leave the Faith.[72]

Pilgrims from California and elsewhere

Another group of pilgrims, including Ella Cooper, Helen Goodall, Georgie Ralston and Kathryn Frankland, all from California, arrived on 21 October. In one of her first diary entries, Kathryn recounted Lotfu'lláh Hakím saying that the British planned to turn the Barracks into a prison, but that the authorities emphasized that Bahá'u'lláh's rooms would not be touched.[73]

On the 24th, they were taken to the Shrine of the Báb in 'Abdu'l-Bahá's little Ford car. Two days later, Elizabeth Stewart arrived from Tehran where she had been working with Dr Susan Moody for the previous nine years. On 30 October, Ella, Helen and Georgia, joined by Emogene and Hovieh Khánum, the 'prospective bride of Mírzá Badi Bushrui, the private secretary of the Governor of Haifa,' Rúḥí Effendi and his sister Sorayah, and Fujita, went to the Shrine of Bahá'u'lláh. Khusraw, 'Abdu'l-Bahá's Indian servant, drove the Ford car while Arthur Radeen, the normal chauffeur, drove the Cunningham car.[74] When they went into the Shrine, Emogene wrote:

> The experience of this visit is one that can hardly be described even by those who have had the privilege of this visit. To kneel at the Holy Threshold, to ask forgiveness, to beg to become worthy

> of service in the Cause; to pray for the unity of the friends, and strength and confirmation to go forth to serve, with the knowledge that these come only through the bounty of Baha'u'llah, are some of the Heart's consciousness at the time.[75]

From the Shrine, the group went to the Riḍván Garden, where the caretaker 'climbed up a date palm of great height and with a cycle [sickle] cut off a branch hanging full of dates to keep those which ripened first from falling.' One of the participants said that she had 'never before . . . eaten anything so delicious as a ripe date fresh from the tree'.[76]

Arthur Radeen was 'Abdu'l-Bahá's best driver. One day the Master complimented him on his skill driving the beach road on a stormy day, saying 'No other chauffeur could have managed . . . You showed that you were an expert yesterday, but you should make Fujita and Khusraw like yourself.'[77]

On 15 November, Hippolyte and Laura Dreyfus-Barney arrived in Haifa from Port Said. Three days later, all the pilgrims and resident believers gathered at the Shrine of the Báb where 'Abdu'l-Bahá spoke about Niagara Falls in America, saying it was one of the greatest waterfalls in the world, then comparing it with the 'overflowing bounty of the Day of the Manifestation'. It was recounted how many military men had attained the presence of 'Abdu'l-Bahá in the previous year. Some had even gone with Him to the Tomb of Bahá'u'lláh.[78]

Rosa and George Winterburn were in Haifa on 21 November on their second pilgrimage. Ella, Helen, Georgie and Kathryn ended their pilgrimage on 24 November, departing by train.

1921: JANUARY–JUNE

Mason Remey and Marjorie Morten

Mason Remey, Marjorie Morten, Mrs Van Patten and her son, Bill, reached Haifa on 14 January. With them was Garibaldo Federici, a friend of Mason's, but not a Bahá'í. Unfortunately, the Van Pattens didn't have their visas and it took Mason's acquaintance with the British officer in charge of the port to clear the way for them to just come ashore briefly. Before any of them could land, however, they all had to go through a quarantine examination for smallpox, which consisted of an inspector in a small cabin looking for a vaccination scar. Mason had the scar, but when he went to show it, he inadvertently displayed a dog bite scar. Before he could remedy his error, the inspector had passed him and sent him out. Mrs Van Patten was next. While she was inside,

> a half-grown Arab urchin from the wharf crowd peered into the window and grinning at Mrs Morten went through the movements of sticking a lancet into his arm, as if being vaccinated, screwing his face up in mock grimaces of pain and pointing toward the door of the cabin to suggest that that was the fate of Mrs Van Patten within – all the time laughing with glee. His little game worked to his satisfaction for Mrs Morten became frantically excited over the fate of Mrs Van Patten and insisted that I [Mason] go to her rescue (I had laughed with the boy taking it all as his joke but I found that Mrs Morten was serious and would not take it as a joke). So I banged the door which was opened as the lady stepped out – she had not been subjected to vaccination. Then seeing how well his little act had taken Mrs Morten that little urchin laughed and roared, rolling over on the ground as he did so, fairly hugging his sides. I laughed also, but to myself.[1]

The Van Pattens were turned back, however, and had to continue to Beirut for their visas. During their delay, they were able to visit with the Bahá'ís in Beirut.

When Mason and Garibaldo stepped ashore, they were met by a group of Bahá'ís who rushed forward and, to Mason's acute embarrassment in front of Garibaldo, kissed him on both cheeks. But when Garibaldo was treated in similar fashion, everyone thinking he was a Bahá'í as well, it turned out well because Garibaldo's heart was touched by their friendliness. A short while later, Mason, Marjorie and Garibaldo were summoned by 'Abdu'l-Bahá. To Mason, He said 'We have been expecting you for a long while. It is about six or seven months since you started from America.' Mason then was asked to tell Him about his almost six months of travel-teaching in Germany.[2]

'Abdu'l-Bahá then greeted Marjorie and Garibaldo. When He welcomed Garibaldo and was told about all the trouble and danger he had faced during the war, 'Abdu'l-Bahá responded by saying that 'he was saved in order that the call of the Kingdom might reach his hearing. Everybody is not fitted to hear the call of the Kingdom. It is only the chosen ones . . .'[3] Later in the afternoon they all went out in 'Abdu'l-Bahá's Cunningham automobile. After a drive up Mount Carmel, they took Garibaldo back to the ship where he rejoined the Van Pattens.[4]

Dinner that night was a great challenge for Marjorie because she suffered greatly from ulcers. When 'Abdu'l-Bahá placed a plateful of pilau in front of her, she wondered if she should eat it. But since He had given it to her, she struggled and managed to eat it all. No sooner was her plate empty then the Master filled it again and told her to eat. Greatly worried about what her ulcer was going to do later, she obeyed. Then He filled her plate a third time and she thought, 'I will surely die obeying my Lord!' In the morning, however, she was pain-free and her ulcers had disappeared.[5]

After dinner that night, 'Abdu'l-Bahá wanted to know all about Mason's German trip. He praised his efforts and the German Bahá'ís, then with His tongue firmly in his cheek, He told Mason:

> I want to send you to exile. I want to write to the German Government to say that he [Mason] has made a revolution in Germany. If he goes again send him out of there. No doubt the result of this journey will be known later on. There is a story in Persia which is told that a thief went to break through the wall of a house in order to enter and steal. The owner of the house saw from a window that the man was digging. It was night. He said, 'What are you doing?' the man replied, 'I am drumming.' He said, 'Where is the sound?'

'Oh,' the man replied, 'you will hear it tomorrow.' Now the voice of your drumming will be heard tomorrow. The Cause will be very much strengthened in Germany, and they will become great friends with the Americans.[6]

Then the Master compared Germany with France: 'France has not this capacity. The capacity for which the Cause should grow, in France does not exist, because France is engaged in pleasure and luxury, theatres, dances, etc. Their spiritual susceptibilities are but little . . . They always think of theatres and dances. They worship women.'[7]

Later, Marjorie asked the Master about inter-marriage between whites and blacks and whether that would increase or decrease the troubles. 'Abdu'l-Bahá replied that in the beginning, there would be a lot of noise, but later when the offspring came, things would be better. Mason mentioned that Louis Gregory, an American black, considered his white English wife to be a great inspiration to him. Things were very difficult for her, but she understood and was strong.[8]

'Abdu'l-Bahá met with the pilgrims on 16 January and told them the story of a man who wanted to be a Bahá'í:

> About fifteen years ago, a Persian merchant came to me and said 'I want to be a Baha'i.' I saw him to be a worldly man, not knowing anything about being a Baha'i, or about the Kingdom, and that he was not thoughtful of God. I said 'Come, you are my friend, but do not say you are a Baha'i . . . I asked him, 'Now tell me the truth, why do you want to be a Baha'i?' He said, 'In every city where one goes there are Baha'is, and as soon as they know I am a Baha'i they will receive me as their own relative and friend. Once I travelled with a Baha'i. We went to Port Said. No one knew me, but they came to receive him. I asked him if they were his relatives. He told me they were not relatives but Baha'is. From Port Said we went to Cairo. They came to meet him at the station, and they gave feasts for him. Being his friend, I was also invited. Then we went to Bushire, then to Shiraz and then to Abadie [sic], then to Kashan and to Teheran. In every city there were Baha'is and no one came near me for my own sake, although I was a Persian, and they were all Persian.'
>
> Among the Baha'is of God there is a divine brotherhood. There is a brotherhood of the heart, an eternal brotherhood.[9]

On 19 January, Mason and Marjorie took a walk down the Jaffa Road and then up to the promontory, where they came to a cave 'known as the School of the Prophets, or Elijah's Cave'. After visiting the cave, Mason and Marjorie returned to the nearby Bahá'í cemetery.[10]

'Abdu'l Bahá held a feast for some notables in Haifa on 23 January. Actually, the Master said that the guests 'themselves asked me to invite them to the Tomb' for the Feast. Preparations began the day before. Mason Remey remembered that there was

> a sheep roasted whole, basted during the process with milk. The cooking of this carcass was done very slowly and lasted the entire night, one of the Master's daughters remaining on watch to direct the servants and see that they did not fall asleep and allow it to burn.
>
> The moslem notables of the town, the white turbaned muftis, and other men in the Arab dress of the country, arriving at the Master's house and going from there up the mountain in the automobile . . .
>
> The feast lasted all day from morning until night . . . In the Orient a feast is a feast. Arthur Radeen who ran the guests up and down the mountain in the automobile gave us a vivid description of how those men of Haifa ate and of the quantities of food they consumed.[11]

The stress of the feast activities exhausted 'Abdu'l-Bahá. He said that his guests were, from morning to evening, 'occupied in smoking, eating and drinking tea. I had to entertain them myself, and therefore, I became very tired.' That evening, however, he still met with the pilgrims. Mrs Van Patten, returned from Beirut and meeting the Master for the first time, said to Him: 'I have many questions but when I come to the presence of the Master I become empty.' 'Abdu'l-Bahá answered, 'God willing, you, yourself will find the answers to these questions in your own heart. The confirmation of the Blessed Beauty, Baha'u'llah will enable your heart to discover the answers.'[12]

Because of His exhaustion at the feast on the 23rd, 'Abdu'l-Bahá fell ill the next day and did not see any pilgrims again until 1 February, when He called for Mason to come. After that visit, He again retired to recover for another week.[13]

Four American pilgrims arrived in Haifa on 7 February 1921. They were Arna Perron (formerly True), Mrs Houser, Will Remey, Mason's brother, and Jane Appel. Jane wrote that as they approached Haifa on the train,

> Mrs. Houser and I were so excited with the realization that we had reached at last after over a month's travel our destination that we were in a tremble all over. We lost the first view of the Bay but not of the friends. We all saw Mason Remey first and we were all so glad on account of Will's pleasure in finding him. Then Fugeta, Arthur Radeen, A. Zizullah [sic] who took care of everything, bags and all, brought us up in the car to the Pilgrim House.[14]

After a drive around Haifa, Arna, Mrs Houser and Jane went to meet 'Abdu'l-Bahá, Who was resting in bed after suffering for two weeks with a bad cold. They were the first pilgrims other than Mason to see Him in that time and that gave them a great sense of honour. Their visit was short, but they still left overcome with emotion.[15] They were in His presence again the next day and Jane thought He looked better. He told them He would like them to return home via Paris and London.

That afternoon Rúhá Khánum took them for a drive up Mount Carmel to the Shrine of the Báb. When they arrived, they first had tea and talked about the education of children. Jane said that Rúhá was 'so unlike an Oriental woman – so progressive – so anxious that her children receive the best education and that they should be free. Her little girls will never wear the veil . . .'[16]

After their tea, they went to the Shrine. Jane wrote that 'after removing our shoes and washing our hands with Rose water, we entered and stood facing the room of the tomb. Someone chanted a prayer after which we each knelt and prayed at the door. It was all so simple, quiet and peaceful. A wonderful calm spell hard beyond words to explain.'

On the 12th, the pilgrims took the train to 'Akká, no more splashing horses and waves threatening to break into the carriage. They first visited the Most Great Prison, which the British were cleaning and remodelling. Then it was on to the Shrine of Bahá'u'lláh, the 'tomb no words can describe . . . The beauty – simplicity – fragrance – majesty.'[17]

The ladies spent most of the day with Rúhá Khánum and were shown the pictures of the Báb and Bahá'u'lláh by the Greatest Holy Leaf. Jane noted that 'a little of the intense feeling one has at the tomb is felt as one studies the picture of Baha-ullah, the wonderful face is so intense and so fine. Eyes are so clear and piercing.' The Greatest Holy Leaf also showed them a coloured picture of the Master and some of Bahá'u'lláh's hair, 'black and still full of life'.[18] On the 18th, the four women left 'Abdu'l-Bahá's presence for the return home.

Mountfort and Adele Mills arrived in Haifa on 21 February. The first afternoon, 'Abdu'l-Bahá told them that the only way to love Bahá'u'lláh was to love the other Bahá'ís. The more they loved the friends, the more they loved Bahá'u'lláh. Afterwards, 'Azízu'lláh Bahádur told them that

> the Master suffers more from inharmony among the friends than from any other cause. This is not a pretty figure of speech, it is an actual fact and news of this kind makes him really ill . . . When the friends are martyred in the Cause, he is sad, but not sickened. He realizes that these things are in the pathway of service and help the Cause. But differences among the friends take his very life.[19]

While they were there, 'Abdu'l-Bahá related the story of His conversation with Dr Van Dyke, a Protestant Christian and one of the founders of the College in Beirut. The Master asked Dr Van Dyke how he expected Christ to return.

> 'We believe He will come from heaven.' I asked, 'Do you expect Him to come from this heaven?' (pointing to the sky). 'You are skilled in the science of mathematics and astronomy and well know that this sky is infinite and that there is no such physical heaven from which Christ could descend. Let us consider the matter further. When Christ came the first time, He came from Heaven. He, Himself, said 'I am come from heaven.' He further said that none goes to heaven save him who comes from heaven. The reality of Christ did come from heaven. It is written in the New Testament that the Son of Man descended from heaven. But apparently He came from the womb of Mary. In reality, however, He came from heaven and His second coming will be the same.'
>
> Dr Van Dyke replied, 'No, no, He must come this way,' (pointing to the sky). I said, 'If an illiterate person should say that I should understand, but that you who are a scholar so speak, astonishes me.' The doctor then began to laugh.[20]

A few days later, Mason made the mistake of calling 'Abdu'l-Bahá the 'real sun'. The Master was quick to correct him, saying, 'My title and name is Abdul-Baha. This name is beloved to me. Neither sun nor moon or stars, only Abdul Baha.'[21]

Mason recounted the story of how several men came to 'Abdu'l-Bahá to ask Him about a transaction they were unable to resolve amongst themselves. After listening to their problem, He suggested a solution. Some accepted it, but others objected. So He offered another solution with the same result. This went on for much of the morning until the men left with the problem still unresolved. 'Abdu'l-Bahá wearily turned to the Bahá'ís and said, 'Verily it is easier to please God then to please some people.'[22]

Covenant-breaking and the ego

There was problem concerning disunity in the American Bahá'í community which Mason wanted to ask the Master about in private, but he had a difficult time getting the meeting arranged. In 1917, a group of people associated with Luella Kirchner had begun to create a division within the Chicago Bahá'í community. Initially, the group had opened, with 'Abdu'l-Bahá's approval, what they called the Bahá'í Reading Room, a library where Bahá'ís could read about the Faith and discuss what they read. Later, because of a struggle for power within the Bahá'í community, the Reading Room renamed itself the Chicago Bahá'í Assembly, claiming that the elected House of Spirituality was not valid. This group, with Kirchner at its centre, began to promote teachings by a Mr W. W. Harmon, who claimed that 'through [his] interpretation of Baha'o'llah's Word . . . the Bahais would receive divine illumination'. All of this created disunity and split the Chicago Bahá'í community in two.[23]

When the Bahá'ís gathered in November 1917 to mark the Birth of Bahá'u'lláh, Mason wrote that one morning in his mind he saw 'a map of this country with the various Bahá'í Centers marked, and on it a huge black octopus with its head in Chicago and its tentacles reaching out into the various Bahá'í Centers.' Mason managed to get a committee of investigation appointed, with himself as the chairman, and which included Emogene Hoagg, George Latimer and Louis Gregory, to look into the matter.[24] The committee took a very wide definition of what 'violation' was and tarred many people with its brush, however long ago their association with the Reading Room group had been. This was, unfortunately, during the time when communications between America and the Master had been cut off by the war, so they had no guidance from the Centre of the Covenant. After communication was restored, 'Abdu'l-Bahá declared that Kirchner was a Covenant-breaker, but did not include many of those who had been accused by association. This created quite a commotion and there was much criticism of Mason. Years later, he bitterly wrote about the episode and accused many prominent Bahá'ís of supporting the Kirchner group of violators, including Agnes Parsons, Juliet Thompson, Mountfort Mills, Roy Wilhelm, Harry Randall, Mary Hanford Ford and Edward Getsinger.[25]

Mason was further crushed in 1920 at the National Convention when Louis Bourgeois's design for the House of Worship in Wilmette was selected over his own. Mason wrote that some of the Bahá'ís, with 'personal antagonism' towards him, had lined up their forces to

> espouse the cause of Bourgeois and his temple design against the architectural ideal that I was trying to put before the people; namely that of a temple design after the lines of the Taj Mahal which the Master wanted. Now I can see quite clearly that the Master's wish for the architecture of the temple was sacrificed because of this condition of violation which condition so blurred the vision and the minds of the Bahá'ís in this country that they could not see nor understand His wish in this matter . . .
>
> The fact that the Master wished me to design the Baha'i Temple for Mount Carmel in Palestine, is proof to me that He preferred the Indian Style in which I worked to any other style.[26]

Mason summed this up by stating that 'Although the outer struggle in that convention had been upon the grounds of the Architecture of the Temple, yet in reality the inner struggle of souls had been upon quite a different plain. It was the conflict of understanding of the Teachings.'[27] Mason obviously believed that he knew what the Master wanted and that the others did not.

Finally, Mason had his private interview with 'Abdu'l-Bahá, but it was constantly interrupted. First a telegram arrived, then a pilgrim came from Persia followed by a Turkish man. The Master welcomed the Turk, ordered coffee and a water pipe, then had a long conversation with him. Finally, an old Bahá'í came with his head tied up with a handkerchief because of a severe toothache. The man wanted 'Abdu'l-Bahá to have someone come with him to the dentist. Mason's interview ended without really having started.[28]

Then on 3 March, 'Abdu'l-Bahá told them that He was going to Tiberias to arrange for the protection of the Bahá'í farmers there; they were being attacked by bandits who were stealing their crops and terrorizing people. He said that the pilgrims could come with Him, some immediately and some later, but cautioned everyone, however, that there were some missionaries there who were opposed to the Faith, so they had to use caution while in Tiberias. He suggested that they go as ordinary tourists and see the sights during the day, while coming to Him at night. Mountfort and Adele Mills travelled with the Master and Mason came a few days later.[29]

The trip didn't start well. Between Haifa and Nazareth, the roads were deeply rutted and suddenly the car, driven by Arthur Radeen, fell into deep ruts and broke the case covering the bearings. A carriage was found and 'Abdu'l-Bahá returned to Haifa, arriving at dusk. The next morning, the party again set out for Tiberias, this time in the Master's dependable carriage,[30] and they were soon ensconced in the Tiberias Hotel overlooking the Sea of Galilee. After they were settled and had gathered in the Master's room, He pointed out at the lake, mountains and sunshine and said that the whole countryside was filled up with spirituality because Christ had walked in the area. He said: 'It was just there (pointing to a church by a palm tree near the shore) that His Holiness met Peter and others and asked what they were doing. They answered, 'Fishing,' and Jesus replied, 'Throw away your nets and follow me. I will make you fishers of men.'[31]

Shortly after 'Abdu'l-Bahá left for Tiberias, Louis Bourgeois, his wife Alice, Willard Ashton and Mr Pemberton arrived in Haifa. Amid all the noise of their arrival in the port, the natives kept yelling out one word at Louis which he asked about later: 'What is this Basshish [baksheesh or begging] that I hear all these people talking about? They talked about it all the time in Egypt, too!' Mason wrote that he greeted Louis, his architectural rival, warmly because he had 'always liked him personally although we differ radically in our architectural ideals'. Later that evening, when Mr Pemberton was recounting the 'heroic sacrifices'

Louis had made to design the Temple and how Bahá'u'lláh 'had chosen him as the instrument' to design it, Mason wrote, 'I was a bit bored because I knew that Bourgeois had already been many times paid in money for this work.'[32] The professional rivalry contained a bit of jealousy too, it appeared.

The day after the Bourgeois' arrival, Mason and his brother Will left for Tiberias and Mason at long last had his private interview with 'Abdu'l-Bahá. The Master spoke strongly against those who violated the Covenant, saying that all America's problems stemmed from this. He named Ibrahim Kheiralla and Ameen Fareed, but no others. 'Abdu'l-Bahá concluded that in reality,

> It is of no importance. These violations cannot achieve any results. They cannot attract nor hold any souls. They simply poison some souls and cause them to wither. But it is temporary. In a short time you will see no trace will be left of them. Observe the life of Ibrahim (Kheiralla), how he was, and how he is. They themselves and their damage to the Cause are like the foam of the surf of the sea – ephemeral.
>
> I have adopted you as my own son. You have to appreciate this favour very much indeed. One should see that you are living according to the requirements of this sonship. You should be aware of your responsibilities. At present take a new spirit to the German friends.[33]

Mason apparently took this to be praise of his steadfastness, but it might have been a warning for him to check ego. Mason was obviously beginning to believe that he knew what 'Abdu'l-Bahá wanted and that few others did. This attitude would reach its zenith in 1960 when he declared himself the second Guardian.

Professor and Anna Kunz

Professor and Anna Kunz arrived in Haifa at midnight on 22 March. 'Abdu'l-Bahá was still away in Tiberias so the Kunzes enjoyed Haifa and 'Akká while awaiting His summons. Their first day was spent visiting the Shrine of the Báb. On the second, they went to 'Akká, the Garden of Riḍván and Bahjí. When they entered the Shrine of Bahá'u'lláh, 'the place was filled with the fragrance of Jasmine blossoms' and 'a heavenly light filled the room'. When they left, they found several Hindu soldiers talking with the caretaker. The soldiers, who were not Bahá'ís, would often come to the gate and kiss the wall, explaining that they 'felt and knew they were on holy ground'.[34]

On 25 March, they took the train to Tiberias, a three-hour ride. On Easter morning, they entered the presence of 'Abdu'l-Bahá in His room on the top floor of the hotel. Anna wrote:

> To us his outward appearance seemed similar to that of the old Hebrew Prophets; his humility, his simplicity and love were like that of the Christ. This boundless love conquered the hearts at once. Abdul Baha talked to us with a ringing, piercing voice which will forever sound in my ears. His words would come forth with that unique simplicity, then he would pause for a while, often closing his eyes. His spirit, it seemed when I dared look at him, had left his body; he was looking into infinitude, communing with that world for which we long. Having seen him, we could understand well what he meant when he said to us, 'the prophets discern by sight.' We came before him, my husband especially, with many, many questions in our minds, but sitting in his presence we seemed to forget them, or better, there did not exist any unsolved problems. He said, 'God has created a remedy for every disease,' and while in his presence, we tasted of this remedy.[35]

They spent the next three days in Tiberias and saw 'Abdu'l-Bahá as much as possible. They followed Him as He strolled, unrecognized, through a nearby garden and in the hotel. When they followed Him back to the hotel, He climbed the many steps to His room with a surprising vigour, and Professor Kunz said, 'It looks as if he were carried over these flights of steps by hands unseen.'[36] Professor and Anna Kunz's daughter, Margaret, later married David Ruhe, who became a member of the Universal House of Justice.

Eastern pilgrims

Seven pilgrims from Nayríz, Persia, arrived in Haifa on 20 April, including Muḥammad-Shafí' Rouhani, a young man of about 27 years. On Riḍván, 'Abdu'l-Bahá sent the group to Bahjí on a bus which dropped them about a kilometre from the Shrine. The group was singing a song whose verses ended with 'Alláh'u'Abhá!' When they met the Master, he laughingly chastised them saying, 'You have publicly disgraced Us! There was a time when no one dared say "Alláh'u'Abhá". Now you raise the cry of praise and glorification and openly utter the greeting of "Alláh'u'Abhá" as you come to the Blessed Shrine.'[37]

Soon after Riḍván, Muḥammad-Shafí'and another pilgrim, Ḥájí Amru'lláh, fell ill. For Muḥammad-Shafí', 'Abdu'l-Bahá ordered that a litre and a half of milk be boiled and that Muḥammad-Shafí' was to drink it when it was cold. The cure was quick and effective. Ḥájí Amru'lláh, however, rapidly grew worse. Dr Lotfu'lláh Hakím and a German doctor were caring for him and on 1 May, a greatly perturbed Dr Hakím told 'Abdu'l-Bahá that Ḥájí Amru'lláh was in a critical condition. The Master simply said, 'He will be all right.' Dr Hakím replied that 'even the German doctor has no hope for him . . .' Muḥammad-Shafí' reported,'With a special gesture, which is His alone, and with considerable force, 'Abdu'l-Bahá repeated His assurance, saying, "He will be all right" . . .' He then took some candy from the table and told the doctor to give it to his patient. By the twelfth day of Riḍván, Hájí Amru'lláh was up and walking around.[38]

Ḍiá'u'lláh Asgharzádih (Asgharzadeh) made his second pilgrimage at some time during the year. During his first pilgrimage in 1903, he had been allowed to stay in 'Akká for several months. On his second pilgrimage, he brought a silk carpet. This carpet had been specially made for the Emir of Bokhara, but because of the Russian Revolution, it could not be delivered. Instead, Asgharzadeh gave it to 'Abdu'l-Bahá, who laid it in the inner room of the Shrine of Bahá'u'lláh. The carpet was later sent to Wilmette for the House of Worship. After his pilgrimage, Asgharzadeh moved to London and became a good friend of Shoghi Effendi who was studying at Oxford. He later, at the age of 73, pioneered to the English Channel Islands for which he was named a Knight of Bahá'u'lláh.[39]

One day the Governor of Palestine asked 'Abdu'l-Bahá for the loan of His car. The British Prince of Wales (who became Edward VIII) was coming to Haifa and evidently 'Abdu'l-Bahá's car was the best one available.[40]

Nell and Stuart French

Nell and Stuart French and their sons arrived in Haifa on 25 April by train. Unusually, no one was there to meet them: 'We secured a carriage and with some difficulty made the driver understand that we wished to go to the home of Abbas Effendi. We drove through the town and I was at a loss to know what to do, but the carriage pulled up before a house and on the gate post a bright brass nameplate bore the magic name of "Abdul Baha Abbas" in English and Arabic.' No sooner had they left the carriage when Lotfu'lláh Hakím, Arthur Radeen and Fujita ran up and escorted them to the Pilgrim House. Later, they walked up to the Shrine of the Báb: 'To get to the Tomb we walked up a little path, quite steep, but with flowery grass, almond, fig and other fruit trees. On the level of the Tomb building there is a lovely garden and the view of Haifa, the Bay and Acca are superb.' When they arrived, there were many Persians sitting there and, at the Frenches' request, one of them chanted. Lotfu'lláh then took them into the Tomb for a short visit.[41]

For the next four days, they remained in Haifa with no word from the Master. One day, they went into town and bought a bathing suit for Stuart and some dark glasses for Nell, as well as candies, preserves and cakes. When they returned, Nell was taken to meet the Greatest Holy Leaf. Entering a room, she saw '"Khanum" as the Greatest Holy Leaf is called sitting alone on one side & the others on the other side. All rose and shook hands. The Greatest Holy Leaf kissed me on both cheeks.' Nell gave the ladies some small gifts and stayed for about a half an hour.[42]

On another day, Nell met the Holy Mother, Munírih Khánum, 'Abdu'l-Bahá's wife. She was not well and lay propped up with pillows. Nell wrote, 'I never saw a more beautifully sweet expression. Beside her sat "Khanum" and the daughters were all near. We visited for an hour, the conversation being devoted to ways of argument and approach in teaching certain individuals.'[43]

Finally, on 29 April, the call came for them to go to Bahjí the next afternoon. It was an interesting trip. They were accompanied by a Mírzá Jalál, whom Nell identified as the grandson of the Covenant-breaker Mírzá Yahyá and who she said 'has come and thrown himself on the Master's mercy incurring expenses and being generally unworthy and unpopular'. This Mírzá Jalál is different from Mírzá Jalál (the Master's son-in-law) who had helped 'Abdu'l-Bahá begin His trip to the West. Nell tried to keep this Jalál away from her husband. She wrote, 'We took third class in order to see the people. No glass in car windows. Many laborers returning to Acca from Haifa after work.'[44]

They arrived at the 'Akká station at 6:15 p.m. and, as in Haifa, there was no one there to meet them, so she was grudgingly forced to turn to Mírzá Jalál for directions:

> He said he was going and would accompany us!!! Nothing else to do. In two minutes we saw Haleel coming with Master's white donkey. He had put cushions on saddle for me. I declined, not thinking I could sit astride with my tight skirt. Haleel said 'It is the Master's wish', so of course I climbed on by getting up on a stone wall first. Haleel guided donkey with bridle and I sat passive very thankful I have means of transportation in growing darkness and country road. Air fresh and lovely, hills green and rolling and here and there ruins of walls & fortresses of uncertain antiquity. Off to the left the white walls of the fortress, the 'Most Great Prison' some little distance away. 1½ miles. My riding left Stuart to walk with Jalal but I kept close watch. We met some stray Arabs – first and then small groups of Persian Pilgrims. I shall never forget the reverence with which they stopped and with bowed heads and hands crossed on breast they greets us 'In the Name of God'. It was wonderful!!!
>
> When the night was almost entirely closed in we saw lights ahead and knew we were near the end of our journey. The end indeed! A large house showed at first and I thought it the Master's abode but was deceived. It is the home of the half-brother Mohammad Ali. The Master's house adjoins it but is only a series of one storey rooms. At one corner of this quadrangle thus formed is the Tomb of Bahá'u'lláh.[45]

They had arrived at Bahjí. When they stopped at a door, they were told that 'Abdu'l-Bahá was waiting for them. About meeting 'Abdu'l-Bahá, Nell wrote:

> The low door thru which we stepped gave into a small, low ceilinged square room. Hard rough dirt floor, table with lamp. As I entered I saw the beloved figure not a few feet away sitting in the very corner

of the room on a divan on which was a cushion and a rug. He rose and I saw the picture which I had always known come to life before me. The white turban, the brownish abba and the Being they enclosed. My presence of mind came to me most wonderfully and instead of falling at his feet as I felt I must I went forward to receive his greeting. He said 'Oh Mrs French, welcome, you are very welcome, and Mr French, come, you are very welcome.'

He then sat down and Stuart sat beside him while I sat directly in front in a chair which Aziz placed . . . Haleel brought Persian tea in small glasses and cakes to go with it. Three glasses were on the tray. I took one, Stuart one, and the boy Haleel looked at the Master to know for whom the 3rd was intended. The Master raised his hand and in a very positive manner indicated Jalal . . . the Master said a few words more then he arose and accompanied us to a room further down the hall. There he stopped and apologized for the simplicity and lack of comfort of the room. He said I might remain there or if I preferred I might go to the other house and share the room with Monevar Khanum (the youngest daughter). I said at once I would prefer the latter so I left Stuart to wash up and I went to meet Monevar Khanum . . . The second house was where the Master slept, where Monevar Khanum was and where the food is prepared. It is as simple as the first but larger. A large high hall (dirt floor) which served as dining room, the Master's bedroom on one side, Monevar's on the other. A very small inner court where were growing a small orange tree and some flowers. And from the court the little primitive kitchen, servant's rooms and simple toilet which is quite the most primitive variety I have ever seen. I greeted Monevar and then went to her room, which I found we were to share together. This room was perhaps 25 x25 ft, rough floor, divan . . . along the side . . . A bed with close mosquito covering in one corner of room, a table in middle – nothing else. A shallow brass basin was brought for me to wash in and a tin kerosene can served as pitcher.[46]

Interestingly, in light of Nell's hostility to Jalál and her discomfort with simple living, she concluded her diary writing: 'This account was never finished. I found myself so engulfed in the mystery of the experience that I could write no more.'[47] The words of May Maxwell in 1899 loomed large: 'The pilgrimage to the Holy City is naught but a crucible in which the souls are tried; where the gold is purified and the dross is consumed.'[48]

On 1 May, 'Abdu'l-Bahá specifically asked Nell if she wished to tell Him anything. Nell had been bothered by the way some groups at home celebrated the Feast. Some groups did 'number reading' at the Feast. When this was translated, the Master simply said, 'Ask them where, in the writings of Baha'Ullah they find these things.'[49]

The Frenches spent only three days with 'Abdu'l-Bahá. Her later articles in *Star of the West* make no mention of any negativity – or of having to ride a donkey.[50] Nell became a Knight of Bahá'u'lláh to Monaco at the beginning of the Ten Year Crusade over thirty years later.

One day, an Egyptian believer, Áqá Shaykh Faraju'lláh, arrived and requested permission for the Mufti of Egypt, Shaykh Muḥammad, to attain the presence of the Master. Áqá Shaykh Faraju'lláh had spoken to the Mufti about the Faith and the Mufti now wanted to pose some unresolved questions to 'Abdu'l-Bahá. After dinner, the two Egyptians met with the Master for some time. Finishing their interview, the two men spoke animatedly as they walked to the Pilgrim House, awakening Muḥammad-Shafí', who happened to understand Arabic. He wrote:

> I understood what they were talking about. In but one meeting 'Abdu'l-Bahá had subdued the heart of the Shaykh in such wise that he had become an ardent lover. Their discussion was so intriguing, and the description of their visit with 'Abdu'l-Bahá so exciting, that I lost my power to resist. I left my bed and with their permission sat on a chair next to them.
>
> They continued their conversation. Shaykh Muḥammad addressing Shaykh Faraju'lláh said, 'I had worked hard for several years and had selected some very difficult questions which I had noted down to ask. When I decided to accompany you to Haifa, I was thinking that my encounter with 'Abdu'l-Bahá would take a long time before settlement could be reached. However, after discussing one of my problems during the first meeting, the response was so comprehensive and all-embracing that I feel all my difficulties have been resolved. 'Abdu'l-Bahá has answered all my questions. For example, the problem of fate and free will which seemed to be very complicated and which I thought would have needed a long time to resolve, was disposed of in one meeting. As soon as the first question

was discussed, the response was such that my other questions were also answered.'[51]

'Abdu'l-Bahá brought the pilgrims, including Shaykh Muḥammad, to Bahjí for the commemoration of the Ascension of Bahá'u'lláh. When 'Abdu'l-Bahá and the pilgrims gathered by the entrance to the Shrine, the Covenant-breakers watched from the Mansion evincing 'signs of immense envy and rancour. They tried to attract attention by pretending that since they were the occupants of the Mansion, they were Bahá'u'lláh's true heirs. When 'Abdu'l-Bahá was giving a discourse, one of them started chanting one of the prayers of the Blessed Beauty's with a very loud voice, so that it could be clearly heard.'[52]

Before midnight, the pilgrims gathered at 'Abdu'l-Bahá's Tea House. Just at midnight, Muḥammad-Shafí' Rouhani saw Khusraw, the Master's faithful servant,

> descending from the steps of the upper chamber with a lantern in his hand. 'Abdu'l-Bahá followed him down the steps . . .
>
> We set off walking behind 'Abdu'l-Bahá until we reached the entrance to the Shrine of Bahá'u'lláh, the Qiblih of the people of Bahá. As I approached the outer Threshold, I beheld 'Abdu'l-Bahá standing in the vestibule holding a large bottle of attar, with which He anointed those who entered. We stood in a line and went in one by one. As my turn came to be anointed, I stretched out my hand in such a way that my palm was flat. 'Abdu'l-Bahá lovingly pressed the palm of my hand with His thumb in order to make a hollow. He then poured the perfume generously into it . . .
>
> After all the friends were anointed, they stood in rows facing the Inner Shrine. The Master, Who was in front, with a movement of His Hand and in a very quiet voice, instructed one of the resident friends to recite the Tablet of Visitation. At that time the learned man from Egypt [Shaykh Muḥammad], who was the travelling companion of Shaykh Faraju'lláh. . . and who had been completely transformed in one meeting with 'Abdu'l-Bahá, was standing in front of me. He was weeping profusely as He supplicated at the Threshold of the Blessed Beauty.
>
> After the recitation of the Tablet of Visitation, 'Abdu'l-Bahá kissed the Threshold of the Sacred Shrine and backed away . . . the

Master sat on a chair outside facing the Sacred Spot. For about half an hour He was fully wrapt in meditation in absolute silence and complete lowliness. During that time we were all standing behind Him in utter humility and supplication. When the morning light broke, we were dismissed and proceeded to our rooms.[53]

1921: JULY–NOVEMBER

Edward Mattoon and Professor Johannes Pederson

On 1 July, Edwin Mattoon, his wife Annie and their two children, Florence, age six, and Zievar, age four months, arrived on pilgrimage and stayed for three weeks. They were the only Western pilgrims at that time; pilgrims from Malaya, India, Persia, Russia, Turkey and Egypt were also there.

In their first meeting with 'Abdu'l-Bahá, while He was asking them about certain American believers, they noticed that He seemed very tired and suggested that they leave Him to rest and not trouble Him more. 'Abdu'l-Bahá responded, 'you are not the cause of trouble, but you are the cause of comfort'.[1] Then, after asking about the Convention in Chicago, He asked,

> Have not the people arisen against you yet? Are not the preachers crying aloud? It is good that they have not yet excommunicated you. No doubt it is hard for the (Christian) ministers. The missionaries come here. They receive salaries so that they may convert one to their religion. They do not succeed. Now they see that you (the friends) gather together in such a way that they become angry and bitter against you. They will attack you; they will excommunicate you; they will rise up causing trouble for you . . .
>
> The more these people rise against it, the more the Cause will spread. The more they arise to extinguish this lamp, the more brilliant it becomes . . .[2]

Also arriving in July was Danish Professor Johannes Pederson. The Professor had visited Ignatius Goldziher in Budapest in 1913 and heard much of 'Abdu'l-Bahá's visit to the city from one who had been there. Then in 1920, Pederson went to Egypt and met some of the Bahá'ís. Leaving Egypt, the Professor then went to Beirut and encountered Bahá'í students at the college. Everything he heard so impressed him that he sailed to Haifa to meet 'Abdu'l-Bahá. There were many visitors when he arrived, but the Master graciously took him aside so that they could talk. The two were able to speak in Arabic. 'Abdu'l-Bahá said that if people had 'not forgotten their religion, there would have been no war' and that a unified humanity was necessary or they would destroy each other. The Professor later said,'I felt that 'Abdu'l-Bahá was a very great figure, and he was very kind to me.'[3]

Marie Watson and Fáḍil-i-Mázindarání

On 9 July, a very hot day of 49°C (120°F), Marie Watson and the eminent scholar Fáḍil-i-Mázindarání (Jináb-i-Fáḍil) arrived in Haifa from America. Jináb-i-Fáḍil was returning from a two-year teaching trip to America at the request of 'Abdu'l-Bahá.

Marie was there because on previous 27 April, 'Abdu'l-Bahá had sent a cable to Agnes Parsons in Washington DC that read: 'Send immediately Mrs. Watson in utmost comfort to Holy Land.' Disunity in Washington had made Marie ill and she was glad for this opportunity to visit the Master.[4] This was Marie's first time in Haifa and she was mesmerized by the people:

> 'Haifè, Haifè, all out for Haifè!' cried the guard, and everybody scrambled, collecting baggage, and endeavoring to get a carriage. We were fortunate in securing a vehicle and, our baggage beside us, we proceeded on our way through the narrow streets and stony road leading to the House of the Master, 'Abdu'l-Bahá.
>
> What strange sights greeted our eyes! The people seemed clothed in fantastic garb, and every color of the rainbow was flaunted before one; a red fez, a purple scarf, a green head-shawl, a yellow sash, a white or creamy coat, and a gunny-sack on the form of a black boy mingled in kaleidoscopic fashion among the chattering throng. And quaintly worded signs fastened on doors and window blinds – these also varied in color from gaudy pink to cerulean blue and saucy reds and henna, with old grey weatherboards showing here and there.
>
> Advertising in western fashion was attempted heroically. Here was the 'new' struggling with the 'old.' In bold black lettering in English the advantages of the Hotel Jerusalem were announced. The hotel was an old stone house with a narrow, arched door, before which stood a donkey laden with formidable sacks, containing,

no doubt, the provender for this hotel; patiently it waited to be relieved of its burden, meanwhile flicking off the troublesome flies buzzing about it. In front of the hotel small tables were arranged at which men were seated, laughing and talking in loud voices, and drinking thick, black coffee from tiny cups, eating and smoking between times, and clapping their hands when anything was to be replenished.

Our carriage wound its way slowly in and out of the melee of animals, carts and human beings on the main street until at last we turned the corner, and this varied picture, like a 'movie screen,' vanished from sight. The sun, the brightest and hottest we had ever known, greeted us with an intensity characteristic of the East, making us burn with impatience to get to our journey's end. Five minutes more and we were at the Master's House. Being informed that 'Abdu'l-Bahá was not in just then, we went with Dr. Lotfullah to the Pilgrim House across the way. Here we found Fugeta in charge. We were greeted most heartily and shown to our rooms, where we removed the dust of travel, and after changing our garments, we joined the friends in the dining-room where we were refreshed with tea.[5]

Fáḍil-i-Mázindarání was the centre of attention at the Pilgrim House because of the two years he had spent in America. Suddenly, in the midst of their tea and talk, Fujita rushed in to say that 'Abdu'l-Bahá was coming. After a warm greeting, the Master sent them to rest. That evening, the Master sat in a chair at the top of the steps of His house to give His talk. Marie described it:

View with me that majestic Figure in white flowing garments seated before us, a white turban crowning the wonderful head with its long silvery locks lifted gently by the breeze; the beautifully moulded hands emphasizing the discourse with impressive gesture. After the address a Russian refugee Bahá'í teacher chants in exquisitely modulated tones, the prayers of Bahá'u'lláh. It is impossible adequately to describe this scene. [I] became conscious of new emotions, the awakening of something so subtle, so elusive, that one could not capture it, yet so impressive that everything was cast into oblivion except the immediate present. The fragrance from the gardens on either side wafted a different scent on each breath of the night air. Roses, orange blossoms, lemon buds, tuberoses, jasmine, honeysuckle, each in turn left its definite sweetness as a fresh odour entranced one and vanished.

O that I might impress this scene upon the heart of the world! To me it is as though all eternity could not efface it; that majestic white Figure seated on the broad stone platform like a king enthroned, the setting of natural beauty so befitting His spiritual station, the gardens, the sea, the starry heavens, and the millions of gleaming points of light reflected below . . . The murmur of the sea is just beyond, the waves in ever repeating undulations, coming nearer and nearer to caress the shore. The melodious chanting, the deep silences, the seated figures with bowed heads and devoted hearts.

The chant ends. In a few moments the Master rises and goes into the house. Everyone rises also and salutes in the beautiful eastern fashion, hand touching the forehead and then the heart. The spell is broken![6]

Then 'Abdu'l-Bahá went to Marie and motioned her to

precede Him into the dining-room, an addition built recently for the entertainment of guests. This is a large room having a very high ceiling, as have all the rooms in the East, and there are seven large windows. Everything is white. A long table is in the centre of the room laid for fifty or more people. The Master placed me at the head of the table on the right, and thus He placed me throughout my visit. He always inquired in English after my health and would urge me to eat more, saying again and again: 'Too little, much too little,' when I assured Him I had eaten abundantly.

On several occasions my replies to the Master's loving solicitations in English were in Persian, a few sentences, but He was pleased and amused, I think, judging by the merry light in His eyes. He said to the big Arabian official, who spoke only Arabic: 'See, here is an American lady who speaks correct Persian. You say you cannot learn it and you hear it every day. She does not hear it often but she has learned.' The Master would ask, 'What is this? What is that?' indicating things on the table, and say approvingly, 'Brava, Brava! You know everything that is useful to know. That is very good.' The big

> man eyed me with astonishment at what seemed to him a wonderful performance, but he was not aware of my limitations, nor of the fact that in asking His questions the Master chose only such things on the table, the names of which I knew in Persian![7]

The following Sunday, 'Abdu'l-Bahá took Marie to the Shrine of the Báb, having her sit beside him in His car. When they arrived, they found over 50 already there. After tea, the Master spoke of prejudice and sincerity:

> 'Take prejudice, how it grows. First a few people say something disparaging about a person, and, generally there is a fragment of truth in what they say. The story grows, is spread, the circle widens, discussions are indulged in, inharmony results, schism takes place, what a waste of precious time that could and should be used for constructive work!'
>
> Then He spoke of sincerity. 'There are degrees always in everything. Until a man is freed from ego he may be positive and certain about many things *that are not so.*' He spoke of tests. 'Tests are not sent as punishment, but to reveal the soul to itself. Suffering unfolds both the strength and the weakness. Tests are sometimes creative of grateful surprise also; for in the midst of our trials we are amazed at the fulness of our strength and our resources, and so the heavy discipline is creative of assurance; the trial becomes the source of greater confidence, faith and trust. It strengthens and confirms.'[8]

Marie also spent time with 'Abdu'l-Bahá's sister, the Greatest Holy Leaf, and other ladies of the Holy Household. She wrote:

> How can my feeble pen worthily record such a life of untiring service and devotion as that of 'The Greatest Holy Leaf,' sister of 'Abdu'l-Bahá?
>
> From early morning till very late at night she is in demand, and with the assistance of the Master's daughters, she carries out every detail of this formidable household.
>
> The women of 'Abdu'l-Bahá's family are the precious flowering of the spiritual civilization inaugurated at the dawn of the New Age, where every faculty of the mind and heart has been quickened by

> the Divine Breath of the Gardener, who has nourished and sustained them through all the vicissitudes that result from such heroic living. No complaint is ever audible, and yet I read in the depths of their wonderful eyes a real tragedy, and this is unconsciously voiced in their desire for their children; they long for nothing for themselves, but yearn to give the children the advantages of modern knowledge and education, of which they, through long years of exile and confinement behind prison walls, have been deprived.[9]

Before leaving America, Marie Watson had been beset by disunity within her community. One group of Bahá'ís had interpreted a certain Bahá'í teaching one way and another group had interpreted it in another fashion. Both sides demanded that she ask the Master and bring back a 'definite' answer. One morning, 'Abdu'l-Bahá asked if she was happy. She said she was, but admitted to having a question, whereupon she detailed the misunderstanding over the teaching. 'Abdu'l-Bahá seemed to ignore her, pointing to the clouds and saying,

> You must be like these swift-moving, luminous clouds. They move, nothing hinders them. I shall pray for you that you will be like these clouds. Let nothing hinder you. Speak always of the Love of God. Teach the people what the Love of God is. Give them the Glad Tidings. Let nothing hinder thee; let nothing touch thy spirit which is not in conformity with the teachings of the Blessed Beauty. Be ever engaged in the service of the Kingdom. Do not let the unpleasant things annoy you. You must be as far removed from them as these clouds are above us. The important thing is to spread the Teachings, to show love and compassion, to be kind to all, and not wound the feelings of others. If we do not like to associate with some people, very well, it is not compulsory. We can let them alone and become so busy with constructive work, that there is no time to waste upon such matters. We do not waste our time in discussing non-essentials. Neither must you do this. Forget every unpleasantness of the past; speak only of constructive work, of the Love of God, of the compassion and mercy of God. *Seek to make others happy.*[10]

On 9 August, Marie and six others went to the Shrine of Bahá'u'lláh: 'It was late when we reached the house of the caretaker of the Holy Tomb.

The moon had risen and was shining above the mountains, pillowed on a vast bed of fleecy clouds, whose silvery edges appeared as an immense etching against the midnight depths of marvellous blue. Earth and sky literally "embraced like two lovers."' Then they entered the Shrine:

> We entered in single file that Holy of Holies, and each pilgrim knelt in adoration. When we emerged it seemed that hours had rolled on toward eternity! It was long past midnight. We supped lightly and retired. Sleep did not come. The few hours were spent in communion, potent and exhilarating yet conducive to self-examination and repentance. Tears flowed freely as we supplicated for the 'cleansing of the sanctuary' within the self, and many of the beloved friends were remembered in the supplications poured forth that night in the Holy Shrine.[11]

The next morning, the pilgrims again visited the Shine and Marie noted that they were 'Seven pilgrims, each from a different part of the world, strangers before, now bound by the firm rope of Bahá'í love and friendship, realizing their kinship and unity as the children of the Household of Faith in the Revelation of God in this Great Day!'[12]

The chiropractic donkey

Marie had been involved in a severe car accident in 1890 which left her spinal column twisted and out of alignment so that a portion of the vertebrae lay upon her left ribs, 'forming a protrusion the size of an infant's head'. Her right hip was out of its socket and she could only partially raise her left arm. For 19 days, she had lain in a coma, the doctors sure she would die. But Marie's

> soul was very much alive on inner subjective planes. In these experiences I met with a Wonderful Being, – whom I afterwards learned was 'Abdu'l-Bahá, who gave me spiritual instructions and taught me the mysteries of life, saying: 'Many of these things thou dost comprehend only in part, for thou must *live* them and then teach the people of the world. This is for future harvesting.'
>
> For thirty years this crippled body suffered untold agony. For years I had tried to live according to the Divine Teachings of the Bahá'í

> Revelation, before coming, on the outer plane of life, into the knowledge of the actual embodiment of my Lord and Master, 'Abdu'l-Bahá. In 1901 He accepted me as a servant in His Holy Vineyard . . .[13]

Now, as the pilgrims prepared to return to Haifa by way of the Riḍván Garden, no transportation was to be found. The men finally decided to walk. The caretaker of the Shrine, knowing that Marie had difficulty walking, brought out 'Abdu'l-Bahá's white donkey for her to ride. Marie had never ridden an animal before and the thought of riding a donkey, with her bad back, worried her. But since there didn't seem to be any other way, she climbed aboard the patient donkey, sitting on a hard pillow held in place by a rope:

> I braced up as best I could for I did not wish to spoil the trip for the men-pilgrims by my timidity; but oh, the road was so stony, the pillow was slipping and I was doubling up on one side! The donkey went swiftly along, kicking every now and then to rid himself of the flies, while I trembled within, fearing every moment that he would get rid of me too. I prayed, 'O God! help me to keep on,' for now there were strange snappings and crackings in my back, sides and shoulders. Pain, sharp pain, racked my whole body. It was growing unbearable and I was inwardly groaning with every forward step of the donkey, as it stumbled over stones and I grasped its mane. One of the pilgrims approached me and said: 'Wouldn't it be better to rest a while? You are suffering, I see, and we have quite a long distance yet.' I declined, trying to smile, and said: 'I think it is best to go on, it would be too difficult to mount again.' . . . He adjusted the pillow as best he could and . . . we started again. The heat was intense yet I felt cold, every nerve quivering with pain, and there was more snapping and tearing. What was going on, I wondered, in my spine and shoulder-blades? I felt as though I were being dismembered. Did it mean my death? The . . . words of the surgeon were in my ears, – 'Nothing can be done. If force is applied the bones will snap. Death will be the result.' 'Well,' I thought at last, 'what more beautiful could happen, – to die in the Holy Land, to be released from pain and suffering? Evidently my work was finished on this plane. For twenty years my humble service had been given to the Cause, more dear than life and now the Blessed One had sent for me to come to

the Land of Desire; I had visited the Holy Shrines and now I would enter the Riḍván, the Garden of God,' so ran my thoughts.

I felt strangely relieved and calm. I could see the tree quite near that marked the entrance to the garden. The Doctor again approached with Jenáb-i-Fadil and they said: 'We will help you down to rest before going in.' A few minutes more and I stood on my feet, but *not as formerly*! I could breathe deeply, which had not been possible for thirty years. My hip, somehow, was in place, the projecting bow on the left side of my spine had disappeared. In a flash this was all realized. I threw up *both* arms and cried out: 'O God, my God! This is a miracle that God hath wrought! Yá-Bahá'u'l-Abhá!' The other pilgrims were no less astonished than I, and joined me in fervent prayer and thanksgiving at what had been so strangely accomplished by the ride on the Master's white donkey.

I mounted again with ease and sat as straight as a major on dress parade on the back of this white 'surgeon' who was utterly unconscious of the aid he had given me, and of the feeling I entertained for him as I reverently kissed his nose.[14]

While in the Riḍván Garden, Marie

seemed treading upon air, and would ask myself: 'Can it be true? Is this really I, who can breathe and walk without pain, so freed? O God, wonderful are Thy ways!' And there in that garden, hallowed by the footsteps of Bahá'u'lláh and 'Abdu'l-Bahá, we lingered until it was time to leave for the train that was to carry us back to Haifa.

Everyone on the train seemed to stare at me. Was it because I was a stranger, or was it that they read the overwhelming joy of my spirit? I felt so elated, so buoyant, so intensely happy, I could only with difficulty control myself in silence. I longed to shout: 'Glory to God! O people, if you could know the wonderful thing that has happened to me since yesterday you too would shout.' My left arm was now entirely free and, again and again, I raised it above my head in sheer joy and wonder.

That night I lived over again the remarkable occurrences of the last twenty-four hours. The experience at the Holy Shrine of Bahá'u'lláh whither 'Abdu'l-Bahá had sent me and the various phases connected with the 'visit'.

> I did not sleep nor even try to. I realized a change *in my consciousness,* a marked change of attitude in my mind and heart toward former matters. I shouted in the stillness of my being at the glorious realization; I knew that the physical healing was the outer symbol of the emancipation of my soul. I was free not only in body, but what was far more important, I was free in soul, in mind and spirit. O Compassionate God! What a revelation came to my soul! I realized the darkened state of human consciousness, – of even such as believe themselves of the enlightened and faithful servants of God! I thought with pity of the former 'foolishness', – wanting something definite to take home to the friends. *Wanting something which the Master had ignored.* 'The wisdom of man is foolishness unto God' was truly proved. Fervently came the prayer: 'O Lord! Heed us not in our foolish requests. Sever us from our limitations. Bestow upon us the Light of Thy Wisdom so that we may become conscious of Thy Will!'[15]

Marie awoke the next morning in Haifa a different person. At breakfast, she told everyone of the amazing events of the previous day, then asked 'Azízu'lláh Bahádur to explain it all to the Master when He came. When 'Abdu'l-Bahá arrived for lunch, He gave Mírzá Bahádur no chance to explain and said to Marie, 'Brava! Brava! Ah, now you are another Mrs. Watson! Now you are *perfectly happy.* Now you have something definite to take home with you to the friends.'[16] And over the rest of her stay, 'Abdu'l-Bahá in His talks made it clear what she needed to do about the disunity in her community.

Mírzá Siyyid Mustapha, a Bahá'í from India who had witnessed Marie's miraculous cure, had formed a Bahá'í colony with 150 people and he begged her to come and teach there. Marie eagerly said yes, but 'Abdu'l-Bahá said no: 'I have already told Sayyid Mustapha that if I should send you to India now, you would ascend in a short time to the Kingdom of Abhá. No, your body is not strong enough . . . I wish you to go back to America and give the Glad Tidings. Take to them the "definite" things I have given you. You are a living sign of the Love of God.'[17]

'Abdu'l-Bahá went to visit Marie shortly before her departure. He gave her a silver salver covered with white jasmine and said, 'I come to bring you my farewell gift, these fragrant blossoms. May your deeds fill the world with like fragrance!' He then asked her to visit as many of the friends in Alexandria, Port Said and Cairo as possible. She left Haifa early on 28 August.[18]

Inez Cook and Jean Stannard

On 17 September, Curtis Kelsey, Inez Cook and Margaret Marshall, who was usually called Daisy, were staying in the Pilgrim House. Soon afterwards, Jean Stannard joined them. Curtis was there at the request of 'Abdu'l-Bahá to install electric lighting in the Shrine of the Báb.

This was the second pilgrimage for Inez, but she was still enthralled by 'Abdu'l-Bahá. She wrote that

> Those days at Haifa are in memory woven into a pattern of pure bliss – it was of no importance whether it was Monday or Tuesday, March or May. We lived entirely by the sun of the Master's Presence; those moments before we were summoned to His house, to be given a private talk, were full of excitement and those when we caught a glimpse of His turban above the garden wall, as He passed on the road for His daily walk, were full of a glowing and quiet emotion.
>
> When we told the Master how grateful we were for this great privilege of being permitted to visit Haifa, He answered: 'Yes, but your conduct when you leave here will prove your gratitude to God for this bounty.'
>
> One evening at supper I asked the Master why it was that so many pilgrims to Haifa shared the same experience of all they were receiving; that it was only later upon reaching home that the full light seemed to burst over them. The Master answered by pointing to a hanging lamp overhead, which cast a large circle of shadow on the table, and said: 'Directly under the lamp there is always a shadow. It is only when one comes out from under this shadow that one receives the full benefit of the direct rays.'[19]

Like most Westerners, they were full of questions. At one point many scientific questions were being asked and finally 'Abdu'l-Bahá suggested that it might be better if they kept the conversations on more spiritual lines. Inez wrote one day that she met the Master and He spoke to her in English. She found that 'the tones of His voice were so beautiful in this language that my heart dilated with pure joy'. 'Abdu'l-Bahá noticed and promised to speak to her only in English. Later, she encountered 'Abdu'l-Bahá in His garden at sunset. He greeted her, then, pointing to the darkening sky, said, 'Good stars, good heavens, goodnight,' and walked on.[20]

'Abdu'l-Bahá seemed to think that the pilgrims were lonely because there were so few compared to the 19 or 20 when Inez had been there the year before, so He spent a great deal of time with them. For several days in a row 'Abdu'l-Bahá went up to Jean Stannard and told her that He would squeeze her hand to see how well she could resist. She was

> soon jumping around frantically, squealing and laughing at the same time. As she was a tall and dignified person, these unusual girations created a comical sight and we were all convulsed with laughter, in which the Master joined heartily. When Mrs S. could endure no more, the Master released her hand and said that now she must try to do the same to Him. She made a tremendous effort, using both hands in order to produce the same result, but to no avail. 'Abdu'l-Bahá stood smilingly motionless and Mrs S. finally had to admit herself defeated.
>
> Then 'Abdu'l-Bahá turned to me [Inez] and said I must meditate on this when I returned home.
>
> The next day this was repeated – and the next. Each time, He said I must meditate on this.[21]

For 21 years Inez meditated before a solution appeared: 'Abdu'l-Bahá's hand was relaxed and flexible and yielded to the pressure while Jean Stannard's hand was stiff and rigid and was therefore crushed. She decided that the Master had been showing them 'the spiritual value of non-resistance to the painful experiences of our lives – or the real meaning of "radiant acquiescence"'.

Bahá'í love and unity was sometimes strained even there in Haifa. Inez tells of one time when a woman lost a piece of jewellery somewhere in front of the Shrine of the Báb. A large group heard of this and one person said that it was 'symbolic, the meaning was clear that all such silly vanities must be lost at Haifa'. The rest of the group didn't accept his thesis, whereupon he extended it to dress, saying that pilgrims should 'adopt a simple uniform of some cheap material'. The group liked this idea even less and soon a 'verbal battle was in full force'. Of course, that was when 'Abdu'l-Bahá arrived in their midst. The argument was instantly quenched when 'Abdu'l-Bahá pointed to a certain lady and said, 'I find Mrs..... suitably dressed for her position in life.' She was wearing a dress of the best quality and workmanship. Then he noted that Mrs....., who was wearing a simple gingham dress, was also appropriately dressed. 'Abdu'l-Bahá later told Inez, 'When there are so many in one house there is apt to be friction, but you must be the peacemaker. When the conversation turns to war you must lead it back to peace – or leave.'[22]

Curtis Kelsey

Curtis Kelsey had come to Haifa to install electricity in the Shrines of the Báb and Bahá'u'lláh and in the House of the Master. It had all started in New York when Roy Wilhelm asked him if he would like to go to Haifa to do some work for the Master. At first, Curtis thought it was a joke because he had little money to pay for his passage, but when he realized that Roy was serious, he wrote to 'Abdu'l-Bahá. A few weeks later, the reply came: 'Curtis Kelsey permitted.'[23] Going meant selling everything he could, including his new, and highly prized, Model T Ford:

> I stopped at a grocery store where I knew several fellows. It was during the rush hour and I called out to the boys and said, how would you like to buy my Ford. It took them by surprise and they did not answer right away, so I started to walk out. One of the boys came running over and said, wait a minute, Curt, if that buggy of yours can climb a certain hill here in town, I'll give you $150 for it. I said, hop in and over the hill we went in high gear . . . Now I had my first money . . .[24]

Even so, he still ended up being forced to accept $500 from Roy. His last obstacle was his father. Curtis's mother, Valeria, was a Bahá'í and supportive, but his father, Frank, was not and his attitude was summed up when he said: 'Son, you must be taking leave of your senses. Here you are, just getting started in your work and now you plan to make this long trip and do that work for that little old man in Haifa; and they are not going to pay you for it.' In the end, however, he relented and even gave Curtis a sum of money to help with his expenses.[25]

Curtis wanted to reach Haifa in 20 days, but he was told it would be impossible in less than 30. When he arrived in Paris, the shipping company said that there would be no sailings from Naples for two to three weeks. Curtis went to Naples anyway, where they reiterated the delay. Curtis told the agent that he would be back the next morning to check, just in case. That evening, the agent called him at his hotel and asked, 'How did you know that the Esperia was putting into port here?' Curtis said he hadn't known. A passenger had become sick, so the ship landed at Naples and Curtis was given the berth.[26]

On the way to Alexandria, Curtis met Charles Dana, a Presbyterian missionary director in Beirut. Mr Dana knew several Bahá'ís in the Protestant College in Beirut and was impressed with their character. One thing baffled him about the Bahá'ís, and he put his question to Curtis: 'What puzzles me, is how the Bahá'í students are able to persuade Muslims to accept the teachings of Jesus when the missionaries have virtually failed to make any inroads among the followers of Muhammad.' Curtis replied that Bahá'ís accepted the Teachings of Muhammad as sacred and also that the Muslims already accepted Jesus. Mr Dana was amazed that a poorly educated Bahá'í understood things that he, who had lived among Muslims for so many years, didn't. Charles had originally been destined for Beirut, but when the train arrived in Haifa, he disembarked and went up to the Shrine of the Báb.[27]

Curtis wasn't an educated electrician; in fact, he had never finished grade school and he wondered why he was being asked to do the job. Others had offered and been told that the time was not yet right. For Curtis the time was right. When he arrived at the station in Haifa, Fujita and Lotfu'lláh Hakím were waiting for him, recognizing him because he was the only American and because the first thing he did after stepping off the train was to gaze at the Shrine of the Báb. The three men quickly became very good friends and shared a room at the Pilgrim House.[28]

During his first two weeks in Haifa, Curtis was given no work, so he went about fixing anything that needed fixing, including the two cars in the garage, neither of which had been running. He was able to take 'Abdu'l-Bahá out on several drives. There was only one other automobile in Haifa at that time, owned by a young Arab man. One day, Curtis drove 'Abdu'l-Bahá to the Shrine of the Báb. When the Master began to walk back down, the Arab suddenly came careening around a corner at high speed, missing the Master by inches. 'Abdu'l-Bahá never even flinched and kept walking.[29]

Finally one day, Curtis was talking with Rúḥí Afnán, at least 100 feet from the House of the Master, and asked when 'Abdu'l-Bahá might want him to start wiring the Shrines. Before Rúḥí Afnán could respond, 'Abdu'l-Bahá stepped out of His house and said, 'We will start tomorrow.' There was no way 'Abdu'l-Bahá could have heard Curtis's question at that distance. The next morning, before Curtis, Fujita or Lotfu'lláh were out of bed, they were surprised to find 'Abdu'l-Bahá standing in their doorway. The Master said that he was unable to go to Bahjí that day: 'What shall I do about it?' Curtis responded immediately that when the Master was ready, he too would be ready. Several hours later word reached Curtis that the Master was able to go to Bahjí after all that afternoon.[30] Curtis, Rúḥí Afnán and Khusraw went with 'Abdu'l-Bahá to the train station and

> the Master sat down on a bench inside the station house. Outside, the conductor paced the platform. If the train arrived after sunset, the passengers would be unable to enter 'Akká, for the city closed its gates at nightfall. The conductor knew he couldn't leave without Sir 'Abdu'l-Bahá 'Abbás . . . It seemed strange to Curtis but he never questioned the wisdom of the situation. In about five minutes an Arab, leading a camel, approached, tied the animal to a post and entered the station house and headed for 'Abdu'l-Bahá. After a brief conversation, the Arab went his way and the Master boarded the train . . .[31]

Another mysterious delay occurred when they arrived at the station in 'Akká where 'Abdu'l-Bahá went into the station and sat down. A short while later, His servant Khalíd arrived from Bahjí with the Master's white donkey, but still the Master remained seated. Then a man came racing up to the station on a horse and rushed in to speak with the Master. After speaking with the man, 'Abdu'l-Bahá came out and climbed aboard His donkey for the trip to Bahjí.[32]

During dinner that night, a very tall Arab arrived and the Master invited him in and seated him on His right. 'They engaged in an animated discussion, all in Arabic. At that point, the Master pushed His turban back on His head, and He and the man started laughing.' The Master had asked the Arab if he belonged to the tribe where the husband was not allowed by his wife to enter the tent unless he stole something for her. The man admitted that he was. The Master then asked if he had ever been denied entrance to his tent. The man said never. Someone had been stealing 'Abdu'l-Bahá's sweet oranges and He now knew who. So He asked if the Arab had ever tried eating sour oranges. 'When the Arab grimaced, 'Abdu'l-Bahá assured him that they tasted delicious with sugar. The next day 'Abdu'l-Bahá discovered that many of the sour oranges had been stripped from the trees.'[33]

The next morning, 'Abdu'l-Bahá showed Curtis where the electrical generator should be installed and Curtis began to survey the work. Curtis had thought that 'Abdu'l-Bahá might have a relaxed day at Bahjí but that wasn't the case: people kept appearing, including the Governor of 'Akká. The following day, 'Abdu'l-Bahá took Curtis and Rúḥí Afnán into the Shrine of Bahá'u'lláh, where He chanted the Tablet of Visitation.

> Though he couldn't understand a word, Curtis was moved by the emotion of 'Abdu'l-Bahá chanting the Tablet of Visitation. There was no semblance of self from the figure before Curtis – just a total expression of devotion, a surrendering of will, an outpouring of love so intense that it seemed the Master was offering his heart to Bahá'u'lláh.[34]

As they left for 'Akká, 'Abdu'l-Bahá asked Curtis what he would do. With a strange surge of confidence, Curtis said that he would 'place underground lighting in the inner garden of the Shrine so that light would shine up through the flowers; that he would electrify the oil lamps . . . And finally, he would place lights around the cornice of the Shrine.' The Master approved.[35]

Back in Haifa, Curtis was introduced by 'Abdu'l-Bahá to a Persian electrician from India, Ḥusayn-i-Kahrubá'í, a young man who had offered his services when he arrived in Haifa a year before. Now the two men were to work together, though neither knew the other's language. Curtis could say 'yes' in Persian and Ḥusayn could say simple words such as 'okay' in English, so the two set out to build a successful partnership. The first thing they did was to lay out all their tools then go through them one by one with each man saying the name in their respective languages until they knew both names. Then they set to work. 'Abdu'l-Bahá told them to work for two weeks in Bahjí then two weeks in Haifa until the jobs were done.[36]

Working in Bahjí had one big drawback and that was that 'Abdu'l-Bahá wasn't there, so Curtis kept finding reasons for short trips back to Haifa. One day he asked the Master if he might use the Ford car for his trips and the request was confirmed. Bathing after work at Bahjí was a bit rough. Curtis and Lotfu'lláh would go to the aqueduct, strip down and, while one stood on a boulder, the other would pour buckets of cold water down over him.[37]

After two weeks, Curtis was back in Haifa. While working on the Shrine of the Báb, he came down each day to eat lunch with 'Abdu'l-Bahá and Fujita at the Pilgrim House. Curtis had to hurry down, then change out of his work clothes before going to eat. One day, he was late and 'Abdu'l-Bahá asked Fujita why. When told that Curtis was putting on clean clothes, the Master said that he should come without changing.[38]

At one point, 'Abdu'l-Bahá called Curtis to His room. Not knowing why he had been called, Curtis came in with some trepidation. 'Abdu'l-Bahá spoke not a word, simply looked intensely at His visitor. At first, Curtis worried that he had done something wrong, but he couldn't think of anything. The Master quietly continued to stare at him and Curtis couldn't meet that gaze. Finally, feeling that it was 'Abdu'l-Bahá's command that he look at Him, Curtis obeyed. He felt

> stripped of every selfish thought, his reality was utterly exposed to eyes reflecting power beyond human dimension. He couldn't turn away from the Master. There was nothing in that room but 'Abdu'l-Bahá. The Master swept up the lanky, Utah-born young man into a different world, a world of love, of joy. For the first time in his life he had been embraced by ecstasy. He would have stayed in that room forever, because time ceased to have meaning; nothing else mattered but being the recipient of the love flowing from 'Abdu'l-Bahá. Finally, the Master smiled – and said that Curtis could leave.[39]

Fujita had a brown cat which he and Curtis would hide in the kitchen before 'Abdu'l-Bahá arrived. The Master would always say, 'Let the cat out.' When Fujita did so, the cat would race to 'Abdu'l-Bahá to be stroked and fed. Curtis was amazed at how much the Master appeared to enjoy the little game Himself.[40] Shortly before Curtis left (some months after the Master's passing), one of 'Abdu'l-Bahá's daughters told him that she had asked the Master why He always went to the Pilgrim House to eat lunch with Curtis and Fujita instead of resting at home. 'Abdu'l-Bahá responded by saying that 'I like to eat with my friends.'[41]

The future of Haifa and 'Akká

One day while standing on the top of Mount Carmel looking out over the great panorama, 'Abdu'l-Bahá described what would be there in the future:

> In the future the distance between Haifa and Acca will be built up and the two cities will join and clasp hands, becoming the two terminal sections of one mighty metropolis. As I look now over this scene I see so clearly that it will become one of the first emporiums of the world: this great semi-circular bay will be transformed into the finest harbour wherein ships from all nations will seek shelter and refuge; the great vessels of all the people will come to this port, bringing on their decks thousands and thousands of men and women from every part of the globe; the mountains and the plains will be dotted with the most modern buildings and palaces; industries will be established and various institutions of a philanthropic nature will be founded; the flowers of civilization and culture from all nations will be brought here to blend their fragrances together and blaze the way for the brotherhood of man; wonderful gardens, orchards, groves and parks will be laid out on all sides; at night the great city will be lighted by electricity; the entire harbour from Acca to Haifa will be one path of illumination; powerful searchlights will be placed on both sides of Mount Carmel to guide the steamers, and Mount Carmel itself from top to bottom will be submerged in a sea of lights.[42]

1921: THE PASSING OF THE MASTER

Premonitions

Shoghi Effendi remembered that in about 1919,

> the Beloved Master turning to a distinguished visitor of His, who was seated by Him in His garden, suddenly broke the silence and said: 'My work is now done upon this plane; it is time for me to pass on to the other world.'
>
> Did He not in more than one occasion state clearly and emphatically: 'Were ye to know what will come to pass after me, surely would ye pray that my end be hastened?'
>
> In a Tablet sent to Persia when the storm raised years ago by that Committee of Investigation was fiercely raging around him, when the days of his incarceration were at their blackest, he revealed the following:
>
> 'Now in this world of being, the hand of Divine Power hath firmly laid the foundations of this all-highest bounty and this wondrous gift. Gradually whatsoever is latent in the innermost of this Holy Cycle shall appear and be made manifest, for now is but the beginning of its growth and the dayspring of the revelation of its signs. Ere the close of this century and of this age, it shall be made clear and manifest how wondrous was that Springtide and how heavenly was that gift!'[1]

'Abdu'l-Bahá had had two dreams that suggested to Him that His earthly life was nearing its end. In the first, He gave the call to prayer:

> I seemed to be standing within a great mosque, in the inmost shrine, facing the Qiblih, in the place of the Imám himself. I became aware that a large number of people were flocking into the mosque. More and yet more crowded in, taking their places in rows behind Me, until there was a vast multitude. As I stood I raised loudly the call to prayer. Suddenly the thought came to me to go forth from the

> mosque. When I found myself outside I said within Myself, 'For what reason came I forth, not having led the prayer? But it matters not; now that I have uttered the Call to prayer, the vast multitude will of themselves chant the prayer.'[2]

'Abdu'l-Bahá had indeed raised the call to prayer to huge numbers of people in both the East and the West. Now it seemed that they would be given the task of saying the prayer.

The second dream was more obvious: 'I dreamed a dream and behold, the Blessed Beauty (Bahá'u'lláh) came and said unto me, 'Destroy this room!'[3]

Fáḍil-i-Mázindarání was in Haifa when 'Abdu'l Bahá talked about taking a long journey:

> One day, in the Pilgrim House, it was said that the physical appearance of 'Abdu'l-Bahá showed signs of weariness. Some of us thought that this was due to the small amount of food which 'Abdu'l-Bahá ate. He always divided the food among the guests, a symbol of the way in which he distributed spiritual sustenance. He took almost nothing, himself, but a glass of milk or the yolk of an egg.
>
> A group of friends were selected and their spokesman, a very old and spiritual Bahá'í, went to 'Abdu'l-Bahá. Overcome with emotion at the question which he was about to present, he could not speak a word. 'Abdu'l-Bahá took him by the hand, and encouraged him. The old man said: 'The believers feel that there are two reasons for 'Abdu'l-Bahá's weariness. First, he does not eat enough. Secondly, he works too hard.' Then 'Abdu'l-Bahá, very humbly, told him that he was mistaken. 'Do you think,' he said, 'that this material food has any effect upon my body? This food has no effect. Only good news from the believers, the glad tidings which comes from all parts of the world of the advancement of the Cause, of the unity of the believers, this, only, improves my health. As to the second point – I am going to take a long journey and at that time my spirit will rest.'
>
> Later, we understood what the Master had meant. These talks showed that 'Abdu'l-Bahá had finished his work, was preparing for the great journey to the Kingdom.[4]

'Abdu'l-Bahá obviously knew the end was nearing, and one thing that worried Him was the reaction of the Covenant-breakers. On 8 November, He had cabled Roy Wilhelm, asking 'How is the situation and health friends?' Roy's frank reply was, 'Chicago, Washington, Philadelphia agitating violation centering Fernald, Dyer, Watson. New York, Boston refused join, standing solidly constructive policy.'[5] On 14 November, 'Abdu'l-Bahá sent a telegram to Corinne True warning about Covenant-breakers. The telegram read, 'He who sits with lepers catches leprosy. He who is with Christ shuns Pharisees and abhors Judas Iscariots. Certainly shun violators.'[6]

The final pilgrims

Looking back, it appears that 'Abdu'l-Bahá chose those He wished to be there at the end of His earthly life. Some people who had asked for permission to visit Him were gently told no. But 'Abdu'l-Bahá Himself wrote to John Bosch saying, 'I am longing to see you.' When John and Louise wrote back asking if they could have a pilgrimage, 'Abdu'l-Bahá cabled back, 'Permitted.' The Bosches arrived on 13 November.[7] Louise, who had met the Master when He was in America, was strongly affected by seeing Him again:

> One must know that to meet with that great One was a matter quite different from meeting anyone else, kings and princes included. It is almost impossible to describe just what one experienced in being with Him. It is certain that the soul was stirred to its very depths. In His presence the soul realized that it stood in the presence of its real master. His personality was a mirror of holiness and sanctity . . .
>
> As thus we stood in His holy presence we felt aware of our unworthiness; we became conscious of our faults and shortcomings; we saw ourselves in our imperfections. We could only take refuge in the ocean of His understanding and in the sea of His love . . .[8]

Another pilgrim present was Johanna Hauff, from Stuttgart, Germany. She later wrote to her parents that Louise had told her, 'His work is done, completely done, everything has been said. Every further day is a gift of grace.' Johanna wrote, 'We did not dare to ask questions, nor dare to deliver the letters, because we heard four hundred letters were still lying there unanswered, but in his great love and kindness for

Germany he wanted to have them nevertheless and his very last Tablet is going to Germany.'[9]

On 19 November, Dr Florian and Grace Krug arrived in Haifa. After greeting the Krugs, 'Abdu'l-Bahá led them through the gate of His own garden, then up the stairs to a room over the garage, His own room, saying, 'Now I am going to give you and Dr. Krug My room.' Grace had a sudden feeling of apprehension and burst into tears. The next morning, she looked out and watched the Master sitting under the grape arbour in His garden 'so serene, with a sweetness of spirit that I had never noticed before. There was an air of finality and completeness around Him.' 'Generals in gaudy uniforms', Arabs and poor people asking for alms came to see Him.[10]

Not all pilgrims who were in Haifa in late November were of 'Abdu'l-Bahá's choice. Curtis Kelsey relates the following story. 'Abdu'l-Bahá told a group of pilgrims:

> Tomorrow an American lady is coming here and I don't want anything said to her about the Bahá'í teachings. So, sure enough, the boat docked the next day and this American lady came up to the pilgrim house. 'Abdu'l-Bahá sat her at the right-hand side of the table and she began to tell the Master who He was. He was Elijah, he was this and he was the everything else. She had him all wrapped up and everything. And He just nodded at every statement she made. He never talked; He just nodded at her statements. She had a nice dinner. After the dinner was over, she asked if she could have a private interview with 'Abdu'l-Bahá and He said yes she could. She walked over to the house with Him and we didn't see her again.
>
> Two days later, Mrs White (who was the one who challenged the Will of the Master) arrived at Haifa. One day she came up to the pilgrim house and she was all excited and she went to 'Abdu'l-Bahá and said that she had met an American lady down at the hotel and 'she was so interested that I had to tell her about the Bahá'í Faith.' 'Abdu'l-Bahá said, 'Did she ask you for money?' Mrs White said, 'Yes, how did you know?' 'I saw this lady two days ago and she asked me for money, too.' Then 'Abdu'l-Bahá said, 'How much did you give her?' 'She told me a hundred bucks and said she was stranded and she needed a hundred dollars to get back to America so I let her have a hundred dollars.' 'Abdu'l-Bahá said, 'Had you obeyed my

instructions, you would still have your hundred dollars.' He had given her money, too.

Shortly afterward, her pilgrimage was over and He sent her away. Two days after she left, when she reached Cairo, that was when the Master passed. She came rushing back, disappointed that the Master hadn't let her stay to witness His passing.[11]

Shortly before the Master's passing, Mírzá 'Abdu'l-Ḥasan Afnán walked down to the sea, folded his clothes, then walked into the water and drowned himself. This elderly man had settled all his affairs before taking this final action. He had spent a great deal of time with 'Abdu'l-Bahá and such had been his suffering in life that when the funeral procession passed in front of the Master's house, 'Abdu'l-Bahá came out and put a corner of the casket on His own shoulder. That night He talked about suicide, saying,

> You must not injure yourselves or commit suicide . . . Should anyone at any time encounter hard and perplexing times, he must say to himself, 'This will soon pass.' Then he will be calm and quiet. In all my calamity and difficulties I used to say to myself, 'This will pass away.' Then I became patient. If anyone cannot be patient and cannot endure, and if he wishes to become a martyr, then let him arise in service to the Cause of God. It will be better for him if he obtains to martyrdom in this path.'[12]

When the Master passed away a few days later, the Bahá'ís realized that Mírzá 'Abdu'l-Ḥasan had known what was coming and did not want to witness it.[13]

The passing of the Master

Around this time, 'Abdu'l-Bahá was in His garden with His faithful servant, Ismá'il-Áqá. The Master said:

> 'I am sick with fatigue. Bring two of your oranges for me that I may eat them for your sake.' This I did, and he having eaten them turned to me, saying 'Have you any of your sweet lemons?' He bade me fetch a few . . . Whilst I was plucking them, he came over to the tree,

saying, 'Nay, but I must gather them with my own hands.'

Having eaten of the fruit he turned to me and I asked 'Do you desire anything more?' Then with a pathetic gesture of his hands, he touchingly, emphatically and deliberately said:

'Now it is finished, it is finished!'

These significant words penetrated my very soul. I felt each time he uttered them as if a knife were struck into my heart. I understood his meaning but never dreamed his end was so nigh.[14]

On 25 November 'Abdu'l-Bahá suddenly insisted that the wedding of Khusraw, one of His most trusted servants, must be held that day, even saying to His daughters that if they couldn't do the preparations, He would. The wedding was held that night. Khusraw had long served the Master. While 'Abdu'l-Bahá still lived in 'Akká many years before, a Bahá'í from India on his way to the Holy Land passed through a slave market and saw a 'forlorn child, aged six years, standing on the block to be sold'. He was so moved by the sight that he bought the boy and took him with him. 'Abdu'l-Bahá had the boy educated and brought him up in His own family. This was Khusraw, who was a most dedicated servant, and his wife-to-be was the daughter of a martyr.[15]

John Bosch described that day in his diary:

> The last time Abdul Baha spoke to me was in the morning of Nov 25th 1921, when I entered the Garden near His House, when he gave instructions to the Gardener and then He walked up and down the lane on the north side of the House taking exercise like most any morning then picking a few oranges and Mandarin oranges with his own hands, giving them to the visitors there – several Persians, Hindus and Arabs were standing there and when he came to me he gave me one Mandarin and said in English – eat – good and smiled at me. I wondered then if I was worthy of that smile of our Master, not knowing then that I would be called to help laying his material Body in the casket in the morning of the Fourth day from this occurrence. He then walked into his House and at the same day at noon He came to lunch in the Pilgrim House, where He spoke to several of the guests and when serving rice when we only took a small portion He always said, 'again, again', meaning that we should again take rice and eat plenty.

How wonderful it was to be a guest of the Host of the World during His last days on earth.

Never shall I forget the farewell of the Master when He rose from the table and turned to us, directing His hands in upward position to us, His face illumined saying in a smiling way to all of us three times Good afternoon, Good afternoon, Good afternoon. How happy we were to see Him happy & how little we knew then that these were His last words to us.[16]

Louise Bosch noted:

While some conversation went on, yet that lunch was passed in comparative silence. Our Lord would lean back in his chair every time after he had had a few mouthfuls of food, and would gaze upwards. When He had finished His meal and had washed His hands, as is the Oriental custom, He stood near the door and said good-bye three times, 'Good-afternoon; good-afternoon; good-bye'. And then He turned and walked out with his grandson down the stairway and out of the compound; and little did we dream that we would see Him no more. The pilgrims looked at one another, and none of us could understand why He had done this – said good-bye three times; only we were satisfied that whatever He did was right and had a perfect wisdom behind it.[17]

On 26 November, 'Abdu'l-Bahá was feverish and cold. 'Cover me up. I am very cold. Last night I did not sleep well, I felt cold. This is serious, it is the beginning,' He said to those around Him. Dr Krug asked Him to rest more. He begged Him not to make the effort to walk over to the Western Pilgrim House for meals and 'Abdu'l-Bahá agreed.[18]

But by the next morning, He was much better. John Bosch wrote:

We expected to see Abdul Baha on Sunday afternoon as on most of the Sundays, he went to the Tomb of the Báb, when from 75 to 100 Believers, of all nations, assembled. This time a Hindu, a new arrival, gave a feast, at which all kinds of fruits, crackers, sweets and tea were served . . . Prayers were chanted and afterwards the men visited the south-west room of the building and a few of the Western ladies joined the Eastern ladies in the south east room. In both rooms prayers were chanted, the middle room being the tomb of the Báb.

This very same Room, in which this feast was held, the middle north room of the Tomb of the Báb, is where the remains of Abdul Baha are resting. The north west room being used for worshipping for the men & the north east room for the ladies.

During the time of this feast Abdul Baha had callers, one of them being the Chief of the Arab Police of Haifa, who called about 6 o'clock and it is said had a long interview with Abdul Baha. The very same Chief ordered about a dozen of Police in less than 14 hours after this interview to guard the home of the Holy family for protection on account of the passing away of Abdul Baha early in the morning.[19]

That night, 'Abdu'l-Bahá went to bed at 8 p.m. He awoke at 1:15 a.m., got up and drank some water, saying, 'I am too warm.' A short while later He said, 'I have difficulty in breathing, give me more air.' After sitting up and drinking some rose water He lay down again and, when He was offered something to eat, 'he remarked in a clear and distinct voice, "You wish me to take some food, and I am going?" He gave them a beautiful look. His face was so calm, his expression so serene, they thought him asleep.'[20]

Dr Krug had had a premonition that he would be called to the Master's bedside so he was ready when the call came: 'Come Dr. Krug, the Master, the Master!' The doctor was dressed in a flash and dashed to 'Abdu'l-Bahá's bedroom, a short run from the Master's room over the garage. Grace was initially petrified with fear, but then quickly dressed and followed her husband. As she entered, Dr Krug stood in the middle of the room with his hand raised, saying 'Silence, our Beloved Master has ascended.' Grace ran to His bedside and

He lay there in the majesty of death. His lovely eyes were still open, but the light of love and understanding that had for so many years cheered the souls of men was gone! My first thought was, my Adored One is freed from our endless questions, freed from His life of servitude and headaches. I turned and knelt at the feet of His sister, the Greatest Holy Leaf, put my head in her lap and in that agonized moment, she stroked my head and tried to comfort me . . . not one thought of herself![21]

Dr Krug closed the Master's eyes.[22]

Fujita told the story from his viewpoint:

> You know, before 'Abdu'l-Bahá passing away, it was on a Friday, we went visit the mosque in Haifa, Friday morning. That day return from mosque, He had to walk up the step. He says, 'I am tired,' went into the room. Then Friday, Saturday, Sunday! Three days. Sunday night, He passed away. Those days we had many American pilgrims there . . . Mrs. Hoagg, Boschs were there. I heard the cry, deafening noise. So immediately I went up this gate, there's many collected and mourning, the Eastern believers very demonstrative, you know. I said 'What is it?' 'It's 'Abdu'l-Bahá has passed.' So immediately I come back to Pilgrim House, informed them. And some of them come out, come now. That day. It's one o'clock, and all the family are all together there. Can't help. Doctor just left, Dr. Habib, that Christian Arab, that's their family doctor.[23]

John Bosch recounted that night, as well:

> On this Sunday night, after midnight we were awakened by a few hard knocks in rapid succession on the Pilgrim House door and we wondered what had happened. My watch pointed to 1.20 o'clock.
>
> My wife said something must have happened to Abdul Baha, let us hurry and find what the unusual call was. In a few minutes we were running to the House of Abdul Baha and found that it was only too true, that our Master just had passed away.
>
> The doctors were leaving the house and we entered the room finding all of the Holy family there with Abdul Baha resting in bed as if he still were alive. I took his hand, it was still warm and touched his forehead and hoped that He still may offer a word, but his spirit had departed. The Greatest Holy Leaf kindly reached her hand to me and motioned to sit beside her, which I did.
>
> The room became filled with friends and people from the town, the outside rooms were full of people. It is really indescribable, the sorrow and weeping of the people at that hour. It seems that thousands of thoughts went through my mind at that moment. Sometimes there come to all of us feelings in our heart that sigh for expression when only our silence really registers the depth of our

emotions and our moist eyes suggest what the word could never reveal.

So I cannot tell you about the deep stirrings within me. When all was deep silence again I arose and touched the hand and forehead of Abdul Baha, still warm but lifeless. I said, 'Oh, Abdul Baha,' and Rizwania said how she loved it that in this deep silence someone called the name of our Master. Again I was seated alongside of the Greatest Holy Leaf.

A change of relief came over me. And tonight at last our Master is relieved, relieved from all the persecutions and the answering the questions of all the friends, enquirers and curiosity seekers.

I felt that his body is now at rest, that his spirit is alive, that we are all equal now, regardless of position and in His teachings that each and every one of us can find Him & serve Him only in Spirit and in His teachings.

The greatest privilege and a great obligation. Why was it for my wife and myself to be here at His Ascension, the only ones from Western America.

A little before four oclock we returned to the Pilgrim House, felt like a lost sheep . . .

Sohrab and Dr Lotfullah sent messages all over the World of the passing of Abdul Baha. We sent a telegram to Mrs Cooper to our Western Region to inform all the friends. Replies of condolence from prominent [people] from all parts of the world were received very quickly.

Hundreds of people of all nationalities called during the day. In the evening Rouhi called us to permit us to have the last look at the Body, Johanna, Mrs Krug, Mrs Bosch and myself.[24]

Calmly sitting at the centre of these events was 'Abdu'l-Bahá's sister, Bahíyyih Khánum, the Greatest Holy Leaf:

The Most Exalted Leaf wept far less than the others, at all times maintaining her great dignity and composure. But many times she sighed, through the night, and many times uttered the words, *Yá Iláhí* – 'O God, my God!' Two years younger than her beloved Brother, Bahíyyih Khánum was the 'most precious great Adorning' of Bahá'u'lláh's house. '. . . all her days she was denied a moment of tranquillity,' 'Abdu'l-Bahá had written; 'Moth-like she circled in adoration round the undying flame . . .' Her life had spanned the Conference at Badasht, the martyrdom of the Báb, the birth of the Bahá'í Faith as her Father lay chained in the Black Pit of Ṭihrán, the peril, destitution and humiliation of years of captivity and exile, the death of Bahá'u'lláh in 1892, the Great War – when the enemy had determined to crucify 'Abdu'l-Bahá and all His family on the heights of Carmel. She had stood by her Brother when their Father left the world, and 'Abdu'l-Bahá, because He was named the Successor, was deserted by His people, 'Forsaken, betrayed, assaulted by almost the entire body of His relatives . . .' Now, for a brief period Khánum at seventy-five was the *de facto* head of the Bahá'í world; she was the custodian of 'Abdu'l-Bahá's Will and Testament, and her loving, sorrowing messages rallied the grief-obliterated Bahá'ís of East and West.[25]

Louise Bosch also described the scene immediately after the Master ascended:

One other thing I noticed, and this was that the head of my Lord was in a very uncomfortable looking position . . . I stood at the back of the bed, and while I gently moved his head I felt the bodily warmth of his head, and face, and neck. And then Rouah Khanoum said to someone, as I held his head, to remove an extra pillow that had been slipped under it during a vain effort of the doctors to retain his life. Someone slipped away the pillow, and this gave me the wonderful privilege of holding his head just one moment longer, and I felt then, near to him in soul and body.

When I looked up again, I saw that the room had filled with believers. They had all come in noiselessly. Most of them were kneeling at the foot of his bed. At that time I did not perceive anyone weeping; the consternation was so great, it was expressed upon all faces. But as I knelt there, I felt that we believers, myself included, only the Holy Family excepted, had by no known privilege found entrance to that room. I felt that we were standing on burning ground. I felt the fire of the burning bush; that we must retreat or be consumed. I felt that the sudden shock of the death of Abdul Baha had removed restrictions and barriers. But I felt that now we must go. And all the believers must have felt the same, because they knelt, one after another, in front of the bed – at the foot of the bed – and kissed the covering where our Lord's blessed feet rested, and then they quietly went away.

It was then that I could not go. When the majority of the believers had left, the Holy Mother shut the doors of that holy room and locked them, and then, from inside of the room she opened another door, leading into the room of the greatest Holy Leaf, and the Holy Ladies went in there, and before the Holy Mother went in, she motioned me to go in, too. I was glad to go in; I was glad for the privilege. I think the Doctor and Mrs. Krug went in (I have no recollection). Johanna [Hauff] followed me and my husband, and when we were all in the room of the Greatest Holy Leaf that door, too, was shut and locked.

And when we were seated inside, the full grief of the tragedy of the other room came to the surface. It is impossible to describe it – the grief! . . .

And now . . . we were in the room of the Greatest Holy Leaf, and the sorrow and the pain was simply indescribable. It would be impossible for me to tell what I witnessed in that room of grief, pain and sorrow. The Greatest Holy Leaf was the calmest; she did not break down as much as did the other holy ladies. But the Holy Mother was ineffable . . . Her bitter pain exalted her. Her superlative grief transfigured her, and it seemed as if the spirit of Abdul Baha came into her. I felt it every day after that. Afterwards it always seemed like being with Abdul Baha when being with her. Always she was a woman of unparalleled dignity and refinement and beauty; but now it was simply indescribable, the way she became. Her bitter pain exalted her above all words.

We sat in that room until we could no more. We sat – Johanna, my husband and I – until we felt we had no right to be any longer witnesses to their grief and to such pain. I felt as though the fire of the other room had come into this. The Greatest Holy Leaf was holding the hand of my husband and the Holy Mother was holding my hand. There was no one there to speak English, but we spoke the universal language of pain.[26]

Curtis Kelsey watched the Greatest Holy Leaf go about the room comforting the grief-stricken, moving from person to person. He felt compelled by an inner voice to observe and saw that she had, he sensed, the same kind of strength that 'Abdu'l-Bahá had. She then looked at Curtis and came over to him, asking him to take Fujita and Khusraw and drive to 'Akká to inform them of the Master's passing.

The trio left at 2:30 a.m. in the little Ford. Curtis had been very calm at the House of the Master, but in the car driving along the beach, he broke down and cried. The crying stopped when they had to cross the first stream. Khusraw waded around until he located the sandbar over which Curtis drove. Arriving in 'Akká, they had to awaken the residents and then give them the bad news. With their task completed, the three men headed back to Haifa. They passed the first river by following their tracks, but at the second, following their tracks got them into trouble. The tracks were still visible –

> But the sandbar wasn't where it was before; it had shifted and the car began to sink. All three scrambled out of the Ford, with Curtis yelling, 'Do what I do!'
>
> Curtis, with water up to his hips, was lifting one of the front wheels, trying to keep it from touching the mucky stream floor. Fujita and Khusraw were beside him, having difficulty with their footing. The water was up to Fujita's neck and Khusraw's shoulders; and when they tried to lift the wheel, their legs gave way and they ended up floating and clinging to the running board. That wasn't going to be much help, Curtis thought. He couldn't allow the car to settle into the mud, yet he couldn't continue to bear most of the weight of the vehicle.
>
> Remembering that before approaching the stream, about two miles away, he had noticed several husky Arab fishermen casting nets into the sea, Curtis asked Khusraw to fetch them. While Khusraw was gone, Curtis and Fujita moved from wheel to wheel . . . trying to keep them from becoming captives of the mud . . .
>
> In about thirty minutes Curtis noticed the fishermen coming, with Khusraw leading the way; all of them talking loudly in Arabic and gesturing freely. They ran into the water, joining the weary Curtis and Fujita. With great ease, they lifted the car from the water and onto the shore pointing toward Haifa. After drying the carburettor, the three young Bahá'ís resumed their trip back to Haifa.[27]

The rest of the night was chaotic. Crowds surged through the house until Dr Krug finally took the Americans – the Bosches, Curtis and Grace – and had Fujita fix them a cup of tea. At least 40 women with their babies slept on the floor of the Master’s house that night.[28]

Johanna Hauff wrote to her parents in Stuttgart:

> He is no longer among us! Oh, no, we must not say this; His spirit is perhaps a thousand times nearer to us; but it is incredible, unbelievable, because this great loss came so swift – so unexpected. We are all as stunned. I cannot say anything; I do not know what will happen!
>
> Rouha Khanum told me – weeping at his bed where he lay still, unspeakably beautiful and as if sleeping – that she had asked him only in the evening whether I might stay here for some time and that he had replied: ‘She may stay; she will be a beautiful teacher.’ But I don’t know what will happen now; the heart, the mind, the spirit of this town, this country, our whole world is no longer in a human body![29]

All of the work now fell upon the Greatest Holy Leaf. Her first task was to inform the world. To Roy Wilhelm, she wrote: ‘His Holiness Abdul-Baha ascended to Abha Kingdom.’[30] From Tehran came the message to the American Bahá’ís: ‘Light of Covenant transferred from eye to heart, day of teaching, unity, self sacrifice.’[31]

The funeral of the Master

The funeral began on 29 November at 9 a.m. John Bosch wrote in his diary:

> Early in the morning some people arrived and already at 7:30 a police force of about 40 men marched up the street and lined up in front of the house. The Chief of Police was one of the last callers on Sunday evening . . .
>
> By 8 o’clock the house, the yards, the garden were full of mourners . . . Mírzá Jalal, the son of the King of the Martyrs, called me to help him to carry the casket, of white wood and zinc lined, from the north room into the room where Abdul Baha was and four of us lifted the body of the Master into the casket. The body was wrapped

in four or five thicknesses of most beautiful white silk. First in casket was placed a silk comforter of the finest quality with a small pillow for his head to lay on.[32]

Louise added:

His body seemed natural, John said, not rigid. John helped the others to close the coffin down. He said he knew the living Master was there. 'I felt He was there. Not in the body – even now I feel that again – His presence. I am sure He was there.' When others started to raise the casket up, John didn't understand at first, but did as they did, and lifted it to his right shoulder. Then all at once he remembered that time in New York, long past, when 'Abdu'l-Bahá had leaned down on his left shoulder and gone to sleep.[33]

And John continued:

The best Attar of Roses was sprinkled over the white silk and the two ends of the comforter were laid over the body and then the cover was placed on the casket. At 5 minutes to 9 o'clock we picked up the casket and carried it on our shoulders to the center room of the house, where a short talk was given by a Mohammedan priest and at 9 silently the funeral procession started, taking about an hour and a half walking up the Mount Carmel road to the Tomb of the Báb.

Never has there been such a procession, comprising of men of all nations of all walks in life, rich and poor, representing all creeds.

About 40 carriages were waiting but only 5 were occupied, as everybody wanted to honor in walking after the remains of the Master . . . Arriving at the tomb several speeches were given in four languages. Real Bahai speeches.

The casket was brought within the tomb about 11:30.[34]

Fujita added his thoughts:

All the notables from Haifa and Jerusalem, all were collected here . . . for [the] funeral. Even Herbert Samuel, walked right up, passing Master. Just out from this room, Number seven, and go around, Rahmatu'llah turn corner, in front of center of church, then go up,

> up, up, up, up to the Shrine. Everybody carrying casket up to the resting-place.[35]

Every notable in Palestine, it seemed, was at the funeral. The mourners included:

> The High Commissioner of Palestine, Sir Herbert Samuel, the Governor of Jerusalem, the Governor of Phoenicia, the Chief Officials of the Government, the Consuls of the various countries, resident in Haifa, the heads of the various religious communities, the notables of Palestine, Jews, Christians, Moslems, Druses, Egyptians, Greeks, Turks, Kurds, and a host of his American, European and native friends, men, women and children, both of high and low degree, all, about ten thousand in number, mourning the loss of their Beloved One.
>
> This impressive, triumphal procession was headed by a guard of honour, consisting of the City Constabulary Force, followed by the Boy Scouts of the Moslem and Christian communities holding aloft their banners, a company of Moslem choristers chanting their verses from the Qur'án, the chiefs of the Moslem community headed by the Mufti, a number of Christian priests, Latin, Greek and Anglican, all preceding the sacred coffin, upraised on the shoulders of his loved ones. Immediately behind it came the members of his family, next to them walked the British High Commissioner, the Governor of Jerusalem, and the Governor of Phoenicia. After them came the Consuls and the notables of the land, followed by the vast multitude of those who reverenced and loved him.[36]

Again, Curtis Kelsey's inner voice told him it was a time to observe and record, so he put the Graflex camera his mother had given him when he left New York to use. He scrambled up and down the Mount Carmel hillside trying to get the best photos of the procession.[37]

When the procession arrived at the Shrine of the Báb, the casket was placed in front of the Tomb and all of those involved gathered around. Then nine speeches were made, none by a Bahá'í, but by Muslims, Christians, Jews and others. When the speeches were over, Sir Herbert Samuel, the British High Commissioner for Palestine, 'holding his hat in his left hand, knelt down and kissed, for the last time, the shawl that covered the casket, and all those who were present did the same.'[38]

The Greatest Holy Leaf, Bahíyyih Khánum, examined 'Abdu'l-Bahá's Will to see if there was any reference to where He should be interred. She found none, but 'Abbás-Qulí told her:

> On the day you came up to the shrine for the interment of the remains of the Báb, 'Abdu'l-Bahá indicated a place for Himself. After He interred the holy remains in their eternal place, He stepped from the vault into a passageway and ordered the opening to be closed and, pointing to the passageway, said, 'And this should be a place for Us.' The Greatest Holy Leaf said, 'Very well.' She blessed him for what he said and stated: 'This is where it will be.'[39]

Emogene Hoagg wrote:

> When they expected the remains of the body of the Bab a resting place was made in the center of what is now the middle front room; but for some reason the Master had another place prepared in the room where the remains now rest. When it was necessary to find a place for the blessed body of the Master they thought of the place already prepared in the front room, and as the Master loved so much that position on the mountain, his remains were placed in that room. You will remember the front room of the Tomb where the believers always gathered and where the Master would speak to them when he went to the Tomb? It is in this middle front room that the Beloved body rests. It is hardly yet possible to believe that we shall not see him walking in and saying 'Marhaba, Marhaba!'[40]

The caretaker of the Shrine of the Báb, Raḥmatu'lláh, was a strong man. The day before 'Abdu'l-Bahá passed away, He asked him a strange question: 'You are a strong man. Could you not carry me away to a place where I could rest? I'm tired of this world.' When the casket was taken into the Shrine, there was only room for one person to descend into the crypt. The casket was placed on Raḥmatu'llah's shoulders and he, alone, carried it down to its final resting place.[41]

The Master's coffin was placed, not under the centre of the room, but under the southeastern part of the room, so that it would not be between the sarcophagus of the Báb and Bahjí.

After the passing of the Master, food was distributed to between

50 and 100 of the poor at the Master's house, the same place where 'Abdu'l-Bahá had met the poor every Friday. Then on the seventh day, 4 December, corn was passed out to a thousand of the poor in His name.[42] Everyone who asked was given forty pounds of corn.[43]

1922: SHOGHI EFFENDI, THE GUARDIAN OF THE FAITH

When 'Abdu'l-Bahá's Will was brought out, it was found to be addressed to Shoghi Effendi, who at that time was studying at the University of Oxford in England. Because of passport problems, Shoghi Effendi was not able to return to Haifa until 29 December, when he arrived in the company of Lady Blomfield and his sister Rúhangíz. That Shoghi Effendi was not in Haifa at the time of 'Abdu'l-Bahá's ascension was not the fault of the Master. A few weeks before His passing, 'Abdu'l-Bahá had gone to Shoghi Effendi's father and told him, 'Cable Shoghi Effendi to return at once.' Unfortunately, Shoghi Effendi's parents decided to write a letter instead of sending the cable because they were afraid a cable would be too alarming. The letter did not arrive until after 'Abdu'l-Bahá's passing.[1] Second-guessing 'Abdu'l-Bahá was never a good idea.

Before leaving England, Shoghi Effendi wrote a letter that suggested he knew that a change was about to happen in his life, with 'Abdu'l-Bahá gone:

> The terrible news has for some days so overwhelmed my body, my mind and my soul that I was laid for a couple of days in bed almost senseless, absent-minded and greatly agitated. Gradually His power revived me and breathed in me a confidence that I hope will henceforth guide me and inspire me in my humble work of service. The day had to come, but how sudden and unexpected. The fact however that His Cause has created so many and such beautiful souls all over the world is a sure guarantee that it will live and prosper and ere long will compass the world! I am immediately starting for Haifa to receive the instructions He has left and have now made a supreme determination to dedicate my life to His service and by His aid to carry out His instructions all the days of my life.[2]

It was a heartbroken Shoghi Effendi who arrived in Haifa on 29 December 1921. 'Abdu'l-Bahá was not there to meet him. Louise Bosch, however, was and heard his arrival:

> Then I heard what must have been his footsteps coming up to the front door and coming in; when he gave – I don't know how to describe that cry – an outcry of greatest grief – pain – *ache*. It was *loud*. And then I remained in the room. Although I did not see Shoghi Effendi I knew for certain it was he . . .[3]

When Shoghi Effendi arrived in Haifa, the Greatest Holy Leaf didn't immediately tell him of the contents of his Grandfather's will, wishing him to have some time for himself. Louise Bosch wrote that when he came to lunch at the Pilgrim House just after having returned, he was 'full of plans of what needed to be done at that crisis in the Faith'. She said, 'He was all right.' Then, on the third day after his arrival, he learned the contents of 'Abdu'l-Bahá's Will. The blow sent him reeling to bed feeling 'frail' and 'unworthy'.[4] Louise wrote that she didn't see him again until two days later when he entered the room of the Greatest Holy Leaf 'like an old man, bent over' and hardly able to speak, 'wholly changed and aged and walking bent'.[5]

When the Will and Testament was read to him, it was the first time that he had heard of the Institution of the Guardianship and the first time he heard that he was to be that Guardian. In a letter, Shoghi Effendi wrote: 'Moments of gloom, of intense sadness, of agitation I often experience for wherever I go I remember my beloved grandfather and whatever I do I feel the terrible responsibility He has so suddenly placed upon my feeble shoulders.'[6] Later, Rúḥíyyih Khánum wrote of Shoghi Effendi's bewilderment when he 'found that the burden which had rested first on the Báb, then on Bahá'u'lláh, and then on his beloved Grandfather, 'Abdu'l-Bahá, had fallen with all its weight on his shoulders . . .'[7] He said, 'when they read the Master's Will to me, I ceased to be a normal human being.'[8] He had expected that 'as he was the eldest grandson, it might fall to his lot to be requested by the Master, posthumously naturally, to open any documents of instruction and communicate them to the Baha'is'.[9] The task he had been given was much greater.

The appointment of Shoghi Effendi as the Guardian wasn't a

complete surprise to everyone. The Tehran Spiritual Assembly had previously asked 'Abdu'l-Bahá in whose name the property held by the Bahá'í community and legal deeds should be registered. He had replied, 'They should be registered in the name of Mirza Shoghi Rabbani.'[10] On a number of occasions, 'Abdu'l Bahá openly spoke of His successor. Florence Khan recounted that one of His daughters remembered Him as saying:

> 'You wonder who will carry on my work when I am gone? Such a soul exists. He is capable. He is wonderful! Marvelous! He is indeed worthy! But he is not here now, he is at present in Europe.'
>
> 'In Europe!' they would think to themselves. 'Who could this soul be?'
>
> 'Is he a Bahá'í?' they asked the Master.
>
> 'Yes, he is a Bahá'í.'
>
> And although they knew very well that Shoghi Effendi was then away at Oxford, 'None of us ever dreamed that it was he.'[11]

Feast and public reading of the Will and Testament

On 3 January, in the presence of nine others, mostly men of 'Abdu'l-Bahá's family, the Will was read aloud for the first time. Three days later, and 40 days after His ascension, a memorial feast was given by the Master's family. There were tables in every room and over 600 people, including the Governor of Phoenicia, other officials and a few Europeans, were present. Long tables were set up, decorated with purple bougainvillea and white narcissus. The food was prepared by members of the household. Every person, whether rich or poor, famous or unknown, all received the same welcome and took whatever place was available at the table.[12]

Emogene Hoagg wrote:

> After the feast, as is the custom, all the guests gathered to give speeches in memory of the Master. The large central room of the Master's House had been prepared with beautiful rugs and with draperies, even the two end rooms of glass were thrown open and chairs and couches placed there, while at the windows were Persian draperies. Chairs were brought from the town so that all were seated. A

small raised place was made for the speakers. About twelve speeches were given, and some were most remarkable. Mohammedan, Jew and Christian seemed to vie with each other in proclaiming the virtues and in expressions of admiration and love for the Master . . . The Bahá'ís had no chance to enlarge upon the speeches made by the others, for they expressed all there was to be said. One man proved by reference to the Koran, all the Twelve Principles as given in America. Often these men gathered would weep when one would give praises of Abdul Baha, or express his love and admiration. It was most touching to be present, even if one did not understand all that was said.[13]

The Governor of Phoenicia said:

Most of us here have, I think, a clear picture of Sir 'Abdu'l-Bahá 'Abbás, of his dignified figure walking thoughtfully in our streets, of his courteous and gracious manner, of his kindness, of his love for little children and flowers, of his generosity and care for the poor and suffering. So gentle was he, and so simple that, in his presence, one almost forgot that he was also a great teacher and that his writings and his conversations have been a solace and an inspiration to hundreds and thousands of people in the East and in the West.[14]

At 9 a.m. on the morning of 7 January 1922, all of the friends gathered at the House of the Master for the reading of the Will. Fujita remembered:

Then up memorial day, we had biggest service here in Number seven. Then we had biggest dinner, luncheon served in . . . Number nine. That one of the daughter's family, Ruha Khanum.

Will of . . .'Abdu'l-Bahá read in Number seven. In the center of the hall! That room! Oh, we had the biggest . . . meeting there. All sitting on floor. A prominent Bahá'í, from Egypt, he read the Will, right in the corner, and everybody faced, and everybody sat around, even the Nakazeen, some of the Nakazeen was among us, violator. Very touching ceremony. Oh, from early in morning, we had a meeting . . . to go some time, to circulate all the Will of 'Abdu'l-Bahá. Every time mention . . . Shoghi Effendi's name, everybody arise . . .

> Shoghi Effendi is be Guardian of the Cause. That day family, back in that tea room now. See, the gentlemen and the ladies are all segregated. They know, behind the curtain, they all know. The Will of 'Abdu'l-Bahá was read, everybody consented, Shoghi Effendi is the Guardian of the Cause. That's final, nobody object, and then after the passing 'Abdu'l-Bahá, the reign of Guardian, Shoghi Effendi.[15]

John Bosch also described the meeting in his diary:

> First Júsef Khan of Tehran, Persia, started to chant the first part of the testament in Arabic at 9.55 & finished at 10.50, then the second part was read (chanted by Mohammed Taki of Cairo) 10.55 to 11.20, then followed the third part by Júsef Khan at 11.25 and ended at 11.45. Afterwards letters were read and speeches made to 12.20 and then all about 120 reviewed the room [where] Abdul Baha passed away. 6 Americans present, Mr Krug, Mrs Krug, Mrs Hoagg, Mrs Bosch, Mr Bosch, Curtis Kelsey of New York, from Germany Miss Johanna Hauff, from England Lady Blomfield and Ethel Rosenberg. Friends present from Cairo, Bombay, India, Persia, Port Said, Damascus, Beyrout, Acca, Jerusalem.[16]

Ethel Rosenberg had left England for Haifa before 'Abdu'l-Bahá's passing. During the voyage, she had the strange feeling that she wouldn't be seeing the Master. When she arrived in Port Said on 1 December, she was met by Mírzá Maḥmúd who helped her through customs and got her on the train that night. He said nothing about 'Abdu'l-Bahá. At about midnight, a man came through the train checking passports and asked her where she would be staying in Haifa. When she responded, 'With Sir 'Abdu'l-Bahá', the man replied, 'Oh! The one who has just died!' Ethel was shocked to the core and seeing her reaction, the man suggested that he may have been wrong. When Ethel arrived in Haifa the next day at noon, she saw Lotfu'lláh Hakím at the station and, from his expression, immediately knew that it was true. Mírzá Maḥmúd had not wanted her to travel with the awful news, but had informed Lotfu'lláh Hakím that he had not told her.[17]

A few years later, Ethel spoke about her experience when the Will was read:

. . . the Will was left sealed up in a packet, and addressed in ‘Abdu’l-Bahá’s own hand to Shoghi Effendi and nothing could be done until Shoghi Effendi came and opened the packet. A very solemn meeting was appointed for the reading of the Will. There were old gray-headed men present, who had been in the Movement for many years, and if there had been the slightest doubt of the authenticity of the Will, they would have known it. The whole document was in His own hand-writing. There were at least 200 people present at the reading of the Will, and it was an impressive ceremony. Every time Shoghi Effendi’s name was mentioned, the whole assembly arose and made obeisance.

The original appointment of Shoghi Effendi was made when he was only 9 and ‘Abdu’l-Bahá was in great danger. The three parts of the Will have different dates. There was not the slightest question at the time as to the validity and the very oldest members there acknowledged it. They had the Will photographed, Miss Rosenberg examined the Will and could see, that it was old, as it is stained from the dampness, as it had been put in a strong box and buried . . .

A Persian believer who had been with ‘Abdu’l-Bahá many years said that he was sitting by the Master at one time, when He was writing a Tablet for this believer to take to Persia, and he began to think, how everything depended upon the Master and it came into his mind ‘Whom can we have to succeed Him?’ – And ‘Abdu’l-Bahá called aloud ‘Shoghi Effendi’ and he came running very quickly to the Master, and the Master said to Shoghi Effendi ‘Here is a friend who very much wishes to see you.’ He said that after ‘Abdu’l-Bahá’s death he understood this incident.[18]

General Sir Ronald Storrs, who had visited ‘Abdu’l-Bahá many times, later wrote:

I met ‘Abdu’l-Bahá first in 1900, on my way out from England and Constantinople through Syria to succeed Harry Boyle as Oriental Secretary to the British Agency in Cairo . . . I drove along the beach in a cab from Haifa to ‘Akká and spent a very pleasant hour with the patient but unsubdued prisoner and exile.

When, a few years later, He was released and visited Egypt I had the honour of looking after Him and of presenting Him to

Lord Kitchener who was deeply impressed by His personality, as who could fail to be? The war separated us again until Lord Allenby, after his triumphant drive through Syria, sent me to establish the Government at Haifa and throughout that district. I called upon 'Abbás Effendi on the day I arrived and was delighted to find Him unchanged.

I never failed to visit Him whenever I went to Haifa. His conversation was indeed a remarkable planning, like that of an ancient prophet, far above the perplexities and pettiness of Palestine politics, and elevating all problems into first principles.

He was kind enough to give me one or two beautiful specimens of His own handwriting, together with that of Mishkín-Qalam, all of which, together with His large signed photograph, were unfortunately burned in the Cyprus fire.

I rendered my last sad tribute of affectionate homage when in 1921, I accompanied Sir Herbert Samuel to the funeral of 'Abbás Effendi. We walked at the head of a train of all religions up the slope of Mt. Carmel, and I have never known a more united expression of regret and respect than was called forth by the utter simplicity of the ceremony.[19]

Shrine lights are turned on

Inspired by the encouragement of the Greatest Holy Leaf, Curtis Kelsey and Ḥusayn-i-Kahrubá'í redoubled their work on the lighting of the Shrines and finished on 21 March. One night after the work was done, Shoghi Effendi asked Curtis to go for a walk. As they walked toward the Shrine of the Báb, watching children play at making shadows in one of Curtis's lights, Shoghi Effendi praised his efforts.[20] Mason Remey described that what Curtis and Ḥusayn had done was

> quite in harmony with the style and character of the buildings. The black iron lamps hang as formerly, suspended from the high, vaulted ceiling, but he has reversed the shades, thus giving the effect of an indirect lighting system.The venetian iron candelabra, in the inner shrine of the Báb . . . is still hanging as before, with its nine tall candles, save that in the central sanctuary lamp, where formerly there hung a glass oil container with a floating wick, there is now an

> electric bulb. A very powerful electric light is placed on the exterior of the tomb, directly above the main doorway to the north. This is lighted every evening and it forms a focal point on the mountain-side and is visible for many miles out at sea.[21]

Effie Baker wrote that the external light initially created a small problem. Some ships coming into port

> were so confused with the light. Looked on their chart and couldn't pick it up. They had the lighthouse on Mount Carmel and the one at Acca, but not this new one, so they were afraid to come in and stayed out at sea till daylight. They complained about the confusion, but the British Government instead of ordering the light to be removed had it marked on the chart.[22]

With his work complete, Curtis began to prepare to leave. He had arrived with little money and had only enough to pay for passage to Istanbul, but that didn't bother him; he could find work in Turkey. Then the Greatest Holy Leaf summoned him and insisted that he accept sufficient funds from her to pay his passage home. As he left her presence, Curtis wondered how she had known his financial condition since he had told no one.[23]

The rough path ahead

On 14 December 1921, with the spectre of the Covenant-breakers in view, the Greatest Holy Leaf began to rally the faithful, cabling the American Bahá'is, 'Now is period of great tests. The friends should be firm and united in defending the Cause. Nakeseens [Covenant-breakers] starting activities through press other channels all over the world. Select committee of wise cool heads to handle press propaganda in America.'[24] On 21 January, Shoghi Effendi wrote his first letter as Guardian to the American Bahá'ís, saying, 'At this early hour when the morning light is just breaking upon the Holy Land, whilst the gloom of the dear Master's bereavement is still hanging thick upon the hearts, I feel as if my soul turns in yearning love and full of hope to that great company of His loved ones across the seas.'[25] The great majority wrote expressing their unfettered support.

Shoghi Effendi's first challenge, other than assuming the mantle of Guardian, came from the usual source: Mírzá Muḥammad-'Alí, the Arch-breaker of Bahá'u'lláh's Covenant. Shortly after 'Abdu'l-Bahá's passing, Mírzá Muḥammad-'Alí had been so bold as to go to the Master's house. The Greatest Holy Leaf turned him away, saying, 'Our Beloved does not allow and does not like you to come in, and if you come in you will add to our sorrows.' The disgruntled Muḥammad-'Alí then wrote to various newspapers 'calling the Bahais to turn to him, quoting extracts from the Covenant of His Holiness Bahá'u'lláh. The Bahai Assembly of Cairo answered him, and exposed his claim to leadership . . .'[26] His agitations with the British authorities for a portion of the estate of the Master, which he based on Islamic law, caused Sir Herbert Samuel to write to Shoghi Effendi on 24 January asking what he was doing to keep the Bahá'í Cause stable. A week later, after Mírzá Muhammad-'Alí's request had been denied by the British, he sent his younger brother, Badí'u'lláh, with some others to the Shrine of Bahá'u'lláh where they forcibly took the keys to the Holy Tomb, claiming that he was the lawful custodian to his Father's tomb. This caused such an uproar that the Governor of 'Akká demanded the keys himself and put a guard on the Shrine, yielding to the entreaties of neither side. An American pilgrim said that in March he was able to enter the 'court of the tomb – the inner sanctuary being sealed . . .'[27] Disregarding his inner turmoil over this act, the young Guardian acted like his Grandfather, calmly proceeding with work already started. A year of careful, steadfast negotiating later, the keys were finally returned to the Bahá'ís.[28]

In March 1922, Shoghi Effendi gathered a group of the strongest and most faithful Bahá'ís from around the world, including 'Abdu'l-Ḥusayn Avárih (later to become a Covenant-breaker) and Fáḍil-i-Mázindarání from Persia; Siyyid Muṣṭafá Rúmí from Burma, Lady Blomfield and Ethel Rosenberg from England, Emogene Hoagg, who had been living in Haifa, Roy Wilhelm, Mountfort Mills, Mason Remey and Corinne True from America, Laura and Hippolyte Dreyfus-Barney from France, Consul and Alice Schwarz from Germany, and Major Wellesley Tudor Pole, who was serving in the British Army in the area. The consensus seemed to be that he should quickly establish the Universal House of Justice. Instead of taking the advice of these wise, older Bahá'ís, Shoghi Effendi instead acted as the infallible Guardian of the Cause of God: he began building the Administrative Order set out in his Grandfather's *Tablets of the Divine Plan* and the *Will and Testament.*

The Centre of the Covenant, 'Abdu'l-Bahá, was gone, but the Covenant itself remained, with Shoghi Effendi as its Guardian.*

* The story continues in *Shoghi Effendi Through the Pilgrim's Eye*, a two-volume set which tells of the struggles of the Guardian to build the Bahá'í Administrative Order and prepare the world for the election of the Universal House of Justice.

BIBLIOGRAPHY

'Abdu'l-Bahá. *Memorials of the Faithful.* Trans. M. Gail. Wilmette, IL: Bahá'í Publishing Trust, 1971.

— *Selections from the Writings of 'Abdu'l-Bahá.* Comp. Research Department of the Universal House of Justice. Haifa: Bahá'í World Centre, 1978. Wilmette, IL: Bahá'í Publishing Trust, 1997.

— *Tablets of the Divine Plan.* Wilmette, IL: Bahá'í Publishing Trust, 1993.

Abu'l-Faḍl-i-Gulpáygání. *The Brilliant Proof.* Los Angeles, CA: Kalimát Press, 1998.

Appel, Jane. United States Bahá'í National Archives, True Family Papers, 1921.

Aṣdaq, Rúhá. *One Life, One Memory.* Oxford: George Ronald, 1999.

Ashbee, C. R. *A Palestine Notebook, 1918–1923.* New York, NY: Doubleday, Page & Co., 1923.

The Báb. *Selections from the Writings of the Báb.* Haifa: Bahá'í World Centre, 1978.

Bagdadi, Hassan Safa, The Heritage Project of the National Spiritual Assembly of the United States, 1919.

Bagdadi, Zia. *History of the Violation of I. Khairallah.* United States Bahá'í National Archives, Emogene Hoagg Papers, 1920.

Bahá'í News. Periodical. National Spiritual Assembly of the Bahá'ís of the United States and Canada, 1924–.

The Bahá'í World: An International Record. Vol. III (1928–1930), Wilmette, IL: Bahá'í Publishing Committee, 1932; vol. VIII (1938-1940), Wilmette, IL: Bahá'í Publishing Trust, 1942; vol. IX (1940 1944), Wilmette, Bahá'í Publishing Trust, 1945; vol. XIII (1954-1963), Haifa, The Universal House of Justice, 1970; vol. XIV (1963-1968), Haifa: The Universal House of Justice, 1974; vol. XVIII (1979-1983), Haifa: Bahá'í World Centre, 1986; vol. XIX (1983–1986), Haifa, Bahá'I World Centre, 1994.

Bahá'u'lláh. *The Kitáb-i-Aqdas: The Most Holy Book.* Haifa: Bahá'í World Centre, 1992.

Bahádur, A. S. United States Bahá'í National Archives, Mary Rabb Papers, 1915.

Baker, Effie. United States Bahá'í National Archives, Mary Rabb Papers, 1925.

Balyuzi, H. M. *'Abdu'l-Bahá.* Oxford: George Ronald, 1971.

Barnitz, Leone and Agnes Parsons. United States Bahá'í National Archives, Leone Barnitz Papers, 1919.

Bell, Archie. *The Spell of the Holy Land.* Boston: The Page Company, 1915. Available at: https://case.edu/ech/articles/b/bell-archie.

Blomfield, Lady. *The Chosen Highway.* London: Bahá'í Publishing Trust, 1940. RP Oxford: George Ronald, 2007.

Bosch, John. United States Bahá'í National Archives, Bosch Papers, 1921.

Bosch, Louise. United States Bahá'í National Archives, Bosch Papers, 1921.
— *Bahai Teaching Conference and Congress, in San Francisco, California, Nov. 26, 1922*, talk, in Merrick (comp.), *Passing of 'Abdu'l-Bahá*, q.v.

Chant, Frank. The Heritage Project of the National Spiritual Assembly of the United States.

Chapman, Anita Ioas. *Leroy Ioas: Hand of the Cause.* Oxford: George Ronald, 1998.

Coy, Genevieve. 'A week in 'Abdu'l-Bahá's home', in *Star of the West*, vol. 12 (1921–22, various dates), no. 10, pp. 163–7; no. 11, pp. 180–83, 186–8,; no. 12, pp. 195–9, 203–4; no. 13, pp. 211–14.

Day, Michael. *Journey to a Mountain: The Story of the Shrine of the Báb*, vol. 1. Oxford: George Ronald, 2018.

Fáḍil-i-Mázindarání. "Abdu'l-Bahá and Shoghi Effendi', in *Star of the West*, vol. XIV, no. 6 (Sept. 1923), pp. 180–81.

Foster, Zachary J. *The 1915 Locust Attack in Syria and Palestine and its Role in the Famine During the First World War*, abstract. Available at: http://www.tandfonline.com/doi/full/10.1080/00263206.2014.976624?scroll=top&needAccess=true.

Frankland, Kathryn. United States Bahá'í National Archives, Kathryn Frankland Papers, 1920.

French, Nell S. United States Bahá'í National Archives, Nellie French Papers, 1921.

Fujita, Sachiro. *Talks of Abdul Baha: Notes of H.S. Fugeta,* 1919, in Merrick (comp.), *Passing of 'Abdu'l-Bahá*, q.v.

Gail, Marzieh. "Abdu'l-Bahá: Portrayals from East and West', in *World Order*, vol. 6, no. 1, Fall 1971.
— *Arches of the Years.* Oxford: George Ronald, 1991.
— *Dawn Over Mount Hira.* Oxford: George Ronald, 1976.

Garis, M. R. *Martha Root.* Wilmette: Bahá'í Publishing Trust, 1983.

Gray, Cora. United States Bahá'í National Archives, Albert Vail Papers, 1920.

Greeven, Inez. United States Bahá'í National Archives, Inez Greeven Papers, 1920, 1921.

Harper, Barron. *Lights of Fortitude.* Oxford: George Ronald, RP 2007.

Hoagg, Emogene. United States Bahá'í National Archives, Hoagg Papers, 1920.
— United States Bahá'í National Archives, Mary Rabb Papers, 1913–14.
— 'Letter from Haifa in the time of mourning, 1922', letter from Emogene Hoagg to Nell French, in *World Order*, vol. 6, no. 2 (Winter 1971–72). Also in Merrick (comp.), *Passing of 'Abdu'l-Bahá*, q.v.

Hofman, Marion. Marion Hofman Papers, private collection now in the Afnán Library.

Holbach, Maude M. 'The Bahai Movement, with some recollections of meetings with Abdul Baha in the nineteenth century and after', in *The Nineteenth Century and After*, pp. 452–66. London, 1915. Available at: https://bahai-library.com/holbach_bahai_movement.

Ioas, Sylvia. Interview with Fujita, 1965, in Merrick (comp.), *Passing of 'Abdu'l-Bahá*, q.v.

Iṣfáhání, Mírzá 'Isá Khán. *With 'Abdu'l-Bahá: The Diary of Mírzá 'Isá Khán Iṣfáhání*. Trans. and ed. Ahang Rabbani. Published in *Witnesses to Bábí and Bahá'í History*, vol. 11, 2008, first written or published 1919. Available at : http://bahai-library.com/isfahani_rabbani_with_abdul-baha.

Kelsey, Curtis. Audio recording. Available at: http://web.archive.org/web/20090213152355/http://www.bahaistudy.org/audio-talks.html.

— *Statement by Curtis D. Kelsey of Experiences in which he Participated, A Part of the Early Days of the Bahá'í Faith in America* (14 July 1955). United States Bahá'í National Archives, Curtis and Harriet Kelsey Papers.

Khadem, Riaz. *Prelude to the Guardianship*. Oxford: George Ronald, 2014.

— *Shoghi Effendi in Oxford*. Oxford: George Ronald, 1999.

Khianra, Dipchand. *Immortals*. New Delhi: Bahá'í Publishing Trust, 1988.

Krug, Grace. *Account of the Passing of 'Abdu'l-Bahá by Grace Krug*, Presented at 'The Cabin' in West Englewood, New Jersey. United States Bahá'í National Archives, Charles (Carl) Krug Papers, 1934.

Kunz, Anna. United States Bahá'í National Archives, Albert Vail Papers, 1921.

Latimer, George. United States Bahá'í National Archives, George Latimer Papers, 1914.

— United States Bahá'í National Archive, George Latimer Papers, 1919.

— *The Light of the World*. Boston, MA, 1920.

Maude, Roderic and Derwent. *The Servant, the General and Armageddon*. Oxford: George Ronald, 1998.

Maxwell, May. *An Early Pilgrimage*. Oxford: George Ronald, 1953.

Mattoon, Edwin & Mrs. Excerpts from the Notes of Mr. and Mrs. Edwin Mattoon taken in Haifa, July 1 to 23, 1921. United States Bahá'í National Archive, MacNutt Papers, 1921.

Merrick, David. *Passing of 'Abdu'l-Bahá*. Compilation of sources, available at: paintdrawer.co.uk/david/folders/spirituality/bahai/abdulbaha/passing-of-abdul-baha.pdf.

Metelmann, Velda Piff. *Lua Getsinger*. Oxford: George Ronald, 1997.

Mills, Mountfort. United States Bahá'í National Archives, Mountfort Mills Papers, 1921.

Momen, Moojan (ed). *The Bábí and Bahá'í Religions, 1844–1944*. Oxford: George Ronald, 1981.
— *Dr. J. E. Esslemont*, London: Bahá'í Publishing Trust, 1975.

Nakhjavani, Violette. *Notes from the Archives Building, in Haifa*. United States National Bahá'í Archives, 1965.

Paine, Mabel Hyde. United States Bahá'í National Archives, Rexford and Sylvia Parmalee Papers, 1920.

Parmalee, Sylvia. *My 3 Years Pilgrimage*. 17 January 1975, The Heritage Project of the National Spiritual Assembly of the United States, audio recording ARC T-1651.
—United States Bahá'I National Archives, Parmelees, Box 6: Sylvia Paine (Parmelee).

Poirier, Brent. 'Story of gate of the garden'. Available at: http://bahai-storytelling.blogspot.com/2010/07/story-of-gate-of-garden-quote-from.html.
— 'Abdu'l-Bahá's use of storytelling'. Available at: https://bahai-storytelling.blogspot.com/2010/02/abdul-bahas-use-of-storytelling.html, 2010.

Poostchi, Iraj, 'Adasiyyah: A study in agriculture and rural development', in *Bahá'í Studies Review*, vol. 16 (2010), pp. 61–105.

Rabbani, Ahang. "Abdu'l-Bahá in Abu-Sinan: September 1914–May 1915', in *Bahá'í Studies Review*, Association for Bahá'í Studies, English-Speaking Europe, no. 13 (2005), pp. 75-103. The extracts quoted here are translated from the diary of Dr Habíb Mu'ayyad, *Kh̲átirát-Habíb* (Memoirs of Habib).

Rabbaní, Rúḥíyyih. *The Priceless Pearl*. London: Bahá'í Publishing Trust, 2000.

Randall-Winkler, Bahíyyih. *My Pilgrimage to Haifa*. Wilmette, IL: Bahá'í Publishing Trust, 1996.
— with M. R. Garis. *William Henry Randall*. Oxford: Oneworld, 1996.

Redman, Earl. *Shoghi Effendi Through the Pilgrim's Eye*. Vol. 1: *Building the Administrative Order, 1922–1952*. Oxford: George Ronald, 2015; vol. 2: *The Ten Year Crusade, 1953–1953*. Oxford: George Ronald, 2016.

Remey, Charles Mason. *A Comprehensive History of the Bahá'í Movement*. United States Bahá'í National Archives, 1927.
— *Through Warring Countries to the Mountain of God: An Account of Some of the Experiences of Two American Bahais in France, England, Germany, and Other Countries, on Their Way to Visit Abdu'l Baha in the Holy Land*, facsimile of author's manuscript, University of California Archives. Available at: http://hdl.handle.net/2027/uc2.ark:/13960/t5x63bd5p, 1915.
— United States Bahá'í National Archives, Charles Mason Remey Papers, 1921.
—, Emogene Hoagg, George Latimer and Louis Gregory. *Report of the Bahá'í Committee of Investigation 1917–1918*, http://www.h-net.org/~bahai/docs/vol5/RCI/RCI.html.
— United States Bahá'í National Archives, Mary Lucas Papers, 1921.

Root, Martha. 'An audience with King Feisal', in *The Bahá'í World*, vol. III, pp. 354, 356.

— *Martha Root, Herald of the Kingdom.* Comp. Kay Zinky. New Delhi: Bahá'í Publishing Trust, 1983.

Rosenberg, Ethel. United States Bahá'í National Archives, Revells, Box 7: Ethel Rosenberg.

Rouhani, Muḥammad-Shafí'. 'Glimpses of 'Abdu'l-Bahá', in *The Bahá'í World*, vol. XIX, pp. 745, 746.

Ruhe, David S. *Door of Hope: The Bahá'í Faith in the Holy Land.* Oxford: George Ronald, 2nd rev. ed. 2001.

Rúḥíyyih Khánum. Audio recording of a talk in Wilmette, Riḍván 1960.
— *Tribute to Shoghi Effendi,* talk at Kampala Intercontinental Conference, 26 January 1958.

Rutstein, Nathan. *Corinne True: Faithful Handmaid of 'Abdu'l-Bahá.* Oxford: George Ronald, 1987.
— *He Loved and Served.* Oxford: George Ronald, 1982.

Sharpe, Victor. 'The ship that changed the Middle East', online article, 31 July 2010. Available at: http://www.renewamerica.com/columns/sharpe/110731.

Shirazi, M. A. *Twenty-one Days with 'Abdu'l-Bahá in the Holy Land.* The Sind Observe Press, 1914.

The Heritage Project of the National Spiritual Assembly of the United States.

Shoghi Effendi. *Directives from the Guardian.* Comp. Gertrude Garrida. New Delhi: Bahá'í Publishing Trust, 1973.
— *God Passes By* (1944). Wilmette, IL: Bahá'í Publishing Trust, rev. ed. 1974.
— *Messages to America 1932–1946.* Wilmette, IL: Bahá'i Publishing Trust, 1947. Published online by the Project Gutenberg.
— *Messages to the Bahá'í World, 1950–1957.* Wilmette, IL: Bahá'í Publishing Trust, 2nd ed. 1971.
— *The World Order of Bahá'u'lláh: Selected Letters by Shoghi Effendi* (1938). Wilmette, IL: Bahá'í Publishing Trust, rev. ed. 1991.

Shoghi Effendi and Lady Blomfield. *The Passing of 'Abdu'l-Bahá.* Haifa: Rosenfeld Brothers, 1922.

Sohrab, Ahmad. *Ahmad Sohrab's Diary.* United States Bahá'í National Archives, 1913–1914.

Star of the West: The Bahai Magazine. Periodical, 25 vols. 1910–1935. Vols. 1–14 RP Oxford: George Ronald, 1978. Complete CD-ROM version: Talisman Educational Software/Special Ideas, 2001.

Taherzadeh, Adib. *The Revelation of Bahá'u'lláh.* 4 vols. Oxford: George Ronald, 1974–1987.

True, Corinne. 'In Memory of Munírih Khánum', in *The Bahá'í World,* vol. VIII, p. 266.

Tudor Pole, Wellesley. United States Bahá'í National Archives. Agnes Parsons Papers, 1918 (name given as Wesley Tutor Pole).
— *Writing on the Ground.* London: Neville Spearman, 1968.

Vail, Albert. United States Bahá'í National Archives, Albert Vail Papers, 1919.

Watson, Marie. *My Pilgrimage to the Land of Desire.* New York: Bahá'í Publishing Committee, 1932.

Weinberg, Robert. *Ethel Jenner Rosenberg: England's Outstanding Bahá'í Pioneer.* Oxford: George Ronald, 1995.

Whitehead, O. Z. *Some Bahá'ís to Remember.* Oxford: George Ronald, 1983.

Whitmore, Bruce W. *The Dawning Place: The Building of a Temple, the Forging of the North American Bahá'í Community.* Wilmette, IL: Bahá'í Publishing Trust, 1984.

Wichhart, Stefanie. 'The 1915 locust plague in Palestine', in *Jerusalem Journal*, Issue 56, (Winter/Spring 2014). Available at: https://oldwebsite.palestine-studies.org/sites/default/files/jq-articles/JQ%2056-57%20The%201915%20Locust.pdf.

NOTES AND REFERENCES

Preface

1 Shoghi Effendi, *The World Order of Bahá'u'lláh*, p. 5.
2 Shoghi Effendi, *Directives from the Guardian*, no. 147, p. 54.

1913–1914

1 *Bahá'í News*, no. 511, Oct. 1973, p. 8.
2 For further information about his life, see Taherzadeh, *The Revelation of Bahá'u'lláh*, vol. 4, pp. 301–4.
3 Aṣdaq, *One Life, One Memory*, pp. 11–21.
4 ibid. p. 21.
5 ibid. pp. 22–3.
6 *Bahá'í News*, no. 511, Oct. 1973, p. 8.
7 Sohrab, *Ahmad Sohrab's Diary*, 25 Nov. 1913, p. 516.
8 ibid. 27 Nov 1913, p. 519.
9 Aṣdaq, *One Life, One Memory*, p. 24.
10 Sohrab, *Ahmad Sohrab's Diary*, 5 Dec. 1913, pp. 533–4.
11 Aṣdaq, *One Life, One Memory*, p. 25.
12 *Star of the West*, vol. IX, no. 2 (9 April 1918), p. 17.
13 Aṣdaq, *One Life, One Memory*, pp. 27–8.
14 ibid. p. 28.
15 ibid. p. 29.
16 Garis, *Martha Root*, p. 211.
17 USBNA, Violette Nakhjavani, *Notes from the Archives Building, in Haifa*, p. 5.
18 Aṣdaq, *One Life, One Memory*, p. 32.
19 ibid. p. 33.
20 ibid. pp. 35–6.
21 ibid. pp. 36–7.
22 Sohrab, *Ahmad Sohrab's Diary*, 11 Dec. 1913, p. 541.
23 ibid. 14 Dec. 1913, pp. 551–2.
24 *Star of the West*, vol. IX, no. 2 (9 April 1918), p. 23.
25 Aṣdaq, *One Life, One Memory*, pp. 39–40.
26 Sohrab, *Ahmad Sohrab's Diary*, 23 Dec. 1913, p. 574.
27 USBNA, Rabb, Box 7: Emogene Hoagg, p. 3.
28 Sohrab, *Ahmad Sohrab's Diary*, 24 Dec. 1913, pp. 576–7.

1914: January to June

1 Holbach, 'The Bahai Movement, with some recollections of meetings with Abdul Baha'.
2 Sohrab, *Ahmad Sohrab's Diary*, 24 April 1914, p. 900.
3 ibid. 23 Dec. 1913, pp. 574–5.
4 ibid. 13 Jan. 1914, p. 632.
5 ibid. 3 Jan. 1914, p. 607.

6 ibid. 13 Jan. 1914, p. 630.
7 ibid. 25 and 26 Jan. 1914, pp. 655, 657.
8 ibid. 27 Jan. 1914, pp. 659–60.
9 ibid. 30 Jan. 1914, p. 688.
10 USBNA, Rabb, Box 7: Emogene Hoagg, p. 6.
11 Holbach, 'The Bahai Movement, with some recollections of meetings with Abdul Baha', p. 466 (p. 12 in online version).
12 Sohrab, *Ahmad Sohrab's Diary*, 1 Feb. 1914, p. 675.
13 *Star of the West*, vol. V, no. 1 (21 Mar. 1914), pp. 3–4.
14 ibid. vol. IX, no. 3 (28 Apr. 1918), pp. 29, 35.
15 Abu'l-Faḍl, *The Brilliant Proof*, pp. viii–ix.
16 *Star of the West*, vol. IV, no. 19 (2 Mar. 1914), pp. 317–19.
17 USBNA, Rabb, Box 7: Emogene Hoagg, p. 7.
18 ibid. vol. IX, no. 3 (28 Apr. 1918), p. 29.
19 Sohrab, *Ahmad Sohrab's Diary*, 28 Jan. 1914, p. 663.
20 ibid. 15 Mar. 1914, p. 793.
21 ibid. 7 Feb. 1914, p. 687.
22 *Star of the West*, vol. IX, no. 3 (28 Apr. 1918), p. 27.
23 ibid. p. 28.
24 ibid. p. 29.
25 Balyuzi, *'Abdu'l-Bahá*, p. 405.
26 *Star of the West*, vol. IX, no. 3 (28 Apr. 1918), p. 31.
27 ibid. p. 35.
28 ibid. vol. IX, no. 10 (8 Sept. 1918), pp. 108–9.
29 ibid. no. 3 (28 Apr. 1918), p. 37.
30 Sohrab, *Ahmad Sohrab's Diary*, 26 Mar. 1914, p. 825.
31 *Star of the West*, vol. IX, no. 3 (28 Apr. 1918), p. 36.
32 ibid. vol. VIII, no. 2 (9 Apr. 1917), pp. 19–20.
33 Sohrab, *Ahmad Sohrab's Diary*, 1 Mar. 1914, p. 759.
34 *The Bahá'í World*, vol. IX (1940–1944), pp. 639–40.
35 Sohrab, *Ahmad Sohrab's Diary*, 27 Mar. 1914, p. 828.
36 ibid. 7 Apr. 1914, p. 855.
37 Khianra, *Immortals*, pp. 27–8.
38 *The Bahá'í World*, vol. IX, p. 638.
39 Sohrab, *Ahmad Sohrab's Diary*, 10 Mar. 1914, p. 782.
40 Shirazi, Twenty-one Days with 'Abdu'l-Bahá in the Holy Land, pp. 2–3.
41 ibid. p. 4.
42 Khianra, *Immortals*, p. 13.
43 ibid. p. 72.
44 Sohrab, *Ahmad Sohrab's Diary*, 30 Mar. 1914, p. 833.
45 ibid. 4 Apr. 1914, p. 847.
46 *Star of the West*, vol. V, no. 5 (5 June 1914), pp. 73–4.
47 Sohrab, *Ahmad Sohrab's Diary*, 23 Feb. 1914, p. 738.
48 ibid.14 Apr. 1914, p. 872.
49 ibid. 16 Apr. 1914, pp. 875–6.
50 ibid. 21 Apr. 1914, pp. 891–2.
51 ibid. 28 Apr. 1914, p. 914.
52 ibid. 1, 2, 3 May 1914, pp. 922–3, 926, 933.
53 ibid. 3 May 1914, pp. 933–5.

54 ibid. 7 May 1914, pp. 946–7.
55 USBNA, Rabb, Box 7: Emogene Hoagg, p. 5.
56 Sohrab, *Ahmad Sohrab's Diary*, 8, 10 May 1914, pp. 949, 956.
57 USBNA, Rabb, Box 7: Emogene Hoagg, p. 4.
58 Sohrab, *Ahmad Sohrab's Diary*, 15 May 1914, p. 971.
59 Poostchi, 'Adasiyyah: A study in agriculture and rural development', pp. 67–8.
60 Sohrab, *Ahmad Sohrab's Diary*, 16, 17 May 1914, pp. 974–5, 977.
61 ibid. 17 May 1914, pp. 978–79.
62 ibid. 28 May, p. 1010; and 3 June 1914, pp. 1026–7.
63 ibid. 5 June, pp. 1030–33.
64 *Star of the West*, vol. IX, no. 10 (8 Sept. 1918), p. 109.
65 ibid. pp. 110–11.
66 ibid. p. 112.
67 Sohrab, *Ahmad Sohrab's Diary*, 13 June, pp. 1053–4.
68 Bell, *The Spell of the Holy Land*, p. viii.
69 ibid. pp. 304, 306.
70 ibid. pp. 306–9.
71 ibid. pp. 311–12.
72 ibid. p. 312.
73 ibid. p. 313.
74 ibid. pp. 316–17.
75 ibid. pp. 320–21.
76 *Star of the West*, vol. IX, no. 10 (8 Sept. 1918), p. 116.
77 Sohrab, *Ahmad Sohrab's Diary*, 15 June, p. 1060.

1914: July to December

1 *Star of the West*, vol. IX, no. 12 (16 Oct. 1918), pp. 133–4.
2 Balyuzi, *'Abdu'l-Bahá*, p. 407.
3 Sharpe, 'The ship that changed the Middle East'.
4 *Star of the West*, vol. IX, no. 12 (16 Oct. 1918), p. 136; Sohrab, *Ahmad Sohrab's Diary*, 29 June 1914, p. 1096.
5 *Star of the West*, vol. VII, no. 3 (28 April 1916), pp. 20–22.
6 Sohrab, *Ahmad Sohrab's Diary*, 5 July, pp. 1110–11.
7 *The Bahá'í Magazine (Star of the West)*, vol. 24, no. 11 (Feb. 1934), pp. 334–7.
8 Sohrab, *Ahmad Sohrab's Diary*, 6 August, pp. 1185–7.
9 USBNA, Latimer, Box 11: George Latimer, p. 160.
10 ibid. pp. 19–20.
11 *Bahá'í News*, no. 511 (Oct. 1973), p. 8.
12 Remey, *Through Warring Countries to the Mountain of God*, pp. 48–9.
13 USBNA, Charles Mason Remey Papers, Diary notes, pp. 1–2.
14 ibid. p. 6.
15 Balyuzi, *'Abdu'l-Bahá*, p. 408.
16 USBNA, Latimer, Box 11: George Latimer, p. 19.
17 Metelmann, *Lua Getsinger*, p. 291.
18 ibid. pp. 294–5.
19 Blomfield, *The Chosen Highway*, p. 191.
20 Sohrab, *Ahmad Sohrab's Diary*, 3 Aug., pp. 1178–80.
21 ibid. 31 July, p. 1172.
22 Remey, *A Comprehensive History of the Bahá'í Movement*, p. 153.

23 USBNA, Latimer, Box 11: George Latimer, pp. 2–3.
24 *Star of the West*, vol. V, no. 15 (12 Dec. 1914), p. 232.
25 ibid. vol. VIII, no. 19 (2 Mar. 1918), p. 241.
26 Sohrab, *Ahmad Sohrab's Diary*, 24 August, p. 1224.
27 *Star of the West*, vol. V, no. 15 (12 Dec 1914)., pp. 232–3.
28 USBNA, Latimer, Box 11: George Latimer, diary pp. 6–7.
29 ibid. pp. 8–9.
30 ibid. pp. 11–12.
31 ibid. pp. 14–16.
32 ibid. pp. 23–4.
33 ibid. p. 25.
34 ibid. pp. 39–40, 48–9, 51–2, 54.
35 ibid. p. 79.
36 ibid. p. 113.
37 ibid. p. 128.
38 ibid. pp. 140–43.
39 ibid. pp. 151–2.
40 ibid. pp. 155–6.
41 ibid. pp. 158–60.
42 ibid. pp. 163–4.
43 ibid. p. 124.
44 ibid. pp. 165–6.
45 *Star of the West*, vol. V, no. 15 (12 Dec. 1914), pp. 232–3.
46 ibid. vol. V, no. 13 (4 Nov. 1914), p. 201.
47 Blomfield, *The Chosen Highway*, p. 189.
48 Rabbani, "Abdu'l-Baha in Abu-Sinan: September 1914–May 1915' pp. 2–3.
49 ibid. p. 5.
50 ibid. pp. 6–7.
51 ibid. p. 7.
52 ibid. p. 8.
53 ibid.
54 Blomfield, *The Chosen Highway*, pp. 209–10.

1915

1 Metelmann, *Lua Getsinger*, p. 303.
2 Balyuzi, *'Abdu'l-Bahá*, p. 412.
3 Metelmann, *Lua Getsinger*, p. 302.
4 *Star of the West*, vol. VI, no. 6 (24 June 1915), pp. 43–4.
5 Rabbani, "Abdu'l-Baha in Abu-Sinan: September 1914–May 1915', p. 10.
6 Metelmann, *Lua Getsinger*, p. 292.
7 ibid. p. 310.
8 Balyuzi, *'Abdu'l-Bahá*, p. 416; Sohrab, *Ahmad Sohrab's Diary*, 6 April, p. 853.
9 Blomfield, *The Chosen Highway*, p. 191; Balyuzi, *'Abdu'l-Bahá*, p. 412.
10 Rabbani, "Abdu'l-Baha in Abu-Sinan: September 1914–May 1915', translated from the diary of Dr Habíb Mu'ayyad, *Khátirát-Habíb* (Memoirs of Habib).
11 ibid.
12 ibid.
13 ibid.
14 ibid.

15 Balyuzi, *'Abdu'l-Bahá*, p. 411.
16 Metelmann, *Lua Getsinger*, p. 301.
17 Balyuzi, *'Abdu'l-Bahá*, p. 411.
18 USBNA, Clark, Box 3: Henrietta Clark Wagner, pp. 6–7.
19 Balyuzi, *'Abdu'l-Bahá*, p. 412–13.
20 USBNA, Latimer, Box 11: George Latimer, 1919, p. 29.
21 ibid. p. 93.
22 *The Bahá'í World*, vol. XIV, pp. 348–9.
23 Quoted in Wichhart, 'The 1915 locust plague in Palestine', p. 30.
24 Foster, *The 1915 Locust Attack in Syria and Palestine and its Role in the Famine During the First World War*, abstract.
25 *Star of the West*, vol. VI, no. 12 (16 Oct. 1915), pp. 89–90.
26 ibid. vol. IX, no. 17 (19 Jan. 1919), p. 190.
27 ibid. vol. VI, no. 6 (24 June 1915), p. 43.
28 Sohrab, *Ahmad Sohrab's Diary*, 18 May, p. 1492.
29 ibid. pp. 1493–4. These are the words of 'Abdu'l-Bahá as reported by Sohrab; they do not carry the authority of authenticated Writings.
30 *Star of the West*, vol. VIII, no. 19 (2 Mar. 1918), p. 244.
31 Taherzadeh, *The Revelation of Bahá'u'lláh*, vol. 2: *Adrianople 1863–1868*, pp. 438–50.
32 *Star of the West*, vol. VI, no. 10 (8 Sept. 1915), pp. 73–4.
33 ibid. p. 77.
34 ibid. p. 80.
35 ibid. no. 12 (16 Oct. 1915), p. 90.
36 ibid. pp. 89–90.
37 'Abdu'l-Bahá, *Memorials of the Faithful*, p. xi.
38 USBNA, Rabb Papers, Box 6: A.S. Bahadur.

1916–1918

1 Blomfield, *The Chosen Highway*, p. 205.
2 Letter from Shoghi Effendi, 26 May 1942, in Shoghi Effendi, *Messages to America, 1932–1946*, p. 56.
3 Shoghi Effendi, *The World Order of Bahá'u'lláh*, p. 86.
4 Shoghi Effendi, *God Passes By*, p. 305.
5 The Báb, *Selections from the Writings of the Báb*, p. 56.
6 Bahá'u'lláh, *The Kitáb-i-Aqdas*, para. 88, p. 52.
7 Letter from Shoghi Effendi, April 1955, in Shoghi Effendi, *Messages to the Bahá'í World*, p. 84.
8 Shoghi Effendi, *God Passes By*, p. 255.
9 Letter from Shoghi Effendi, 4 May 1953, in Shoghi Effendi, *Messages to the Bahá'í World*, p. 155.
10 *Star of the West*, vol. IX, no. 17 (19 Jan. 1919), p. 189.
11 Blomfield, *The Chosen Highway*, pp. 206–7.
12 Maude and Maude, *The Servant, The General and Armageddon*, p. 87.
13 Blomfield, *The Chosen Highway*, p. 219.
14 Momen, *The Bábí and Bahá'í Religions, 1844–1944*, p. 333.
15 ibid.
16 ibid. p. 334.
17 ibid.

18 Maude and Maude, *The Servant, The General and Armageddon*, p. 116.
19 Tudor Pole, *Writing on the Ground*, p. 157.
20 ibid. p. 158.
21 Momen, *The Bábí and Bahá'í Religions, 1844–1944*, p. 336.
22 *Star of the West*, vol. IX, no. 13 (4 Nov. 1918), p. 142.
23 ibid. no. 16 (31 Dec, 1918), p. 182.
24 Momen, *The Bábí and Bahá'í Religions, 1844–1944*, p. 340.
25 ibid. p. 337.
26 USBNA, Parsons, Box 20: Wesley Tutor Pole [sic], pp. 1–2.
27 *Star of the West*, vol. IX, no. 13 (4 Nov. 1918), p. 142.
28 ibid. no. 17 (19 Jan. 1919), p. 189.
29 Maude and Maude, *The Servant, The General and Armageddon*, p. 116.
30 Blomfield, *The Chosen Highway*, p. 210.
31 *Star of the West*, vol. IX, no. 17 (19 Jan. 1919), p. 187.
32 ibid. p. 192.
33 ibid. pp. 192–3.
34 ibid. pp. 193–4.
35 Tudor Pole, *Writing on the Ground*, p. 163.
36 *Star of the West*, vol. IX, no. 17 (19 Jan. 1919), pp. 194–5.
37 ibid. no. 19 (2 Mar. 1919), p. 219.
38 ibid. vol. X, no. 2 (9 Apr. 1919), p. 19.
39 Khadem, *Shoghi Effendi in Oxford*, pp. 14, 16, 22.
40 ibid. p. 21.

1919: January–November

1 *Star of the West*, vol. IX, no. 19 (2 Mar. 1919), p. 220.
2 ibid. vol. X, no. 11 (27 Sept. 1919), p. 218.
3 USBNA, Parsons, Box 20: Wesley Tutor Pole [sic], pp. 3–4.
4 Rabbani, *The Priceless Pearl*, p. 202.
5 Khadem, *Shoghi Effendi in Oxford*, p. 25.
6 *Star of the West*, vol. X, no. 11 (27 Sept. 1919), p. 217.
7 ibid. p. 217–18.
8 *Star of the West*, vol. XI, no. 3 (28 April 1920), pp. 49–50.
9 ibid. p. 50.
10 ibid. pp. 50–51.
11 ibid. p. 51.
12 ibid. pp. 53–4.
13 USBNA, Parsons, Box 20: Wesley Tutor Pole, pp. 3–4.
14 *Star of the West*, vol. XI, no. 3 (28 Apr. 1920), p. 53.
15 ibid. vol. X, no. 6 (24 June 1919), pp. 104–05.
16 ibid. no. 7 (13 June 1919), p. 136.
17 ibid. no. 18 (7 Feb. 1920), p. 336.
18 ibid.
19 USBNA, various pilgrim notes, Mírzá Badi, 15 Jan. 1920.
20 *Star of the West*, vol. X, no. 10 (8 Sept. 1919), pp. 195–6.
21 ibid. no. 16 (31 Dec. 1919), pp. 291–2.
22 Khadem, *Shoghi Effendi in Oxford*, pp. 48–9.
23 ibid. pp. 50–51.
24 Khadem, *Prelude to the Guardianship*, pp. 91–3.

25 ibid. p. 95.
26 ibid. pp. 96–7.
27 ibid. pp. 101–03.
28 Khadem, *Shoghi Effendi in Oxford*, pp. 57–8.
29 USBNA, Latimer, Box 11: George Latimer, 1919, p. 3.
30 *Star of the West*, vol. X, no. 17 (19 Jan. 1920), p. 312.
31 Rutstein, *Corinne True*, p. 140; Sylvia Ioas, Interview of Sachiro Fujita, p. 3.
32 Rutstein, *Corinne True*, p. 141.
33 ibid.
34 ibid. p. 142; see also *Star of the West*, vol. X, no. 18 (7 Feb.1920), p. 313.
35 Rutstein, *Corinne True*, p. 142.
36 *Star of the West*, vol. X, no. 18 (7 Feb. 1920), p. 313; Rutstein, *Corinne True*, p. 143.
37 Rabbani, *The Priceless Pearl*, p. 29.
38 Rúḥíyyih Khánum, *Tribute to Shoghi Effendi, Kampala,* 1958, pp. 2–3.
39 *Star of the West*, vol. X, no. 18 (7 Feb. 1920), pp. 313–14.
40 Whitmore, *The Dawning Place*, p. 75, 87.
41 Rutstein, *Corinne True*, p. 144.
42 Khadem, *Prelude to the Guardianship*, pp. 108–09.
43 True, 'In Memory of Munírih Khánum' in *The Bahá'í World*, vol. VIII, p. 266.
44 Momen, *Dr. J. E. Esslemont*, pp. 11–12.
45 Esslemont, pilgrim notes, Marion Hofman Papers.
46 ibid.
47 Rutstein, *Corinne True*, p. 145.
48 Chapman, *Leroy Ioas*, p. 185.

1919: November–December

1 USBNA, Latimer, Box 11: George Latimer, 1919, p. 1.
2 Latimer, *The Light of the World*, p. 7.
3 Ioas, Interview of Sachiro Fujita, 1965, p. 3.
4 USBNA, Latimer, Box 11: George Latimer, 1919, pp. 69–70.
5 Randall-Winckler, *William Henry Randall*, pp. 107–8.
6 Latimer, *The Light of the World*, p. 11.
7 Randall-Winckler, *William Henry Randall*, pp. 108–9.
8 Latimer, *The Light of the World*, pp. 12–33.
9 Randall-Winckler, *My Pilgrimage to Haifa*, p. 3.
10 ibid. pp. 4–5.
11 Randall-Winckler, *William Henry Randall*, pp. 113–14.
12 Ioas, Interview of Sachiro Fujita, 1965, pp. 3–4.
13 Latimer, *The Light of the World*, pp. 18–25.
14 Randall-Winckler, *My Pilgrimage to Haifa*, p. 15.
15 ibid. pp. 42–61.
16 Latimer, *The Light of the World*, p. 26.
17 USBNA, Latimer, Box 11: George Latimer, 1919, p. 12.
18 ibid. pp. 24–5.
19 Harper, *Lights of Fortitude*, pp. 288–305.
20 Randall-Winckler, *My Pilgrimage to Haifa*, p. 17.
21 ibid. pp. 15–16.
22 Ioas, Interview of Sachiro Fujita, 1965, p. 1.

23 Rutstein, *He Loved and Served*, pp. 76–7.
24 Ioas, Interview of Sachiro Fujita, 1965, p. 4.
25 USBNA, Latimer, Box 11: George Latimer, 1919, p. 51.
26 Rutstein, *He Loved and Served*, p. 75.
27 Randall-Winckler, *My Pilgrimage to Haifa*, p. 29.
28 ibid. p. 19.
29 USBNA, Latimer, Box 11: George Latimer, 1919, pp. 28–30, 55.
30 Randall-Winckler, *William Henry Randall*, p. 138; *Star of the West*, vol. XII, no. 11 (27 Sept. 1921), p. 184.
31 Ruhe, *Door of Hope*, pp. 180–81.
32 Randall-Winckler, *My Pilgrimage to Haifa*, p. 28.
33 ibid. p. 35.
34 Randall-Winckler, *William Henry Randall*, p. 134.
35 Randall-Winckler, *My Pilgrimage to Haifa*, pp. 43, 49.
36 ibid. pp. 51–2.
37 USBNA, Latimer, Box 11: George Latimer, 1919, pp. 73–4.
38 ibid. pp. 74–5.
39 Randall-Winckler, *My Pilgrimage to Haifa*, pp. 66, 68.
40 USBNA, Latimer, Box 11: George Latimer, 1919, p. 75.
41 USBNA, Vail, Box 8: Albert Vail, pp. 1–2.
42 Randall-Winckler, *William Henry Randall*, pp. 156–7.
43 Randall-Winckler, *My Pilgrimage to Haifa*, pp. 81, 85.
44 *Star of the West*, vol. XXIV, no. 10 (Jan. 1934), p. 304.
45 Latimer, The *Light of the World*, pp. 107–10.
46 Randall-Winckler, *William Henry Randall*, pp. 163–4.
47 Randall-Winckler, *My Pilgrimage to Haifa*, p. 91.
48 Randall-Winckler, *William Henry Randall*, p. 178.
49 USBNA, Latimer, Box 11: George Latimer, 1919, p. 67.
50 Sohrab, *Ahmad Sohrab's Diary*, 14 Nov. 1913, pp. 487–8.
51 USBNA, Latimer, Box 11: George Latimer, 1919, p. 68.
52 USBNA, Leone Barnitz, Box 21: Leone Barnitz/Agnes Parsons, p. 4.
53 Randall-Winckler, *William Henry Randall*, p. 183.
54 *Star of the West*, vol. X, no. 18 (7 Feb. 1920), p. 329.
55 Momen, *Dr. J. E. Esslemont*, pp. 16–17.
56 ibid. pp. 17–19.
57 *Star of the West*, vol. X, no. 17 (19 Jan. 1920), p. 314.
58 Bagdadi, The Heritage Project of the National Spiritual Assembly of the United States.
59 Iṣfáhání, *With 'Abdu'l-Bahá*, 18 Dec. 1919, p. 1.
60 ibid. 25 Dec. 1919, p. 12.
61 ibid. p. 7.
62 ibid. pp. 8–19.
63 ibid. p. 4.
64 ibid. p. 9.
65 ibid. p. 4.
66 ibid. pp. 6–7.
67 ibid. p. 7.
68 ibid. p. 6.
69 ibid. p. 5.

1920

1 USBNA, Leone Barnitz, Box 21: Leone Barnitz/Agnes Parsons; Frank Chant, The Heritage Project of the National Spiritual Assembly of the United States.
2 ibid. Leone Barnitz, Box 21: Leone Barnitz/Agnes Parsons, p. 1.
3 ibid. Leone Barnitz, Box 21-s: Leone Barnitz/Agnes Parsons.
4 ibid. pp. 2–3.
5 ibid. p. 4; see also Momen, *Dr. J. E. Esslemont*, p. 19; USBNA, Rabb, Box 7: H. E. Hoagg.
6 Momen, *Dr. J. E. Esslemont*, p. 21.
7 ibid. pp. 18–19, 31–5.
8 USBNA, Leone Barnitz, Box 21: Leone Barnitz/Agnes Parsons, p. 5.
9 Whitehead, *Some Bahá'ís to Remember*, p. 87.
10 Momen, *The Bábí and Bahá'í Religions, 1844–1944*, p. 340.
11 Ashbee, C. R., *A Palestine Notebook*, pp. 116–20.
12 ibid. p. 173.
13 Poostchi, 'Adasiyyah: A study in agriculture and rural development', pp. 77–8.
14 Poirier, *The story of the 'Gate of the Garden quote from 'Abdu'l-Bahá'*, p. 1.
15 USBNA, Inez Greeven, Box 1: Inez Greeven, p. 1.
16 Poirier, *The story of the 'Gate of the Garden quote from 'Abdu'l-Bahá'*, p. 1.
17 USBNA, Inez Greeven, Box 1: Inez Greeven, p. 4.
18 USBNA, Seto, Box 4: Inez Greeven.
19 Poirier, "Abdu'l-Bahá's use of storytelling', p. 1.
20 Poirier, *The story of the 'Gate of the Garden quote from 'Abdu'l-Bahá'*, pp. 2–3.
21 USBNA, Hoagg Papers, Box 7: H. Emogene Hoagg, p. 1.
22 USBNA, Rabb, Box 6: Effie Baker, p. 6 (pdf p 7).
23 Momen, *The Bábí and Bahá'í Religions, 1844–1944*, p. 344.
24 ibid. p. 343.
25 ibid.
26 Blomfield, *The Chosen Highway*, pp. 214–15.
27 USBNA, Rabb, Box 6: Effie Baker.
28 *Star of the West*, vol. XIII, no. 11 (Feb. 1922), p. 298.
29 USBNA, Nakhjavani, *Notes from the Archives Building, in Haifa*, p. 6.
30 Root, 'An audience with King Feisal'.
31 http://en.wikipedia.org/wiki/Feisal_I_of_Iraq.
32 For further details see Redman, *Shoghi Effendi: Through the Pilgrim's Eye*, vol. 1.
33 *Star of the West*, vol. XII, no. 7 (31 Dec. 1920), pp. 136–7.
34 Khianra, *Immortals*, p. 161.
35 ibid. p. 164.
36 *Star of the. West*, vol. XI, no. 8 (16 Oct. 1920), p. 128.
37 ibid. vol. XI, no. 12 (1 Aug. 1920), p. 209.
38 USBNA, Emogene Hoagg Papers, Box 5, p. 1.
39 *Bahá'í News*, no. 511, Oct. 1973, p. 9.
40 USBNA, Emogene Hoagg Papers, Box 5, p. 3.
41 ibid. p. 4.
42 ibid. p. 7.
43 ibid. p. 8.
44 *Bahá'í News*, no. 511, Oct.1973, pp. 9–10.
45 USBNA, Rexford and Sylvia Parmelee, Box 4: Mabel Hyde Paine, p. 1.
46 USBNA, Vail, Box 8: Cora Gray, pp. 1–2.

47 Coy, 'A week in 'Abdu'l-Bahá's home', in *Star of the West*, vol. XII, no. 10, p. 165. See also nos. 11 and 12 for further instalments.
48 USBNA, Rexford and Sylvia Parmelee, Box 4: Mabel Hyde Paine, p. 2.
49 Coy, 'A week in 'Abdu'l-Bahá's home', p. 165; USBNA, Vail, Box 8: Cora Gray, p. 3.
50 Coy, 'A week in 'Abdu'l-Bahá's home', pp. 166–7.
51 ibid. no. 11, p. 179.
52 USBNA, Vail, Box 8: Cora Gray, p. 4.
53 Coy, 'A week in 'Abdu'l-Bahá's home', p. 180.
54 Parmalee, *My 3 Years Pilgrimage.*
55 ibid. p. 2.
56 USBNA, Parmelees, Box 6: Sylvia Paine (Parmelee), p. 4.
57 Coy, 'A week in 'Abdu'l-Bahá's home', pp. 180–81.
58 ibid. pp. 181–2.
59 Coy, 'A week in 'Abdu'l-Bahá's home', pp. 187–8.
60 ibid. pp. 188, 195–6.
61 USBNA, Vail, Box 8: Cora Gray, p. 11.
62 Parmalee, *My 3 Years Pilgrimage,* p. 2.
63 ibid. pp. 8–9.
64 ibid. p. 9.
65 ibid.
66 Coy, 'A week in 'Abdu'l-Bahá's home', pp. 204, 211.
67 Parmalee, *My 3 Years Pilgrimage,* pp. 9–10.
68 ibid. p. 10.
69 Coy, 'A week in 'Abdu'l-Bahá's home', p. 212.
70 ibid. pp. 213–14.
71 *Star of the West,* vol. XI, no. 16 (31 Dec. 1920), pp. 267–8.
72 Parmalee, *My 3 Years Pilgrimage,* p. 7.
73 USBNA, Kathryn Frankland Papers, Box 1: Kathryn Frankland.
74 ibid; see also USBNA, Hoagg Papers, Box 7: H. Emogene Hoagg, p. 1.
75 USBNA, Hoagg Papers, Box 7: H. Emogene Hoagg, p. 2.
76 ibid.
77 ibid. p. 3.
78 ibid. pp. 4–5.

1921: January–June

1 USBNA, Charles Mason Remey Papers, Box 2, vol.2: Charles Mason Remey, p. 22.
2 ibid. pp. 22–3.
3 ibid. p. 24.
4 ibid. pp. 24–5.
5 USBNA, Mary Lucas, Box 1: Martha Root.
6 USBNA, Charles Mason Remey Papers, Box 2, vol. 2: Charles Mason Remey, pp. 26–7.
7 ibid. p. 27.
8 ibid. pp. 34–5.
9 ibid. pp. 38–9.
10 ibid. p. 45.
11 ibid. pp. 58–9.

12 ibid. pp. 59–61.
13 ibid. pp. 63, 66.
14 USBNA, True Family, Box 9: Jane Appel, p. 1.
15 ibid. p. 2.
16 ibid. p. 4.
17 ibid. p. 7.
18 ibid. p. 8.
19 USBNA, Mountfort Mills, Box 1: Mountfort Mills, p. 3.
20 ibid. pp. 13–14.
21 ibid. p. 23.
22 USBNA, Charles Mason Remey Papers, Box 2, vol. 2, p. 98.
23 Remey et al., *Report of the Bahá'í Committee of Investigation 1917–1918*, pp. 5–6.
24 USBNA, Charles Mason Remey Papers, Box 10, vol. 46: 'The Violation in Chicago', p. 1.
25 ibid. pp. 2–3.
26 ibid. p. 2.
27 ibid. p. 3.
28 USBNA, Charles Mason Remey Papers, Box 2, vol. 2, pp. 99–100.
29 USBNA, Mountfort Mills, Box 1: Mountfort Mills, p. 38; USBNA, Charles Mason Remey Papers, Box 2, vol. 2, p. 124–5.
30 USBNA, Charles Mason Remey Papers, Box 2, vol. 2, pp. 119–20.
31 USBNA, Mountfort Mills, Box 1: Mountfort Mills, pp. 42–3.
32 USBNA, Charles Mason Remey Papers, Box 2, vol. 2, pp. 120–21.
33 ibid. p. 129.
34 USBNA, Vail, Box 8: Anna Kunz, pp. 1–2.
35 ibid. p. 3.
36 ibid.
37 Rouhani, 'Glimpses of 'Abdu'l-Bahá', in *The Bahá'í World*, vol. XIX, pp. 745, 746.
38 ibid. p. 747.
39 *The Bahá'í World*, vol. XIII, pp. 881–2.
40 Rouhani, 'Glimpses of 'Abdu'l-Bahá', in *The Bahá'í World*, vol. XIX p. 750.
41 USBNA, Nellie French, Box 7: Nellie S. French, pp. 3–4.
42 ibid. p. 5.
43 ibid. p. 7.
44 ibid. p. 10.
45 ibid. pp. 10–12.
46 ibid. pp. 12–15.
47 ibid. p. 15.
48 Maxwell, *An Early Pilgrimage*, p. 25.
49 USBNA, Rabb, Box 7: Nellie S. French.
50 *Star of West*, vol. 13, no. 1 (21 Mar. 1922), p. 26.
51 Rouhani, 'Glimpses of 'Abdu'l-Bahá', in *The Bahá'í World*, vol. XIX, p. 748.
52 ibid. p. 754.
53 ibid. pp. 754–5.

1921: July–November

1 USBNA, MacNutts, Box 3: Mr & Mrs Edwin Mattoon, p. 1.
2 ibid.
3 Root, *Herald of the Kingdom*, pp. 219–20.

4 Watson, *My Pilgrimage to the Land of Desire*, p. 11.
5 ibid. pp. 3–4.
6 ibid. pp. 5–6.
7 ibid. p. 6.
8 ibid. p. 7.
9 ibid. p. 9.
10 ibid. pp. 11–12.
11 ibid. p. 15.
12 ibid.
13 ibid. pp. 13–14.
14 ibid. pp. 16–17.
15 ibid. p. 17–18.
16 ibid. p. 19.
17 ibid. p. 20.
18 ibid. pp. 20, 22.
19 USBNA, Inez Greeven, Box 1: Inez Greeven, 1920, p. 9.
20 ibid. pp. 2–3.
21 ibid.pp. 12–13.
22 ibid. p. 11.
23 USBNA, Curtis and Harriet Kelsey Papers: Statement by Curtis D. Kelsey, Sheet 5.
24 ibid. Sheet 6.
25 Rutstein, *He Loved and Served*, pp. 37, 41.
26 USBNA, Curtis and Harriet Kelsey Papers: Statement by Curtis D. Kelsey, Sheet 8.
27 Rutstein, *He Loved and Served*, pp. 44–7.
28 ibid. pp. 47–8.
29 ibid. pp. 52–53.
30 USBNA, Curtis and Harriet Kelsey Papers: Statement by Curtis D. Kelsey, Sheet 10.
31 Rutstein, *He Loved and Served*, p. 55.
32 ibid. p. 56.
33 ibid. pp. 58–9.
34 ibid. p. 61.
35 ibid. p. 62.
36 ibid. pp. 67–8.
37 ibid. p. 71.
38 ibid. p. 73.
39 ibid. pp. 1–2.
40 ibid. pp. 73–4.
41 USBNA, Curtis and Harriet Kelsey Papers: Statement by Curtis D. Kelsey, Sheet 24.
42 USBNA, Bosches, Box 11: Louise Bosch, pp. 8–9.

1921: The Passing of the Master

1 First letter from Shoghi Effendi to the Bahá'ís of America, 21 January 1922, in *Star of the West*, vol. XIII, no. 1, p. 17.
2 Shoghi Effendi, *God Passes By*, p. 310.
3 ibid.

4 Jináb-i-Fádil (Fáḍil-i-Mázindarání), "Abdu'l-Bahá and Shoghi Effendi', in *Star of the West*, vol. XIV, no. 6 (Sept. 1923), p. 180.
5 Harper, *Lights of Fortitude*, p. 137.
6 *Star of the West*, vol. XII, no. 14. p. 233.
7 Gail, "Abdu'l-Bahá: Portrayals from East and West', in *World Order*, vol. 6, no. 1 (Fall 1971), pp. 29–41.
8 USBNA, Bosches, Box 11: Louise Bosch, p. 4.
9 Letter from Joahnna Hauff to her parents, 28 November 1921, translated from *Sonne der Wahrheit*, in *Star of the West*, vol. XII, no. 19 (2 Mar. 1922), p. 299.
10 Krug, *Account of the Passing of 'Abdu'l-Bahá*, p. 1.
11 Kelsey, audio recording.
12 Letter from Ahmad Tabrizi to Dr Zia Bagdadi, 29 November 1921, in *Star of the West*, vol. XII, no. 18 (7 Feb. 1922), p. 280. A photograph of 'Abdu'l-Bahá as one of the pall-bearers appears on p. 281.
13 ibid.
14 Shoghi Effendi and Lady Blomfield, *The Passing of 'Abdu'l-Bahá*, p. 6.
15 Krug, *Account of the Passing of 'Abdu'l-Bahá*, p. 2.
16 USBNA, John and Louise Bosch, Box 11: John Bosch, 1921, pp. 16–19.
17 Louise Bosch, talk at Bahá'í Teaching Conference and Congress, San Francisco, California, 26 November 1922, in Merrick, *Passing of 'Abdu'l-Bahá*, pp. 17–18.
18 Krug, *Account of the Passing of 'Abdu'l-Bahá*, p. 2.
19 USBNA, John and Louise Bosch, Box 11: John Bosch, 1921, pp. 16–19.
20 Shoghi Effendi and Lady Blomfield, *The Passing of 'Abdu'l-Bahá*, pp. 8–9.
21 Krug, *Account of the Passing of 'Abdu'l-Bahá*, p. 3.
22 Letter from Muhammad Said Adham, 1 January 1922, in *Star of the West*, vol. XII, no. 19 (2 Mar. 1922), p. 292.
23 Ioas, Interview of Sachiro Fujita, 1965, p. 6.
24 USBNA, John and Louise Bosch, Box 11: John Bosch, 1921, pp. 19–22.
25 Gail, "Abdu'l-Bahá: Portrayals from East and West', in *World Order*, vol. 6, no. 1 (Fall 1971); also in Gail, *Dawn Over Mount Hira*, pp. 211–12.
26 Louise Bosch, talk at Bahai Teaching Conference and Congress, in San Francisco, California, 26 November 1922, in Merrick, *Passing of 'Abdu'l-Bahá*, pp. 28–30.
27 Rutstein, *He Loved and Served*, pp. 96–7.
28 Krug, *Account of the Passing of 'Abdu'l-Bahá*, p. 4.
29 Letter from Joahnna Hauff to her parents, 28 November 1921, translated from *Sonne der Wahrheit*, in *Star of the West*, vol. XII, no. 19 (2 Mar. 1922), p. 296.
30 *Star of the West*, vol. XII, no. 15 (12 Dec. 1921), p. 245.
31 ibid. no. 16, (31 Dec. 1921), p. 253.
32 USBNA, Bosches, Box 11: John and Louise Bosch, Box 11, John Bosch, pp. 29–30.
33 Gail, "Abdu'l-Bahá: Portrayals from East and West', in *World Order*, vol. 6, no. 1 (Fall 1971), also in Gail, *Dawn Over Mount Hira*, p. 213.
34 USBNA, Bosches, Box 11: John and Louise Bosch, Box 11, John Bosch, pp. 30–31.
35 Ioas, Interview of Sachiro Fujita, 1965, p. 6.
36 Shoghi Effendi and Lady Blomfield, *The Passing of 'Abdu'l-Bahá*, p. 10.
37 Rutstein, *He Loved and Served*, p. 99.
38 Letter from Muhammad Said Adham, 1 January 1922, in *Star of the West*, vol. XII, no. 19 (2 Mar. 1922), p. 293.

39 Quoted in Day, *Journey to a Mountain*, p. 124.
40 Hoagg, *World Order*, vol. 6, no. 2 (Winter 1971–72), in Merrick, *Passing of 'Abdu'l-Bahá*, doc p. 2.
41 Quoted in Day, *Journey to a Mountain*, p. 131; see also Rutstein, *He Loved and Served*, p. 100.
42 Shoghi Effendi and Lady Blomfield, *The Passing of 'Abdu'l-Bahá*, p. 19.
43 Weinberg, *Ethel Jenner Rosenberg*, p. 187.

1922: Shoghi Effendi, The Guardian of the Faith

1 Rabbaní, *The Priceless Pearl*, p. 45.
2 ibid. p. 40.
3 Gail, *Dawn over Mount Hira*, pp. 213–14.
4 Gail, *Arches of the Years*, p. 223.
5 Gail, *Dawn over Mount Hira*, p. 214.
6 Rabbaní, *The Priceless Pearl*, pp. 42–3, 45.
7 Rúḥíyyih Khánum, *Tribute to Shoghi Effendi*, p. 2.
8 Rabbani, *The Priceless Pearl*, p. 148.
9 Rúḥíyyih Khánum, *Tribute to Shoghi Effendi*, p. 2.
10 Rabbani, *The Priceless Pearl*, p. 47.
11 Gail, *Arches of the Years*, pp. 283–4.
12 Shoghi Effendi and Lady Blomfield, *The Passing of 'Abdu'l-Bahá*, pp. 19–20.
13 Hoagg, *Letter from Haifa in the Time of Mourning*, 1922, in Merrick, *Passing of 'Abdu'l-Bahá*, p. 61.
14 Shoghi Effendi and Lady Blomfield, *The Passing of 'Abdu'l-Bahá*, doc p. 20.
15 Ioas, Interview of Sachiro Fujita, 1965, p. 6.
16 USBNA, Bosches, Box 11: John and Louise Bosch, Box 11: John Bosch, pp. 33–4.
17 Weinberg, *Ethel Jenner Rosenberg*, pp. 181–2.
18 Minutes of the London Spiritual Assembly, talk by Ethel Rosenberg, 2 February 1929, in USBNA, Revells, Box 7: Ethel Rosenberg.
19 *The Bahá'í World*, vol. VIII, p. 626.
20 Rutstein, *He Loved and Served*, p. 104.
21 *Star of the West*, vol. XIV, no. 9 (Dec. 1923), pp. 265–6.
22 USBNA, Rabb, Box 6: Effie Baker (1925), p. 3.
23 Rutstein, *He Loved and Served*, pp. 108–9.
24 Rabbaní, *The Priceless Pearl*, p. 49.
25 ibid. p. 52.
26 *Star of the West*, vol. XII, no. 19 (2 Mar. 1922), pp. 302–3.
27 ibid. pp. 53–4.
28 ibid. p. 71.

INDEX

ABOUT THE AUTHOR

Earl Redman is a geologist who worked in Alaska and Chile for two decades. One job was for the US Bureau of Mines, studying mineral deposits in the Juneau Gold Belt, Alaska. In 1999 he moved with his wife Sharon to Ireland, where he has researched and written five books, exploring the gold mines of the stories included in *'Abdu'l-Bahá in Their Midst*, the two volumes of *Shoghi Effendi Through the Pilgrim's Eye*, a book on the Knights of Bahá'u'lláh and a volume on pilgrims who visited 'Abdu'l-Bahá in the Holy Land before His Western journeys. This volume tells the story of pilgrims to the Holy Land after 'Abdu'l-Bahá's return in 1913.

Earl and Sharon have travelled widely and for long periods in recent years and are much in demand as speakers and storytellers.

VISITING 'ABDU'L-BAHÁ

VOLUME 1: THE WEST DISCOVERS THE MASTER, 1897–1911

Among those who visit 'Akká, some have made great forward strides. Lightless candles, they were set alight; withered, they began to bloom; dead, they were recalled to life and went home with tidings of great joy.

'Abdu'l-Bahá

. . . each pilgrim brings back information and suggestions of a most precious character, and it is the privilege of all the friends to share in the spiritual results of these visits. Shoghi Effendi

This two-volume series on pilgrims who visited 'Abdu'l-Bahá in the Holy Land may be seen as a companion to *'Abdu'l-Bahá in Their Midst*, about 'Abdu'l-Bahá's three-year journey to Egypt, Europe and North America. The present volume covers the time from 1897 until the Master's departure on His journey to the West.

Virtually all pilgrims and many other visitors wrote down what 'Abdu'l-Bahá said, including many of His talks, both formal and informal. Their accounts provide a great wealth of stories that help illustrate who 'Abdu'l-Bahá was in the context of history and how he taught and interacted with others. Most of these accounts come from personal diaries and letters initially written in longhand, though many were later typed. They are to be considered 'pilgrims' notes', but are a fascinating and moving testimony to how 'Abdu'l-Bahá affected and transformed those He met, described in their own words.

ISBN: 978–0–85398–617–1

Soft Cover, 304 pages, 23.4 x 15.6 cms (9.75 x 6.25 ins)

‘ABDU’L-BAHÁ IN THEIR MIDST

If the believers . . . establish, in a befitting manner, union and harmony with spirit, tongue, heart and body, suddenly they shall find ‘Abdu’l-Bahá in their midst.
‘Abdu’l-Bahá

‘Abdu’l-Bahá in Their Midst is the story of the journey of ‘Abdul-Bahá to Europe and North America over the period 1911 to 1913. Rather than focusing on the public talks he gave, inspiring though these were, it narrates how ‘Abdu’l-Bahá affected and transformed the lives of those he met, described in their own words.

Time after time, ‘Abdu’l-Bahá would delay his departure to catch a train, meet ‘important people’ or attend a meeting, to the consternation and frustration of those around him, because he ‘knew’ someone who needed to see him was coming to visit him. Many times the ‘someone’ was unknown and poor or roughly dressed, but ‘Abdu’l-Bahá would wait for them, then surround them with his love. There were also stories of those who thought themselves important, but who were reduced to wordlessness in his presence. ‘How gentle and wise he was, hundreds could testify from personal knowledge,’ wrote one notable Christian cleric. And ‘Abdu’l-Bahá himself wrote: ‘If the believers . . . establish, in a befitting manner, union and harmony with spirit, tongue, heart and body, suddenly they shall find ‘Abdu’l-Bahá in their midst.’

ISBN: 978–0–85398–557–0
Soft Cover, 384 pages, 23.4 x 15.6 cm (9.75 x 6.25 in)

SHOGHI EFFENDI THROUGH THE PILGRIM'S EYE

VOLUME 1:
BUILDING THE ADMINISTRATIVE ORDER, 1922–1952

Shoghi Effendi Through the Pilgrim's Eye tells the story of the Guardian's ministry from 1922 when the young Shoghi Effendi, just 24 years old, was charged with guiding the affairs of a worldwide Faith. Rather than a biography, it draws on the diary entries and letters (many now published for the first time) of the many pilgrims and visitors to the Bahá'í Holy Places in Haifa and 'Akká, as well as the accounts of those who worked to assist the Guardian in his many extraordinary achievements.

Volume 1 (1922–1952) covers the years when the Guardian was laying the foundations of the Bahá'í Administrative Order destined to culminate in the World Order of Bahá'u'lláh, while at the same time planning and carrying out the extension and development of the Shrines of the Báb and Bahá'u'lláh, translating the Writings of Bahá'u'lláh as well as *The Dawn-Breakers* and writing his own major works, as well as facing challenges to his authority and responding to the confiscation of the House of Bahá'u'lláh in Baghdad and the persecution of Bahá'ís in Iran and Egypt. The volume ends just before the dramatic decade that was to begin in 1953.

ISBN: 978–0–85398–588–4
Soft Cover, 480 pages, 23.4 x 15.6 cms (9.75 x 6.25 ins)

SHOGHI EFFENDI THROUGH THE PILGRIM'S EYE

VOLUME 2: THE TEN YEAR CRUSADE, 1953-1963

While volume 1 (1922–1952) covered the years when Shoghi Effendi was laying the foundations of the Bahá'í Administrative Order destined to culminate in the World Order of Bahá'u'lláh, volume 2 begins with the opening of the dramatic decade 1953–1963 with the launching of the ten-year worldwide spiritual plan to carry the Faith of Bahá'u'lláh to every place on the planet. That first global teaching plan involved every National Assembly and every Bahá'í in a 'fate-laden, soul-stirring, decade-long, world-embracing Spiritual Crusade'. It was a monumentally incomprehensible leap for the world Bahá'í Community. When Shoghi Effendi announced the plan, there were just twelve National Spiritual Assemblies in the world, formed over a period of 30 years. The Plan ended with 56. In 1952 the Bahá'í Faith had members in 129 countries and dependencies; Shoghi Effendi wanted to open an additional 131 – all in just ten years.

ISBN: 978–0–85398–595–2
Soft Cover, 400 pages, 23.4 x 15.6 cms (9.75 x 6.25 ins)

THE KNIGHTS OF BAHÁ'U'LLÁH

The amazing stories of the Knights of Bahá'u'lláh, whose indomitable spirit, courage and steadfastness brought the Bahá'í message to countries where it was previously unknown.

Why would a legal counsel with the rank of brigadier general in the Department of Defence go to a desolate island with just a few score inhabitants? Where it was so hot that he cooked his eggs on rocks on the beach and so isolated that the arrival of an eggplant on the tide was the cause of celebration?

Why would a young doctor give up a potential job that included a nice house, servants, car and driver and a good salary, for a job paying just $25 a month in a place where the toilet was two boards placed over a stream full of water snakes?

These and other stories of indomitable spirit, courage, steadfastness and self-abnegation are the subject of this book on the Knights of Bahá'u'lláh, those Bahá'ís who left their homes to bring the message to Bahá'u'lláh to countries and territories where it was unknown, and whose names are inscribed on Shoghi Effendi's Roll of Honour. They came from over two dozen countries scattered over the earth representing every continent; 131 of them were men and 126 women. The oldest left home at the age of 85, while the youngest was a youth no older than 14. They endured loneliness and made sacrifices, and in so doing experienced the greatest adventure of their lives.

ISBN: 978-0-85398-605-8
Soft Cover, 512 pages plus photographs, 23.4 x 15.6 cms (9.75 x 6.25 ins)

www.ingramcontent.com/pod-product-compliance
Lightning Source LLC
LaVergne TN
LVHW050952080826
845145LV00005B/1479